HUMAN RESOURCE MANAGEMENT
AND TECHNICAL CHANGE

HUMAN RESOURCE
MANAGEMENT
AND
TECHNICAL CHANGE

edited by

Jon Clark

Professor of Industrial Relations
University of Southampton

SAGE Publications
London • Newbury Park • New Delhi

First published 1993

 SAGE Publications Ltd
6 Bonhill Street
London EC2A 4PU

SAGE Publications Inc
2455 Teller Road
Newbury Park, California 91320

SAGE Publications India Pvt Ltd
32, M-Block Market
Greater Kailash – I
New Delhi 110 048

British Library Cataloguing in Publication data

Human Resource Management and Technical Change
  I. Clark, Jon
  658.3

  ISBN 0–8039–8786–2
  ISBN 0–8039–8787–0 pbk

Library of Congress catalog card number 93–83564

Typeset by Photoprint, Torquay, Devon
Printed in Great Britain by The Cromwell Press Ltd, Broughton Gifford,
Melksham, Wiltshire

Contents

Preface

Academic research, professional training requirements and current practice are apparently at one: human resource management and technical change are separate matters and never – or only exceptionally – the twain shall meet. This volume both confirms and challenges this conventional wisdom.

The origins of this book go back to 1981, when I simultaneously embarked on a seven-year programme of research on technical change at the University of Southampton and was accepted into associate membership of the Institute of Personnel Management (IPM). Until the late 1980s these two events remained quite separate areas of my life, until one day in 1988 one of my IPM colleagues, David Yeandle, Personnel Manager of Pirelli General (now Pirelli Cables), invited me to help him write an article for the IPM monthly magazine *Personnel Management* outlining the new human resource policies he and his colleagues had devised for a new computer-integrated manufacturing plant in Aberdare, South Wales. I accepted, on condition that I was given a guided tour round the factory. Two weeks later I had drawn up an outline proposal to study the practical implementation and effects of the new human resource policies at Aberdare, and after some months, the company agreed.

Having carried out the first main phase of fieldwork in 1990, I was appointed in September 1991 to a two-year research fellowship at the Industrial Relations Research Unit (IRRU), a Designated Research Centre funded by the Economic and Social Research Council and located at the University of Warwick. Knowing that IRRU had a good track record in organizing conferences leading to the publication of edited volumes (see most recently Storey, 1989a; Pollert, 1991a), I suggested to my colleagues that I should organize a workshop around the general theme of my research. This would have a dual function: it would be a kind of 'thank offering' to the Unit, conceived and carried through during my stay at Warwick; and it would stimulate wider academic and practitioner debate about the much neglected links between human resource management and technical change. I received enthusiastic support and encouragement, and proceeded to invite a number of academic colleagues who had a longstanding interest in the field and whose work I knew and respected. Within two months I had secured the participation of the contributors represented in this volume, and within a further two months had persuaded Sage to publish it.

A workshop of the contributors and members of IRRU was held at the University of Warwick in September 1992. This provided a useful deadline, but also a unique opportunity to read and discuss individual chapters and to revise our chapters to reflect common themes and important differences. The concluding chapter would not have been possible in its present form without the stimulating ideas of all the workshop participants.

Special thanks are due, first and foremost, to the ESRC for funding my two-year secondment, and to all my colleagues at IRRU, in particular Keith Sisson and Paul Edwards, who gave invaluable advice and encouragement throughout, and Lesley Williams and Norma Griffiths, who provided administrative support whenever requested and helped make the workshop an organizational success. In June 1992 IRRU gave David Preece and me the luxury of a captive audience at an afternoon research seminar where we could try out our ideas on human resource management and technical change on greenfield sites.

I would also like to thank Susanne Lawrence for permission to reprint Figure 1.2 from the April 1992 edition of *Personnel Management*, and Meg Davies for preparing the index to this volume. Finally, Sue Jones has been an inspiration to the project since I approached Sage in January 1992. She has maintained throughout a delicate balance between intellectual involvement and market realism which has undoubtedly helped to sharpen the focus of the volume and has forced some academics to stick their necks out further than the data strictly allowed. Needless to say, the contributors and the editor alone bear ultimate responsibility for the final product.

Jon Clark
Leamington Spa

About the Contributors

John Bessant is Professor of Technology Management at the Business School, University of Brighton. He has been working in the area of innovation management in manufacturing industry for the past 18 years, joining the School in 1982 from Aston University's Technology Policy Unit. At Brighton he has been responsible for setting up the Centre for Business Research and the development of an industry-based Masters course in the Management of Technology. His current research interests include a major collaborative study on mechanisms for establishing and maintaining continuous incremental innovation, and a programme of work on new organizational techniques including TQM and JIT manufacturing. His most recent book is *Managing Advanced Manufacturing Technology: The Challenge of the Fifth Wave* (NCC/Blackwell, 1991).

Jon Clark studied at the Universities of Birmingham, West Berlin and Bremen and has held research posts at the London School of Economics and the Groupe de Sociologie du Travail, University of Paris. He was appointed in 1978 to the Department of Sociology and Social Policy at the University of Southampton, where he is now Professor of Industrial Relations. He is currently on a two-year secondment to the Industrial Relations Research Unit, University of Warwick. His publications, as sole or joint author, include *The Process of Technological Change* (Cambridge University Press, 1988) and *Technological Change at Work* (Open University Press, 1988; second edition, 1993). He is also Principal Editor of the *Falmer Sociology Series*. In 1992 he completed a three-year study of Pirelli Cables' automated factory in Aberdare, South Wales, and is currently working on a study of the factory from 1982 to the present.

David Collinson is Lecturer in Industrial Relations and Organizational Behaviour in the School of Industrial and Business Studies at the University of Warwick. He completed his doctorate at the University of Manchester Institute of Science and Technology, and taught at the Universities of South Florida and St Andrews before taking up his post at Warwick in 1992. He has conducted research and published papers on shopfloor culture, management control, managerial accountancy, sex discrimination in the recruitment process and the power, role and status of personnel management. He is co-editor of *Job Redesign* (Gower, 1985), author of *Barriers to Fair Selection* (Equal Opportunities Commission, 1988), co-author of *Managing to Discriminate* (Routledge, 1990) and author of *Managing the Shopfloor: Subjectivity, Masculinity and Workplace Culture* (Walter de Gruyter, 1992). He is currently researching workplace culture and safety practices on North Sea oil installations.

Bill Daniel studied psychology and industrial sociology at Manchester University. For most of his working life he has been a professional researcher engaged in studies, principally, of labour markets and labour relations. The large part of that work has been carried out at the independent Policy Studies Institute (PSI) and one of its predecessors, Political and Economic Planning (PEP). He has been Director of the PSI since 1986. His books include *Racial Discrimination in England* (Penguin, 1968), *The Right to Manage?* (Heinemann, 1972) with Neil McIntosh, *Workplace Industrial Relations in Britain* (Heinemann/Gower, 1983/1984) with Neil Millward, *Workplace Industrial Relations and Technical Change* (Frances Pinter/PSI, 1987) and *The Unemployed Flow* (PSI, 1990).

Chris Hendry studied at the University of London followed by work in banking and local government before going to Sheffield City Polytechnic where he took his MSc and PhD. He was a Lecturer, then Senior Lecturer, at Nottingham Polytechnic from 1980 to 1985, and joined the Centre for Corporate Strategy and change at Warwick University in 1985 to undertake full-time research. He is currently a Principal Research Fellow and Associate Director of the Centre. He has co-authored a number of major reports, including *Training in Britain: Employers' Perspectives on Human Resources* (HMSO, 1989), *Corporate Strategy and Human Resource Management* (Employment Department, 1990), and *The Learning Organisation: A Review of Literature and Practice* (Human Resource Development Partnership, 1992). He is currently completing three books to be published during 1993 – a textbook on HRM, a study of small-to-medium size enterprises, and a book on human resource strategies for internationalization.

Karen Legge is Professor in the Department of Behaviour in Organizations, University of Lancaster. Previous posts included Reader in Organizational Behaviour at the School of Management at Imperial College, London, and research and teaching at Manchester Business School and the Medical Research Council/Economic and Social Research Council Social and Applied Psychology Unit, University of Sheffield. She is joint editor (with Geoff Lockett) of the *Journal of Management Studies*. Her major publications include *Power, Innovation and Problem-Solving in Personnel Management* (McGraw-Hill, 1978), *Evaluating Planned Organizational Change* (Academic Press, 1984), *Cases in Organizational Behaviour* (edited with Chris Clegg and Nigel Kemp, Harper and Row, 1985), and *Case Studies in Information Technology, People and Organizations* (edited with Chris Clegg and Nigel Kemp, NCC/Blackwell, 1991). She is currently continuing conceptual work in the areas of human resource management, managerial rhetoric, organizational change, and knowledge-intensive organizations.

an McLoughlin is a graduate of the Universities of Kent and Bath. After holding a research fellowship in the New Technology Research Group at the University of Southampton, he lectured for five years at Kingston University. In 1990 he was appointed to one of four founding lectureships in the Centre for Business and Management Studies at Brunel University in West London. In 1992 he spent a semester as a Visiting Fellow in the Department of Commerce at the University of Adelaide, South Australia. He is co-author of *The Process of Technological Change* (Cambridge University Press, 1988) and *Technological Change at Work* (Open University Press, 1988; second edition, 1993). He is currently writing a book based on the first in-depth study in Britain of industrial relations in non-union firms.

Neil Millward gave up his first career as an engineer to do research on factory wage systems under Tom Lupton at the Manchester Business School in the late 1960s. After a year at Harvard Business School and completing his PhD in organizational sociology at Manchester, he became an industrial relations adviser at the Pay Board in London. Thereafter he joined the research division of the Department of Employment, and in 1979 started on the design of the Workplace Industrial Relations Survey series, which has been the focus of most of his research activity ever since. He co-authored the source books for each of the three surveys: *Workplace Industrial Relations in Britain* (Heinemann/Gower, 1983/1984); *British Workplace Industrial Relations 1980–1984* (Gower, 1986); and *Workplace Industrial Relations in Transition* (Dartmouth Publishing, 1992). The last of these was written while on secondment at the Policy Studies Institute, London, where he is Senior Fellow. He is currently writing a further volume entitled *The New Workplace Industrial Relations?*

David Preece has studied and worked at Manchester Metropolitan University and the Universities of Leeds, Bradford and Coventry. Since 1989 he has been Senior Lecturer in Organization Analysis at the Business School, University of Portsmouth. He is the author of *Managing the Adoption of New Technology* (Routledge, 1989) and a range of papers in journals, edited collections and conference proceedings. He is currently involved in researching social, managerial and technical issues related to the implementation of quality management programmes in organizations. He is Co-Director of the Management and Decision Support Unit within Portsmouth Business School. The Unit is undertaking a number of research contracts, including an examination of social and managerial issues related to information technology and the implementation of quality management in business organizations.

Graham Sewell gained a degree in Town Planning Studies from the University of Wales in 1985. He has recently completed his doctoral thesis on the multinational activities of US microelectronics manufacturers. Currently he is Lecturer in Management Information Systems in the

Manchester School of Management, UMIST. He has also held posts at the University of Liverpool and the University College of Wales at Cardiff and visiting appointments at the University of California's Santa Cruz and Berkeley campuses. His current research is concerned with the impact of new information technologies on organizational design and development, including a long-term study of the disciplinary effects of workplace performance monitoring. He has published widely in social sciences and management journals and edited collections. He is currently completing a book with Barry Wilkinson on the integration of management information systems with new manufacturing and management techniques.

Barry Wilkinson gained a Sociology degree from the University of Warwick in 1978, then completed his doctoral research at the University of Aston's Technology Policy Unit in 1981. He spent three years at the National University of Singapore until taking up a post in 1986 at the Cardiff Business School, where he is currently Professor in Human Resource Management and Co-ordinator of the Japanese Management Research Unit. His main research interest is in the human and organizational implications of new manufacturing systems and technologies. His main publications include *The Shopfloor Politics of New Technology* (Heinemann, 1983) and, with Nick Oliver, *The Japanization of British Industry* (Blackwell, 1988 and 1992). He is currently completing a book on *Labour and Industry in the East Asian NICs* (to be published by de Gruyter). Recent and current research is primarily in the area of Japanese forms of management and organization, and he is cooperating with scholars in other countries to examine their transferability to alien institutional environments.

Abbreviations

AEU	Amalgamated Engineering Union (from 1992, part of AEEU)
AEEU	Amalgamated Engineering and Electrical Union
AGV	automatic guided vehicle
AMT	advanced manufacturing technology
BIFU	Banking, Insurance and Finance Union
BTEC	Business and Technician Education Council
CAD/CAM	computer-aided design/computer-aided manufacture
CAM	computer-aided manufacture
CIM	computer-integrated manufacturing
CIT	computer-integrated technology
CNC	computer numerically controlled (machine tools)
DNC	direct numerical control
DTI	Department of Trade and Industry
EETPU	Electrical, Electronic, Telecommunication and Plumbing Union (from 1992, part of AEEU)
FMS	flexible manufacturing systems
GMB	General, Municipal, Boilermakers and Allied Trade Union
HMSO	Her Majesty's Stationery Office
HRM	human resource management
IPM	Institute of Personnel Management
IR	industrial relations
IT	information technology
JCC	joint consultative/consultation committee
JIC	joint industrial council
JIT	just-in-time
MCI	Management Charter Initiative
MRP	materials requirements planning
NEDO	National Economic Development Office
NTA	new technology agreement
OLP	on-line processing
PC	personal computer
PET	product engineering team
PSI	production, sales and inventory (plan); or Policy Studies Institute, London
SBU	strategic business unit
SPC	statistical process control
SWOT	strengths, weaknesses, opportunities, threats

TASS	Technical, Administrative and Supervisory Staffs union (now part of the Manufacturing, Science and Finance union)
TGWU	Transport and General Workers' Union
TPIP	total productivity improvement programme
TQM	total quality management
TSB	Trustee Savings Bank
TUC	Trades Union Congress
WIRS	(UK) Workplace Industrial Relations Surveys (of 1980, 1984 and 1990)

1

Personnel Management, Human Resource Management and Technical Change

Jon Clark

In the past decade personnel management, human resource management and technical change have been the subject of extensive debate, but the relations between them have rarely been explored systematically. Is technical change within work organizations still seen largely as a technical matter in which there is no established role for the specialist personnel or human resources manager? Does it present particular opportunities and constraints in the management of personnel? To what extent are organization and job design, delayering, total quality management, teamworking, increased flexibility, skills training, employee involvement, central or marginal to technical change? Are these issues now accorded a higher priority or earlier consideration in the management of technical change than in the 1970s and 1980s? Do non-union firms behave differently from unionized ones in relation to technical change? These are just some of the questions discussed in this volume.

This chapter provides an initial introduction to the main themes of the volume. It begins with general definitions of personnel management and personnel issues and explains the crucial importance of distinguishing between the two. It then goes on to examine recent debates about whether human resource management represents a new paradigm in the development of personnel management, suggesting that the adoption of a more strategic approach to the management of human resources *is* likely to encourage organizations to give a greater priority to personnel issues in managing processes of technical change. However, it may not always be specialist personnel managers who are the champions of personnel issues in such circumstances. The second main section turns its attention to technical change, exploring those capabilities of computing and information technologies that influence the way in which organizations manage the human resource. The chapter concludes with an outline of the contents of the following ten chapters.

Personnel Management

Personnel Management and Personnel Issues

Personnel management is not confined to the role of specialist personnel managers in work organizations. It encompasses all those people who are involved in devising personnel policies, as well as all those with direct responsibility for managing personnel. Indeed, one of the most interesting developments in recent years has been the changing role of general managers, specialist personnel managers and line managers in managing the human resource (see Guest, 1991; Millward et al, 1992; Daniel and Millward, this volume). Since the early 1980s, too, external consultants have increasingly been used to design and implement organizational and human resource changes in companies. Finally, experiments in self-regulating or self-managing teams have led to the delegation of some traditional personnel functions to workgroups, particularly in organizations that have introduced advanced technical change (see Chapters 4, 5, 6 and 7, this volume).

In this context it is important to distinguish analytically between personnel management – the actors and actions involved in the management of personnel – and personnel issues – the issues involved in the management of personnel, irrespective of agency (see on this Legge, 1989b; Guest, 1991; Legge, this volume). In recent years many companies have begun to engage strategically with issues such as organizational design, direct employee involvement, performance management and quality management, and this has often led them to develop novel forms of interaction between specialist personnel managers, senior executives and line managers. In fact, some commentators have argued that it is the relative decline of labour as a 'problem' for work organizations in the 1980s – the traditional industrial relations rationale for specialist personnel managers in anglo-saxon countries – which has enabled specialist personnel managers to begin to change the focus of their activity. This is held to involve a reorientation away from industrial relations fire-fighting and guardianship of procedures towards a greater emphasis on 'human resource' issues such as recruitment and selection, training and development, performance appraisal and management, and direct employee communication and involvement (see Fombrun et al, 1984; Walton and Lawrence, 1985; and for similar trends in the UK, Storey, 1989b, 1992a). This reorientation is inextricably linked with the theory and practice of human resource management.

Human Resource Management: a Working Definition

There is no unanimity about how to define human resource management or its implications for the personnel specialist. For some it is an opportunity to raise the status of specialist personnel managers, for others it represents a fundamental challenge to them (see Torrington and Hall, 1987; Tyson, 1987; Torrington, 1989; Guest, 1991). However, most commentators would agree that, in theory at least, it challenges traditional views about who has responsibility for the management of personnel in the organization and what are the most important and relevant personnel issues and approaches.

It may be useful at the outset to provide a simple definition or model of human resource management. A good starting point is Guest's seminal article of 1987, in which he characterizes HRM as a set of interdependent personnel policies to maximize four objectives: organizational integration, employee commitment, flexibility and quality (Figure 1.1 represents an elaboration of Guest's basic model).

Organizational integration refers to the extent to which personnel policies are integrated with other activities within the organization. Strategic HRM implies a planned and coherent strategy towards the management of human resources which is 'owned' by senior management within the organization (see Fombrun et al, 1984; Hendry and Pettigrew, 1986, 1990; Miller, 1989; Purcell, 1989; Storey, 1992a; Legge, this volume;

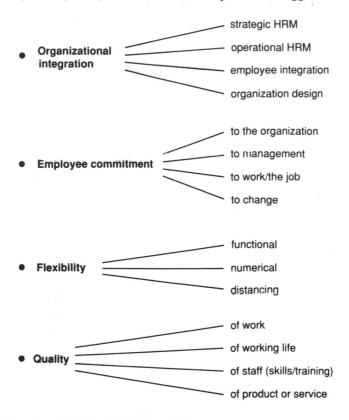

Figure 1.1 *Guest's (1987) definition of human resource management*

Hendry, this volume). In contrast, operational HRM is the province of middle and junior management, involving the translation of HR strategies into operational policies and practices for the day-to-day management of personnel in the workplace. As for employee integration, the aim is to ensure that the work of different groups of employees is coordinated across the organization as a whole, both horizontally – within and between departments – and vertically – between different levels in the hierarchy. Finally, organizational integration requires the design of organization structures which facilitate the development of strategic and operational HRM and employee integration. All four objectives directly involve personnel issues, although no assumptions are made about the relative role of the specialist personnel or HR manager in achieving them. For example, there is undoubted scope for specialist personnel involvement in strategic HRM and organization design, although it is also plausible for other senior managers or consultants to make a major input into both areas. In contrast, the 'traditional' organization would exhibit very little organizational integration on any of the four counts.

Employee commitment is often contrasted with employee compliance in comparisons between HRM and more traditional 'low trust' personnel policies (see Sisson, 1989b: 28–30; Guest, 1992: 151–3). There is now an extensive literature on the theme of employee commitment which distinguishes between various types and forms: to the company or organization, senior management and line management, the profession, occupational group or trade union, to work and/or the job, to the product or service, to the family or local community (see on this Coopey and Hartley, 1991; Guest, 1992; Guest and Dewe, 1991). Personnel or HRM policies can clearly inhibit or promote some or all of these different types of commitment. For example, it is often suggested that employee commitment to the organization will be difficult to achieve if there are strong status divisions between hourly paid manual workers, monthly paid staff, managers and executives, whereas the introduction of some form of single status employment across the organization helps facilitate greater commitment. High organizational commitment is also associated with low labour turnover and absence levels, although there is little evidence as yet that high employee commitment is positively correlated with improved employee or company performance (see on this Guest, 1991).

Another distinctive element of commitment in HRM theory is the emphasis placed on the commitment of *managerial* employees. In contrast, traditional personnel management is held to focus largely on shopfloor and office staff and to neglect middle and junior management. (The changing role of middle and junior management in advanced technical change is one of the main trends identified in many contributions to this volume.) Finally, HRM theory places particular emphasis on the need to generate a more diffuse and general commitment to organizational change, a willingness amongst employees to accept change as a normal part of working life. The traditional personnel approach, it is implied, sees change (including technical change) as something abnormal which will therefore involve a renegotiation of some aspects of terms and conditions of employment.

This brings us directly to the third objective of HRM policy identified by Guest. As with employee commitment, there is now a voluminous literature on **flexibility** (see, for example, Atkinson and Meager, 1986; Marsden and Thompson, 1990; Pollert, 1991a). Pollert has identified a whole range of different aspects and implications of flexibility – task and job range, job demarcations, managerial control, intensification of effort, labour productivity, skill, training, payment systems (1991b). Atkinson and Meager (1986), in contrast, have focused on three main types, associated, in their ideal-typical 'flexible firm', with three different types of employee: functional flexibility, which involves an extension of task and job range and an erosion of job demarcations for core staff; numerical flexibility, which refers to the managerial freedom to adjust the numbers of peripheral staff through flexible working hours and the use of part-time, temporary and fixed term contracts; and distancing, in which an organization no longer employs personnel directly for particular purposes, but buys in the services of external staff (for example, contract cleaners, security personnel, consultants). This is not to imply that the HRM-orientated organization must necessarily introduce high levels of flexibility in all three areas. However, increased functional flexibility does prove to be one of the most important and consistent outcomes of advanced technical change (see Chapters 4–10 below), and there is some evidence that the appropriate mix of enhanced functional, numerical and distancing flexibility can make an indirect contribution to productivity gains (Guest, 1991: 155).

Finally, there is the objective of **quality**. In Guest's model of HRM, quality refers not just to the quality of work and working life – the working environment, the design of jobs, job satisfaction – but to the quality of the workforce itself, in particular the level of skill and training of personnel (a notoriously under-resourced area in many organizations; on UK companies, see Keep, 1989). Interestingly, some of the most advanced philosophies of quality management (such as TQM) tend to focus, like HRM, as much if not more on the quality of managers and managerial performance as on that of non-management employees (see Hill, 1991a, 1991b). They are also strongly associated with the redesign of organization structures, 'delayering' of extended management hierarchies and a redefinition of middle and junior management roles.

Personnel Management and Human Resource Management

Recent debates on the relation between HRM and personnel management have revolved around two main questions: to what extent does the normative model of HRM represent a departure from the dominant orthodoxy in personnel management, or is it simply what good personnel managers have always done; and to what extent have companies and organizations actually adopted the normative model of HRM in practice? Karen Legge has expressed some scepticism about the extent to which normative models of HRM are significantly different from previous normative or idealized models of personnel management. Indeed she has argued that the sharp contrasts often drawn between HRM and personnel management, for example by Guest in 1987, 'appear to owe much to an implicit comparison of the *descriptive practice* of personnel management with the *normative aspirations* of HRM, rather than comparing like with like' (Legge, 1989a: 27; emphasis added). She has nevertheless identified three differences of emphasis which do appear to distinguish HRM from more traditional 'personnel management' approaches:

1 Personnel management is aimed largely at non-managers, whereas HRM treats management development and the management team as equally if not more important.
2 Personnel management views line managers as implementing personnel policy for the employees under their control, whereas HRM views line managers as directing and coordinating a whole range of resources (not just human ones, but also money, machines, materials, information) in order to achieve 'bottom-line' objectives.
3 HRM highlights senior management's corporate responsibility for managing organizational culture and giving a sense of direction and leadership within the organization, whereas personnel management has tended to see this as an activity for a separate department such as Organization Development (OD).

The view that the prime responsibility of senior general managers is to provide an integrated and consistent set of human resource policies through which the 'core values' of the organization can be conveyed to all employees is a common theme in many discussions of HRM. It also encapsulates well the ambiguity of HRM for specialist personnel managers. On the one hand, personnel issues are accorded an enhanced role in the overall management of work organizations. On the other hand, it is often the chief executive officer, and not necessarily the personnel or HR director, who is the champion and embodiment of human resource values. In short, there is a strong element of truth in the claim by Alan Fowler, one of the leading UK practitioner writers on personnel management, that the real difference between HRM and personnel management is 'not what it is, but who is saying it. In a nutshell, HRM represents the discovery of personnel management by chief executives' (1987: 3). This accords with Storey's view that 'what is different . . . is not so much that the message has changed, but that it is being received more seriously' (1989b: 5).

To what extent does HRM represent a 'paradigmatic break' from the prevailing orthodoxy in the management of the employment relationship? According to Storey, unlike more traditional approaches it has a clear philosophical underpinning as a set of interrelated practices whose main aim is to 'free up' managerial initiative (1989b: 3). However, in the UK at least, only a small minority of companies (nearly all foreign-owned) appeared fully to have embraced HRM in practice by the mid-1980s. The vast majority had adopted particular aspects on an ad hoc and piecemeal basis, but certainly not as part of an overall medium-term strategy (Storey and Sisson, 1989: 172).

In 1992 Storey constructed a more elaborate model of the differences between HRM and what he termed the 'personnel and industrial relations' paradigm (see Figure 1.2). Based on evidence from research conducted at Warwick University's Industrial Relations Research Unit in the late 1980s, he suggested that there had been a remarkable increase in the adoption of HRM-type practices in large UK companies (Storey, 1992a; a shorter version has been published in Storey, 1992b). The organizations surveyed – including the Ford Motor Company, ICI, Lucas, Massey–Ferguson, Peugeot–Talbot and Rolls-Royce – were all 'mainstream', in other words what Purcell and Sisson (1983) have called 'standard modern' or 'sophisticated modern' companies. In this sense Storey's findings can be distinguished from studies of leading US and Japanese companies – such as Rank Xerox, Hewlett Packard and Nissan – which are often cited as exemplars of an integrated HRM approach (see Chapters 6 and 7 in this volume for case studies of leading companies from Italy and Japan).

Storey presented his more detailed conclusions under four main headings: prevailing beliefs and assumptions; strategic aspects; line management; and key levers. In looking at **beliefs and assumptions**, he concluded that business need had now become the guide to management action in nearly all the case study companies, while procedures, rules and contractual arrangements were generally regarded as impediments to effective performance. Interestingly, though, the key institutions of the pluralist 'personnel and industrial relations' approach – collective bargaining and trade union recognition – had been maintained in most cases *alongside* a series of more unitarist initiatives such as increased direct communication with the workforce. In summary, in the majority of companies surveyed Storey found 'the co-existence of two traditions' of beliefs and assumptions (1992: 30).

Interestingly, Keenoy had argued two years previously that there was in reality no necessary conflict between HRM and personnel management. Indeed they were:

> complementary rather than mutually exclusive forms of practice . . . A human resources policy may be unitary or pluralistic, collaborative or conflictual, depending upon both circumstances and strategic choice; the role of the personnel or human resource specialist is to translate and implement the strategic HRM decisions into appropriate practices. (Keenoy, 1990a: 6)

In support of Keenoy, it could be argued that procedural fairness and consistency – for Storey archetypal features of the personnel and IR model

Dimension	Personnel and IR	HRM
Beliefs and assumptions		
Contract	Careful delineation of written contracts	Aim to go 'beyond contract'
Rules	Importance of devising clear rules/mutuality	'Can do' outlook; impatience with 'rule'
Guide to management action	Procedures/consistency/ control	'Business need'/ flexibility/commitment
Behaviour referent	Norms/custom and practice	Values/mission
Managerial task vis-à-vis labour	Monitoring	Nurturing
Nature of relations	Pluralist	Unitarist
Conflict	Institutionalized	De-emphasized
Standardization	High (e.g. 'parity' an issue)	Low (e.g. 'parity' not seen as relevant)
Strategic aspects		
Key relations	Labour–management	Business–customer
Initiatives	Piecemeal	Integrated
Corporate plan	Marginal to	Central to
Speed of decision	Slow	Fast
Line management		
Management role	Transactional	Transformational leadership
Key managers	Personnel/IR specialists	General/business/line managers
Prized management skills	Negotiation	Facilitation
Key levers		
Foci of attention for interventions	Personnel procedures	Wide-ranging cultural, structural and personnel strategies
Selection	Separate, marginal task	Integrated, key task
Pay	Job evaluation; multiple, fixed grades	Performance-related; few if any grades
Conditions	Separately negotiated	Harmonization
Labour–management	Collective bargaining contracts	Towards individual contracts
Thrust of relations with stewards	Regularized through facilities and training	Marginalized (with exception of some bargaining for change models)
Communication	Restricted flow/indirect	Increased flow/direct
Job design	Division of labour	Teamwork
Conflict handling	Reach temporary truces	Manage climate and culture
Training and development	Controlled access to courses	Learning companies

Figure 1.2 *Storey's comparison of the differences between personnel management and human resource management* (Storey, 1992b: 28)

– are essential if organizations are to maintain the trust and commitment of their employees. In relation to employee representation, too, both Sisson (1989b) and Guest (1989) have argued that, unlike in the United States, there appears to be no necessary conflict in the UK between HRM and the existence of trade unions, although there is undoubtedly a tension between the 'collectivist' and 'pluralist' values of the personnel management tradition and the more 'individualist' and 'unitary' values of HRM. The tension between these two traditions and sets of values is likely to be a continuing focus of attention in the 1990s, and is one of the central themes of McLoughlin's chapter in this volume on technical change in the non-union firm.

In looking at what he called **strategic aspects**, Storey found that most companies surveyed had moved in recent years from a production or labour-management orientation to a business and customer one. There was little evidence, though, of the strategic integration of personnel policies with corporate plans, indeed, he found that most organizations still operated largely on a 'pick-and-mix' basis. With regard to **line management**, however, the findings were unambiguous: according to Storey's interviewees, general managers and line managers had emerged in nearly all cases as the key players on personnel issues (on this see Daniel and Millward, this volume). Finally, there was a great unevenness in the take-up of what he called **key levers** (harmonization/single status, performance-related pay etc.), despite the fact that many of these issues had been strongly featured in the practitioner literature in the recent past.

Two further findings from Storey's study are of interest in the context of this present volume. First, there was a low correlation between the financial performance of companies and the number of HRM initiatives taken; also, the extent to which companies had taken up HRM initiatives was not closely correlated with increases in employee commitment, trust and satisfaction, a finding consistent with previous studies (see Guest, 1991). Part of the answer to this conundrum lies in the fact that, as Storey himself found, there is not one common approach to HRM in practice, but a number of different versions – 'hard', 'soft', 'strong', 'weak' – which place different priorities on issues such as employee commitment and job satisfaction (see Storey, 1992a: 27ff; also Storey, 1989b: 8). For example, hard HRM involves a more selective, instrumental approach to the management of personnel, while soft HRM lays more stress on an integrated 'total' approach with a strong emphasis on employee involvement and development. In this connection, Schuler has used Porter's typology of business strategies (Porter, 1985) to draw a useful distinction between 'innovation-driven', 'quality-driven' and 'cost-driven' approaches to HRM and company management. According to Schuler (1989), innovation- and quality-driven strategies are more likely to need a strong, sophisticated and integrated HRM policy than the harder cost-driven strategy, which stresses the *efficient* rather than *full* use of human resources (see on this Guest, 1991: 157–8).

Before we turn to the question of technical change, we will conclude this section by looking at specialist personnel/HR managers themselves and evidence of the extent to which they play an innovative role in the management of change. Legge's classic study of 1978 identified two specific roles which personnel managers could adopt in order to increase their power and influence in organizations – 'deviant innovator' and 'conformist innovator' (1978: 79–85). According to Legge, deviant innovators achieve change by actively promoting new values in an organization. Not surprisingly, she found that they were few and far between! Where new values or organization cultures were promoted within organizations, they tended to be initiated by senior general managers, although specialist personnel managers were often able to assist in their implementation. Legge found more examples of conformist innovation, where personnel managers acquired or exhibited expertise which enabled them to demonstrate a close relationship between their specialist activities and business success. In Guest's formulation, the model of conformist innovation implies a 'greater use of those personnel techniques which have a potential organizational pay off' (1991: 161), for example, employee recruitment and selection, training and development, and human resource planning. However, although opportunities were available for personnel specialists to play the role of deviant and conformist innovators, Guest concluded, on the recent evidence from British-owned companies at least, that they were generally failing to play either role:

> This is unfortunate, because the picture appears to be rather different in a number of foreign-owned and apparently successful firms with a reputation for their personnel/HRM policies and in a number of predominantly foreign-owned greenfield sites . . . In these, as in a few British-owned multinationals, the personnel department has a higher profile and greater credibility. Furthermore, where they do play a part, as Daniel in particular indicates, personnel managers can make a useful contribution. (1991: 162)

Interestingly, Guest cited Daniel's research on technical change (1987; see also Daniel and Millward, this volume) as evidence that there can be an identifiable pay-off from specialist personnel intervention. Most of the contributions to this volume will demonstrate that, while advanced technical change does often lead to, even require, changes in areas such as organization design, work structuring and employee relations, it is only under specific circumstances that specialist personnel managers make a strategic contribution. It will be one of the aims of the conclusion (Chapter 11) to specify these circumstances.

Technology and Technical Change

There is now a voluminous literature on technical change at work (see Huczynski and Buchanan, 1991: part III; McLoughlin and Clark, 1993). This short introduction to the debate will begin with an outline of the capabilities and diffusion of 'new technologies'. It will also present some definitions and frameworks which are useful in the analysis of particular technical changes, including a discussion of the concept of technology itself. This will be followed by an outline of the main personnel issues raised by advanced technical change and a concluding section which underlines the importance of processes as well as outcomes of technical change. Throughout the focus will be on production technologies (technology applied to production and administrative processes) rather than product technologies (the application of technologies in new products).

The Capabilities and Diffusion of Computing and Information Technologies

The modern history of electronic computing and information technologies, which are the main focus in this volume, can be divided into three main phases (see on this Friedman and Cornford, 1989). The first can be dated from the 1940s, when the state-sponsored defence industries of the West pioneered the development of large and often unreliable mainframe computers. In the second phase, which lasted from the late 1960s until the mid-1980s, attention shifted from hardware to problems of software. Concurrently, the development of microelectronics – miniaturized electronic components such as the microprocessor or silicon chip – revolutionized the capabilities of computers, making them not only more reliable, but more powerful, speedier, smaller, cheaper and more flexible. According to Friedman and Cornford, by the mid-1980s the problems with the supply side of computing (hardware and software) had been largely overcome, and we are now in a third stage in which user relations and applications (the 'demand side') are the greatest priority. In this phase, the telecommunications infrastructure, which allows links and networks to be established between previously separate computing systems, becomes increasingly important in enhancing real time communication within and between organizations.

The principal capabilities of microelectronics-based computing technologies are the capture, storage, manipulation and distribution of information. It is these capabilities which account for the extraordinarily wide scope of their application, not just to manufacturing (the traditional focus of automation), but to a whole range of administrative processes too. They can be used to automate the control of operations in a number of ways: by allowing the programming of machines to carry out a pre-defined sequence of operations; by automatically measuring deviations from pre-arranged standards and initiating or suggesting corrective action; and by giving automatic feedback on the performance of machines and human beings (for an example of the latter in practice see Sewell and Wilkinson, this volume). Information technologies can also promote organizational integration by improving the accessibility and speed of information capture and display across different levels and areas of operation. As we will see, these capabilities have considerable implications for employees at all levels of the organization.

In assessing the human resource implications of advanced technical change, it is important to distinguish between 'radical' and 'incremental' change, depending on (i) the extent to which the change in technology is discontinuous with previous experience (ii) its magnitude and (iii) the degree of risk or uncertainty associated with it (see Hage, 1980). Many technical changes take place incrementally over many years, and adaptation to change tends not to be seen or experienced as problematic by either management or workforce. In such cases, the management of change remains largely in the hands of line managers as part of their day-to-day operational duties. Radical technical changes, in contrast, are likely to require more concentrated and significant changes in areas such as managerial roles, organization structure, training, skills, staffing levels and employee communications, and specialist personnel involvement thus tends to be more prominent.

Technical change is now a fact of organizational life for employees in most advanced industrial countries. By the late 1980s, it was calculated that over $300 billion per annum were being spent worldwide on the use of computers and communications hardware and software (see Forester, 1989: viii). However, at the same time voices were being raised which questioned the productivity gains resulting from such investments. A number of US commentators became increasingly critical of the 'hype' surrounding computerization and presented data which showed that technological changes in manufacturing, offices and banks had not generally yielded productivity improvements, *at least in the short term* (see the separate contributions of Bowen, Warner and Franke in Forester, 1989: 267–90). In some cases, computerization had simply compounded existing problems. As one office system manager noted: 'If people are doing the wrong things when you automate, you get them to do the wrong things faster' (cited in Bowen, 1989: 269). In other cases computerization had diverted attention away from the need to make fundamental changes in management information systems and management structure (according to Drucker, for example, most US companies in the 1980s had 20–30 per cent more managers than they needed; cited in Bowen, 1989: 271). For Forester, there was one clear conclusion to be drawn from this evidence:

> what decides the difference between success and failure in the implementation of information technology systems is the human factor . . . companies are rediscovering that people and not machines are their most valuable resource and that they can best improve their competitive performance by getting humans and technology working together in harmony. US managers are realizing what the Japanese figured out years ago: that you can have the best gee-whiz technology in the world, but you need to get the people side of the equation right if you want to get the most out of it. (1989: ix, 13)

In this volume we will be examining how far companies based in the UK (including a number of foreign-owned multinationals) have acted on such insights since the mid-1980s.

Concepts, Frameworks and Implications

Existing studies of the implications of new technologies for work organizations operate with very different concepts of technology. It is not possible to discuss these in detail here; an excellent overview can be found in Huczynski and Buchanan (1991: ch. 11). However, there are three main ways in which the term is used: in a narrow *material* sense, as tools, machines and instruments; in a wider *purposive* sense, to refer to 'skills, methods, procedures or routines' performed by people to achieve particular ends; or in an *organizational* sense, to refer to social arrangements such as factories or bureaucracies which have been created to achieve specific planned objectives. Langdon Winner has referred to these three types of use as apparatus, technique and organization (Winner, 1977: 10).

In previous research the present writer and colleagues have found it empirically useful to adopt a narrow concept of technology, but to incorporate within it more sophisticated and precise engineering ideas. On this analysis all technologies are *engineering systems*, i.e. not just pieces of hardware and software, but systems based on certain engineering principles and composed of elements which are functionally arranged (configured) in certain specific ways. An engineering system is composed of two primary and two secondary elements. The primary elements are the *architecture* – the design principles and the way they are configured – and the *technology* – the hardware and the software. The secondary elements are the *dimensioning* – the way in which a system is adapted for a specific customer application – and the *appearance* – the system's ergonomic and aesthetic characteristics. The definition can be illustrated in diagrammatic form (Figure 1.3).

In the study from which this concept was derived, we showed how, contrary to much contemporary argument, technologies (defined as engineering systems) can generate strong imperatives for certain aspects of work and organization, and establish constraints and opportunities for others:

> First, they eliminate or reduce the amount of complex tasks requiring manual skills and abilities; second, they generate more complex tasks which require mental problem-solving and interpretive skills and abilities and an understanding of system interdependencies; third, in order that many tasks can be performed effectively, tacit skills and abilities associated with the performance of work with the old technology are still required; fourth, they involve a fundamentally different relationship between the user and the technology compared to [older] technologies. (McLoughlin and Clark, 1988: 116–17)

Huczynski and Buchanan (1991) have also suggested that, to a greater or lesser extent, technology does make determinate demands on those who work with it, whether they be in hospitals or factories, consultancy firms or coalmines. In fact they have identified six main personnel issues which are

---

Primary elements

Architecture	*Technology*
System principles	Hardware
Overall system configuration	Software

Secondary elements

Dimensioning
Detailed design for a particular
organizational setting

Appearance
Audible and visual characteristics
Ergonomics
Aesthetics

Figure 1.3 *The concept of engineering system* (Clark et al, 1988: 14)

determined to some extent by the technology of an organization (1991: 274):

- The kinds of work tasks that have to be done
- Job design (the horizontal division of labour)
- The organization of work or the grouping of jobs
- Organization structure or the hierarchy through which work is planned and organized (the vertical division of labour)
- The knowledge and skills required to carry out work
- The values, attitudes and behaviour of employees.

The ways in which these issues, separately and together, are determined – or, as some would prefer, shaped – by technology will be a major focus of this volume.

Having concentrated so far mainly on outcomes, we will conclude this section by looking at processes of technical change. Daniel has identified four main stages at which specialist personnel managers may become involved in the implementation of new technology: (i) the decision to change; (ii) immediately after the change; (iii) after the decision to tell the workforce; and (iv) at a later stage (for discussion of findings see Daniel, 1987: 107–10; also Daniel and Millward, this volume). In contrast, Clark et al have presented a more general framework for analysing the introduction of new technology, breaking it down into five main stages: (i) initiation; (ii) decision to adopt; (iii) system selection; (iv) implementation; and (v) routine operation (1988: 31; see also McLoughlin and Clark, 1988: 43–4). Daniel's approach is clearly of direct relevance to the question of specialist personnel management involvement in technical change, while Clark et al's more extended framework provides a more appropriate basis for assessing the importance of different personnel issues at different stages of change.

This more extended framework is in fact made up of three elements: stages of technical change; issues arising during change; and critical junctures in the process of change. The idea of analytically distinct *stages* aims to capture the processual, temporal element of technical change. However, a number of substantive *issues* (financial, technical, personnel) arise in any process of change which requires decisions to be made or policies to be elaborated, either by conscious choice and negotiation or by omission. The importance of different issues (in the personnel field: organization and job design, recruitment, training, remuneration, appraisal, employee representation and involvement, work organization etc.) at particular stages is likely to vary from organization to organization and from technology to technology and therefore needs to be specified from case to case. Finally, *critical junctures* are the points at which temporal stages and substantive issues intersect, for example, where organizational actors seek to influence a particular personnel issue or outcome. In their timing and significance, critical junctures are likely to be unique to a particular organization and innovation.

If we bring all these points together and relate them to the specific concern of the present volume, then we would suggest that, within the constraints and opportunities provided by a number of contingencies (including the capabilities of the advanced technology or engineering system), critical junctures arise at various stages during the process of technical change at which organizational actors are able (or seek) to intervene in order to influence particular personnel issues. The aim of the following chapters is to explore these connections with reference to recent empirical data ranging from large-scale surveys to one-company case studies.

The Structure and Contents of the Volume

The second introductory chapter, by Karen Legge, focuses more precisely on the question as to whether specialist personnel/human resource managers are marginal or central to advanced technical change. She begins by examining some of the reasons for the low profile of personnel specialists in the management of technical change in the 1980s, then looks at more recent developments (including the growth of HRM) to see whether this 'pattern of marginalization' is likely to continue in the 1990s. She then goes on to discuss evidence on the part played by human resource issues in the initiation and implementation of technical change, arguing that they are becoming increasingly important, but as a concern of executives and line managers rather than personnel specialists. She concludes with some reflections on the extent to which UK experience is mirrored in Europe and the United States.

There then follow eight chapters that discuss primary research evidence. In the first of these, Bill Daniel and Neil Millward report on the most authoritative large-scale research evidence available in the UK, the Workplace Industrial Relations Surveys of 1980, 1984 and 1990 (known as the WIRS surveys or WIRS series). They find not only that advanced technical change has become increasingly pervasive in all sectors of the UK economy, but that employees affected by technical change are generally supportive of its introduction because it is associated with progress, competitive advantage and managerial confidence in the future. While personnel specialists play little or no part in the management of technical change in the generality of cases, this is explained principally by the fact that the majority of workplaces still do not employ personnel specialists. Where they are employed and become involved at an early stage, the level of employee support for technical change tends to be stronger.

Chapter 4, by Chris Hendry, provides an interesting methodological and substantive contrast to Chapter 3, tracing ten years of personnel leadership in technical and human resource change in one large manufacturing company, GKN Hardy Spicer. Hendry argues that the single case study can reveal processes of involvement over a period of time which may be concealed by a narrower focus on a 'decision event' such as the decision to invest in new technology. His account shows the leading role played by personnel specialists over an extended period, describing the combination of planning and adaptation to evolving circumstances as 'genuine strategic behaviour'. The Hardy Spicer case also shows that a manufacturing philosophy which allows human beings a significant role in the production process can also be fully compatible with various forms of advanced technical change. The challenge for personnel specialists in espousing HRM is, for Hendry, to plan and act strategically while the operational reins pass increasingly to line managers.

In Chapter 5, David Preece argues that greenfield sites provide a rare opportunity to study what key decision-makers perceive to be desirable HRM policies and practices to underpin the effective utilization of advanced technology. Drawing on a wide literature he provides a detailed summary of the contents of HRM strategies on greenfield sites, suggesting that although many HRM policies are also to be found in brownfield ones, it is the combination and integration of policies driven by an explicit HR philosophy which make greenfield sites distinctive. He illustrates his argument by presenting findings from his own research into one particular company, Venture Pressings Ltd.

Chapter 6, by Jon Clark, discusses evidence from a longitudinal case study of Pirelli Cables' computer-integrated manufacturing plant in Aberdare, South Wales, a region which has achieved the greatest success in attracting inward investment to the UK. This chapter, like Hendry's, also shows under what conditions and on which issues personnel/human resource specialists can play a leading role in managing advanced technical change. The main part of the chapter concentrates on one element of the new human resource strategy for the plant, the contractual requirement on all employees to be 'fully flexible', and identifies six reasons why, after only three years of the factory's operation, the level of flexibility fell short of the original intention. Clark gives a paradoxical explanation of this development, arguing that management has actually achieved its original objective – full flexibility to do what it wants – but to do what it wants, it does not require full flexibility. Nevertheless, he concludes that the degree of flexibility achieved, together with the introduction of a system of self-supervision for production staff, amounts to a significant change in working practices which enjoys the commitment of both management and staff.

In Chapter 7, which provides a clear contrast with many of the findings of Chapter 6, Graham Sewell and Barry Wilkinson examine the theory and practice of HRM in what they call 'surveillance' firms. Using data from a Japanese-owned manufacturing company, they show how the nature of electronic work monitoring supports a form of self-management by shopfloor employees which incorporates many of the traditional personnel management functions. They argue that the professional role of personnel specialists in 'surveillance' firms is marginalized, not only by the use of new technology, but by the fact that the configuration of the surveillance apparatus bypasses personnel specialists and places control firmly in the hands of line managers. So while the case study company has a fully fledged HRM policy, specialist human resource managers are reduced to areas of narrow technical specialization, devising the techniques (psychometric testing, numerical tests) for staff selection, for example, but not involved in establishing the selection criteria.

David Collinson explores the role of personnel specialists in the implementation of on-line processing (OLP) in a major insurance company in Chapter 8. He focuses on two particular HR policies, one concerned with job content, skill and grading, the other with staffing levels, both designed to anticipate and implement the transition to OLP. The first illustrates the positive potential of personnel specialist involvement, showing how the deskilling effects of new technology on largely female clerical jobs were anticipated and overcome by a job enlargement scheme which helped to smooth the way for technical change. In contrast, corporate personnel's policy on staffing levels, which involved a ban on recruitment in order to reduce labour costs, placed enormous pressure and stress on employees who were trying to utilize the new technology, generating inefficiencies, informal resistance and a more negative attitude towards technical change. Collinson argues that there is scant recognition in the HRM literature of how different policies can have opposing objectives and effects, concluding that in this case the contradictions were a direct result of the fact that the company's HRM strategy was driven primarily by accounting preoccupations with minimizing labour costs.

In Chapter 9, Ian McLoughlin discusses data from the first in-depth UK study of employment relations in non-union firms to examine whether the relation between personnel management and advanced technical change differs in unionized and non-union companies. Drawing on survey data from 115 establishments, and interview and questionnaire data from a follow-up study of thirty, he concludes that unionized establishments are more likely to have introduced advanced technical change than non-unionized ones, although union presence appears to inhibit technology-related organizational change, particularly in small establishments. He also found a strong correlation between the adoption of an HRM-type approach to personnel management, specialist personnel involvement in technical change, and the introduction of technology-related organizational changes.

Chapter 10 concludes Part II of the volume with a discussion of the organizational shape of the factory of the future. Using data from a recent study of twenty-eight companies using advanced manufacturing technology, John Bessant argues that AMT represents a new paradigm in organization and work design, marked by flatter management hierarchies, new forms of first-line management, flexible work practices, mechanisms to ensure 'continuous improvement', new reward systems often linked to appraisal, more focused recruitment criteria and high levels of continuous training and development for managers and staff. In his conclusion, he reprises one of the main themes of the volume, the distinction between personnel issues and personnel management. He suggests that, although the *skills* of the specialist personnel manager will be increasingly in demand, the factory of the future is likely to require a 'shared professional perspective' in which HRM may well end up as a central part of the training and practice of all employees in the establishment.

In Chapter 11, Jon Clark uses the findings of the preceding chapters to unpack some of the connections between technical and organizational change, identify the most important issues arising from advanced technical change, and assess the role of general managers, line managers and personnel/HR specialists in managing its introduction and operation. He draws three main practical conclusions. First, if, as appears likely, general and line managers will have primary responsibility for managing the human resource aspects of advanced technical change, then human resource considerations and capabilities will need to be much more prominent in the accountabilities, selection and management of these managers. Second, there is strong evidence to suggest that the benefits of advanced technical change will only be fully realized if appropriate organizational and work arrangements are designed and a strategic approach adopted to the management of human resources. Organizations will therefore need to identify a person, job or mechanism to ensure that there is a 'voice' for HR issues at all levels in the organization. Whoever acts as that voice, their performance and the actual personnel/human resource outcomes will need to be subject to a regular 'audit' within the organization, preferably by someone with a knowledge and experience of personnel issues and practices. Finally, there appear to be two distinct roles open to personnel/human resource specialists in the management of advanced technical change. First, they can become full, recognized members of the management team, strategic change-makers, specialist advisers and monitoring 'auditors' in the planning, implementation and operation of change. Alternatively, they can follow the currently dominant trend in the UK and confine themselves to important but increasingly narrow technical specialisms (employment law, recruitment techniques), acting as reactive advisers and handmaidens to line management. Against this background, the theme of this volume – the relation between personnel management, human resource management and technical change – raises fundamental questions about the future of the personnel profession.

2

The Role of Personnel Specialists: Centrality or Marginalization?

Karen Legge

In the 1980s in the UK survey evidence pointed to a paradox: whereas personnel specialists in a majority of establishments were only marginally involved in the initiation and implementation of advanced technical change, where they *were* involved and at an early stage, employees' reactions to it were much more favourable than in cases of non- or late involvement (Daniel, 1987). At first or even second sight, this marginalization of personnel specialists seems surprising. Not only has information technology (IT) immense implications for employment-related issues, including organizational design and job design, employment, careers and skills (see Legge, 1989b), but ever since Mumford's early and seminal studies (1969, 1972) of the introduction of first-generation computer operations into offices in the late 1960s and early 1970s, it has been conventional in the prescriptive literature to advocate personnel specialists' adoption of a proactive 'organizational diagnostician' or 'collaborative systems designer' role in managing technical change. And yet, if with some notable exceptions (see, for example, Chapters 4, 5, 6 and 8 in this volume), research evidence throughout the 1980s appears to present much the same message: that at best, even when personnel *considerations* in the introduction of new technology are not ignored, the role played by personnel *specialists* appears to be one of late-in-the-day facilitators of implementation, constrained by technical and financial parameters over which they have little say and to which they can merely react (see, for example, Child and Tarbuck, 1985; Rothwell, 1985; Willman and Winch, 1985; MacInnes, 1988; Marginson et al, 1988). In one aptly entitled paper, based on intensive research in CAM-operating companies, Clegg and Kemp (1986) seem to be voicing the finding of many fellow researchers when they ask 'Information technology: Personnel, where are you?'

The objective of this chapter is to explore four interrelated questions. First, how do we account for the low profile or non-involvement of personnel specialists in the management of technical change for most of the 1980s? Second, is this pattern of marginalization likely to continue in the 1990s and with the emergence of HRM? Third, even if personnel specialists are marginalized, what part do personnel (or HRM) considerations play in the initiation and implementation of technical change in the late 1980s and 1990s? Finally, is the UK experience unique or is it mirrored to a large extent in Europe or the United States?

Who Needs Personnel Managers?

Three explanations might be offered for the nature of personnel specialists' involvement – or lack of it – in the 1980s:

1   It might be argued that considerations other than personnel 'naturally' will have a dominant influence over the choice and implementation of IT. Personnel's peripheral and reactive involvement is appropriate and only to be expected, given the focus on *technical* change.
2   This reactive role would have expanded at the implementation stage if employees and their representatives had opposed IT investment and its implications for jobs, pay and so forth. In practice this rarely occurred, as employees welcomed rather than resisted new technology.
3   Where resistance and opposition did occur, the role of personnel specialists was smaller than it might have been owing to the divisions and weakness of the opposition.

Let us examine each of these explanations in more detail.

Choice and the Status Quo

Investment in IT can take two forms. Either it can be regarded as a radical departure in response to prior choices about market positioning and the bases of competitive advantage, or it may be seen as part of an ongoing incremental process in the piecemeal updating of a technical system. British Telecom's investment in System X and Toyota, Nissan or Whitbread's greenfield site investments might be regarded as examples of the former; the addition of a single CNC machine into a conventional engineering job shop, or of a couple of word processors into an office using typewriters, as examples of the latter.

In the first case personnel specialists stand a chance of playing a proactive role, but only if they achieve representation and influence on the committees that are responsible for such strategic decision-making. Purcell, in interpreting the Warwick Company Level Survey data, suggests that personnel considerations appear to have greater prominence in strategic decision-making where *no* corporate personnel department exists, but where a main board director, whose primary responsibility is in personnel/industrial relations, sits on a personnel policy committee whose membership includes non-personnel senior managers, including the chief executive. Ironically, in this situation the management of personnel is vested more in the line than in specialist managers (Purcell, in Marginson et al, 1988: 76, 78–9). In such circumstances it is not surprising that personnel considerations, although more prominent, still weigh rather lightly in capital investment decisions, as most policy committee members, possibly including the personnel director, will have been socialized in the disciplines and concerns of other management functions. And, as Sorge and Streeck (1988: 39–40) point out, managements generally tend to picture a hierarchy of causal determination and decision-making criteria which runs from market to labour, not vice versa.

> For the management of a firm operating in a competitive market environment, product strategies have to follow the signals of the market, technology has to follow both product design and competitive (market) pressures for low production costs, and work organization has to be fitted to the adopted technology so that the resulting products can optimally exploit the opportunity structure of the market. Finally, how much and what kind of labour is hired, and at what price, is determined by the requirements of an optimal organization of work, and it is the task of collective bargaining to ensure that the labour market supplies exactly what the firm needs. Marketing, therefore, governs product and process engineering, and *these together control the manpower function, including collective bargaining, which is relegated to the receiving end of the managerial decision-making process.* (1988: 39; emphasis added)

While recognizing that this represents managements' ideal-typical model of a preferred decision-sequence rather than what always happens in a world of vested interests and political manoeuvre, it does suggest an interesting paradox about the role that personnel specialists are likely to play in strategic decision-making. A personnel director is likely to be most credible and influential precisely when, like colleagues from other functions, he or she has this taken-for-granted perspective of privileging the product market before the labour market and speaks their language. (This, of course, is the central message of 'hard' HRM.) This may well be the situation in those companies where Purcell finds personnel considerations taken most seriously in strategic decision-making. But, consider the evidence from the Warwick Company Level Survey that there seems to be an inverse relationship between the existence of a large corporate personnel department and the importance placed on personnel considerations in strategic decision-making. Apart from the other explanations Purcell offers (Purcell, in Marginson et al, 1988: 76–8), it might be argued, if we can equate such departments with the 'contracts manager' model of personnel management (Tyson and Fell, 1986), that this state of affairs occurs *precisely because* such specialists define their role as negotiators, and hence *place themselves* at the end of the decision-making chain.

Furthermore, evidence from the Warwick Survey suggests that decisions on new technology tend to take place at corporate and establishment levels – the corporate level being more likely to approve investment initiated at establishment level in the manufacturing sector, and actually to initiate the investment in the service sector (Martin, in Marginson et al, 1988: 167–70). Either way, intermediate organizational levels such as divisions appear to play a lesser role in deciding on investment in new technology. Yet, beside this finding, we must place the evidence that the large specialist personnel departments found at corporate and divisional level in heavily unionized firms have least influence on strategic decision-making at corporate level and most influence on decision-making at divisional level. This is precisely the level at which, according to the survey, decision-making about new technology is *least* likely to occur (Purcell, in Marginson et al, 1988: 76; Martin, in Marginson et al, 1988: 167–70). This again is suggestive of the marginalization of personnel specialists in decision-making at the initiation stage.

If, on the other hand, IT innovation is regarded as just part of an ongoing incremental process of technical updating, its choice, as an operating decision, is likely to be decentralized and vested firmly in the hands of the manufacturing or engineering functions (or administration or management services in the service sector) without any perceived necessity for personnel's initial involvement. In some ways such a situation is similar to the introduction of conventional technical change, where the 1984 WIRS survey found the lowest level of personnel involvement (13 per cent) of all the three types of change examined (Daniel, 1987: 109). In both situations, of strategic and piecemeal investment, a further factor may dictate personnel's low and reactive profile. Most managements, in theory, are reluctant to concede the 'right to manage', including the right to introduce new technology and working methods as and when they please. In this they have been supported by the politico-economic climate of the 1980s. Equally, unions seek to curb the unilateral exercise of this prerogative and, depending upon their market power and the organization's industrial relations style (see Price, 1988), have often secured some bargaining over major changes in production methods and, sometimes, even over capital investment. However, the fact remains that managements rarely *look* for an opportunity to negotiate, if change can be introduced unilaterally but without opposition (see, for example, Daniel, 1987: 113). Indeed the WIRS evidence suggests that consultation and negotiation tend to be a response to employee and union opposition to change rather than being initiated by managers to smooth the path of innovation.

The introduction of IT in the early and mid-1980s had precisely this characteristic. Hence a major reason for personnel's involvement – to negotiate – was unnecessary. It might be suggested then that in such circumstances other management groups would be reluctant to involve personnel in the early stages, even in a purely organizational design role, in case this was misinterpreted by the unions as a pre-existing managerial expectation that bargaining over change would inevitably take place.

Finally, if technical change is non-deterministic and choices can be made about appropriate forms of job and organizational design, it is equally possible – either deliberately or by default – to make minimal organizational changes. Child (1987: 121–2), for example, points out that cross-functional integration within or between roles may be discounted for various reasons; it may be thought necessary for legal reasons or those of expertise to leave specialist roles intact; or to retain a distinctive role recognizable in the external labour market for recruitment reasons; or internal opposition to disruption of traditional accountabilities and career paths may inhibit change. Furthermore, organizational inertia may be facilitated by the producers of new technologies and systems marketing their products on the basis of the ease with which they can be adapted to existing structures and systems. When, in spite of IT investment, few organizational changes are made, personnel's role will either appear passive (even if, on the contrary, the function has been a major protagonist for the status quo), or this image may well reflect a real lack of influence, or genuine passivity. Either way, personnel is likely to appear peripheral to IT innovation.

IT: Friend or Foe?

If, for reasons cited above, personnel specialists appear to have played little part in the choice of and planning for IT, nevertheless it might have been expected that a crucial role awaited them at implementation as facilitators or negotiators for the acceptance of technical change at plant level. Such an expectation rests on two questionable assumptions: that most plants introducing technical change possess personnel specialists and that such changes are likely to be negotiated. The evidence does not support either assumption. First, the WIRS surveys reveal that only a minority of establishments possess a designated personnel specialist (15 per cent in 1980 and 1984; 17 per cent in 1990). In this matter there is no difference between workplaces involved in technical change and those that are not, although the chances of a personnel specialist were highest in foreign-owned establishments, in those which recognized trade unions and in those which employed substantial concentrations of non-manual employees (see Daniel and Millward, this volume). If, at operational level, personnel specialists do not exist, their invisibility with regard to the 'grass roots' implementation of technical change is hardly surprising. Nevertheless, if negotiations were routine, the drafting in of personnel specialists from divisional or head office level might have been expected. But both survey and case study evidence would suggest that such traditional involvement has largely failed to materialize (for a summary of the research evidence, see Legge, 1989b: 37–9). Certainly, up to the mid-1980s, management felt little need to negotiate and not always to consult. As Daniel puts it,

> the pervasive management approach to the introduction of change affecting manual workers was quite simply *opportunist*. When managers wanted to make changes they simply set about introducing them and if they could get away with it without consulting anyone they did so. (1987: 285)

Managements' ability 'to get away with it' – so obviating the need for personnel specialists to act as negotiators – stems largely from the popularity of and lack of general resistance to technical change (see, for example, Northcott and Rogers, 1984; Edwards, 1985; Daniel, 1987; MacInnes, 1988; Smith, 1988 – all summarized in Legge, 1989b: 38–9). This may seem surprising at first sight given that such investment raises the *potential* if not the inevitability for deskilling, enhanced management control, truncated careers and loss of employment. However, survey and case study data (summarized in Legge, 1989b: 39–41) suggest in broad terms that for the majority of employees advanced technology has meant little change. Their jobs might have become marginally more skilled or skills may have changed, but little else has changed. Where changes have occurred, they have either been clearly positive (for example, increases rather than decreases in pay, possible enhanced job content) or where negative (as in the case of staffing reductions), at least not resulting in compulsory redundancy.

In a subsequent analysis, Daniel and Hogarth (1990) and Daniel and Millward (this volume) have provided some additional and convincing explanations to account for the popularity of technical change, although admittedly their data source derives from the survivors of technical change rather than the dispossessed. In their view, and in marked contrast with organizational change, the introduction of new technology tended to be associated with success. It was seen as representing

> progress and advance; the benefits of new and improved machines were concrete, manifest and demonstrable; they represented competitive advantage – the modernity of its technology symbolized the standing of a manufacturing workshop to all who knew the industry, both internally and externally; investment in new technology represented confidence in the future and hence improved longer-term job prospects and security; many features of new technology were familiar to workers and valued in their domestic and leisure lives; and, finally, the introduction of new technology tended to be an incremental and continuous process. (Daniel and Millward, this volume, p. 62)

The bare bones and general outlines of the survey data are brought to life by employees' experience as recorded in case studies. Although clearly more typical of non-manual workers' experience than that of manual workers', MacInnes' explanation of non-resistance in a large bank (1988) rings true. Banks have been using electronic technology for more than 20 years, and it was not obvious to staff that the latest introduction of microelectronics technology (for example, 'through the wall' cash dispensers, systems for automatic same-day clearance of cheques, and direct bank-to-retailer fund transfer) should be qualitatively different from earlier applications. Union representatives accepted the bank's arguments (with some scepticism in the light of its record profitability) that new technologies were essential in maintaining competitive advantage in the face of a deregulated financial sector and with increasing competition from building societies, insurance companies and City institutions. Introduction (between 1981 and 1984) came at a time when business levels were rising between 6 and 7 per cent per annum and, in the light of the bank's policy of restricting growth in staff numbers, work pressure in the branches could be intense. New technology – particularly cash dispensers – was welcomed as considerably relieving some of this work pressure. Furthermore, MacInnes reports, rather than deskilling work, new technology was seen as automating the more routine and repetitive aspects such as counting and checking. Perhaps most significantly, bank staff thought cash dispensers, giving a 24-hour service, would help defend existing opening hours under threat from building societies' six-day week, an issue of particular salience given the high number of married female employees. Not surprisingly, then, MacInnes found, via an employee survey, that 73 per cent of staff agreed that 'it's made my job easier', against only 6 per cent who agreed that 'it's made my job more boring'. Few staff felt that new technology threatened either their job security or nature of employment – 98 per cent thought that they had good job security, 77 per cent 'variety and interest'. Representatives on the joint consultation committee (JCC) took an overwhelmingly positive view of new technology: only two members criticized its technical aspects at all – about how staff were called out to refill machines – while an early discussion of cash dispensers in the JCC had union representatives pressing for their more rapid introduction (MacInnes, 1988: 135–6).

Wilson's (1988) account of the experience of CNC machines by apprentice-trained craftsmen in a large engineering company provides further insights from a very different workforce as to why new technology has been accepted with little resistance. Here one might have expected, union and employee opposition to the new technology, as the craftsmen most directly involved perceived that deskilling had taken place. Many operators complained that manual skills were less required, they no longer ground their own tools, or decided which tooling was to be used; on some machines the variety of work had been reduced while pressure had been intensified. Yet, at the same time, they recognized that they had acquired new and sought-after skills that for optimal use required their background knowledge of traditional machining. They now had to know how to prove new tapes; adapt parts of proved programs to new work; write parts of programs either deliberately or unconsciously omitted by the programmer; adjust machine speeds and feeds if quality of work was likely to be affected by those programmed; understand the machine controls and capabilities sufficiently, not only to operate it, but to prevent expensive smash-ups if the machine went wrong. From her rich interview data, Wilson reveals the ambiguous feelings of the craftsmen – of some regret for skill loss, combined with pride in new skills and their responsibilities towards what was perceived to be the company's élite machines and the high value-added components in their charge. Furthermore, the craftsmen recognized that these were the machines of the future, and that the company needed to introduce them to ensure the viability of the business and their jobs. Given the widespread introduction of such technology, operators perceived that learning such skills enhanced their own position in the labour market and increased their bargaining power (Wilson, 1988: 82). Where resistance was mounted it was informal and aimed at maintaining their effort–reward bargain by failing to cooperate fully with management's desire for enhanced flexibility and increased performance.

Opposition to IT: Divided We Fall

A third explanation may be offered for personnel specialists' lack of involvement even in implementing IT during the early to mid-1980s. Such opposition as *did* occur generally reflected union and employee divisions and market vulnerability. As such, resistance was informal and piecemeal, rather than concerted confrontation, calling for accommodations on the part of line management rather than personnel's routine involvement in formal collective bargaining and conflict resolution. Why then has potential union opposition either failed to emerge or remained at best low profile, at worst ineffective?

The Union Challenge   To begin with, it would be a mistake to consider that unions are implacably opposed to new technologies. Potentially, unions may adopt one of at least four stances *vis-à-vis* new technology: total opposition; concerted opposition; bargained acceptance; or total acceptance (Francis and Willman, 1980; see also Davies, 1986). Generally speaking, though, as many commentators have pointed out – citing, for example, the TUC's early document *Employment and Technology* (1979) – the union movement officially takes a positive view about accepting the technology itself. The general position is that investing in new technology to increase productivity (even at risk of short-term job loss) is essential for the long-term good of the economy and the guarantee of jobs. However, as negotiators, unions aspire to influence how IT is introduced. In particular, they are concerned to protect the jobs of existing members, to ensure that the pressure of work is not intensified, to protect and, if possible, enhance skill and pay levels while reducing hours of work, and to ensure that health and safety at work are safeguarded (Francis, 1986: 16). In addition, unions aim to be consulted, granted access to all relevant information and negotiate over new technology from the earliest stages and with the right of veto. Ideally such substantive and procedural aspirations may be pursued by the negotiation of a new technology agreement (NTA) (see, for example, Francis, 1986: 161–2; also Bamber, 1988: 206–8).

The evidence, as discussed earlier, is that it is the exception rather than the rule for managements to negotiate over new technology. Although NTAs have been signed (240 NTAs between 1977 and 1983 in the UK), the signing seems to have peaked in 1980 and at best mainly involved single bargaining units of public sector clerical workers (Williams and Steward, 1985). As Willman (1987a: 12) reports, there can be little doubt that by the mid-1980s the initiative to sign new technology agreements had run out of steam. The failure to achieve ideal-type NTAs in those relatively rare cases where negotiations have taken place can be attributed to the very real obstacles confronting unions in developing and sustaining a strong negotiating posture. Willman (1987b) provides a convincing analysis of some of the strategic and tactical issues involved. First, at the strategic level, there is the question of intra- and inter-union conflict involving issues of union organization and bargaining structure. Employees' lack of opposition to, not to mention positive welcome of, new technology not only undermines what bargaining hand their unions might otherwise have had, but places them in a cleft stick. WIRS 2 found that in a majority of plants where new technology had been introduced it was reckoned to have had no short-term impact on the numbers employed in the sections directly affected. However, when decreases did occur, particularly in manufacturing, they tended to be substantial. Where it had no impact, clearly employee opposition would not be expected on the grounds of job loss. However, even where job loss occurred, and particularly if compulsory redundancies were avoided, surviving employees could welcome the new investment as a guarantee against complete plant closure. As Willman puts it:

> Recessionary conditions highlight the ambivalent nature of trade union resistance to change, particularly cost-minimizing process change . . . wage increases may actually accelerate the rate at which capital is substituted for labour by changing relative factor prices. However, the inefficient retention of surplus labour may discourage investment. In extreme cases such costs may encourage disinvestment, or force closure (Prais, 1981). Where multi-plant firms are considering capacity reductions, plants may be in direct competition for new investment with other UK operations or with overseas plants. In such cases, companies may be in a position to extract concessions in return for 'granting' change rather than to pay a price for it. (1987b: 139)

The varying perceptions of investment or closure by employees and unions in multi-plant organizations are not conducive to intra- or inter-union solidarity. Within a single union the interests of the membership in different plants may vary, if one plant has been selected for investment and the other(s) for partial or total closure. In such circumstances, a divergence of interest is likely to occur, not only between the representatives of the different plants, but between the national leadership concerned with the future of the industry and the necessity to secure a future membership base, and local union representatives concerned with terms and conditions of employment and job security in particular plants. Furthermore, even within a plant designated for investment, and where employers are prepared to negotiate improved terms and conditions for enhanced craft skills, different groups of workers may have different interests. While skilled workers are likely to welcome pay negotiations, non-craft workers are unlikely to favour proposals that widen differentials. Management may exploit such divisions by appealing over the heads of workers' representatives directly to the members concerned, for example, through ballots on draft agreements (Martin, 1988: 111). If all grades are organized by one union, intra-union conflict may emerge or, if organized by craft and general unions, inter-union conflict. The potential for the latter type of conflict also arises over which union has the right to organize the 'new' jobs resulting from IT investment. The erstwhile electricians' union (EETPU) had a policy of resisting the transfer of 'its' work to other unions, while emphasizing its right to represent élite craft grades. The manual engineering union (AEU) stressed the right of its members to program CNC machine tools, in conflict with the position of the erstwhile technicians and supervisory union (TASS), claiming control over such work for its draughtsmen and white-collar grades. Severe inter-union conflict between printing and journalists' organizations has occurred over who has the right to operate new technology in the printing industry, not to mention the conflict between the print workers and the electricians at the new Murdoch plant at Wapping (Martin, 1981; Willman, 1987b: 143).

Investment in greenfield sites again raises the potential for intra- and inter-union conflict. If the investment is by an already established unionized firm, for each union the interests of those employed on the greenfield site have to be weighed against those of existing plants that will not receive new investment and against the risk that investment may not occur at all in the face of hard bargaining. If, however, the greenfield site represents inward investment by overseas companies, inter-union competition in order to secure respective membership bases is likely to occur. In such circumstances, rather than opposing the employer, unions are in competition with each other in offering the appropriate 'sweet heart' inducements (no-strike deals, for example) in order to secure sole negotiating rights (Willman, 1987b: 145). As Willman concludes, not only is it almost impossible for unions to negotiate over process change under the threat of closure or disinvestment (or non-investment), but the plant-level bargaining of the 1970s is highly inappropriate to deal with changes which are company- or industry-wide. Nor was an industrial climate marked by recession and the trumpeting of the virtues of the enterprise culture conducive to union confrontation and solidarity (1987b: 142).

Quite apart from intra- and inter-union divisions weakening the hand of union negotiators in that minority of cases where negotiation over new technology actually occurred, other factors – such as the nature of supplier relations, the technical expertise of managers, the nature of union involvement in innovation decisions and the absence of statutory support for bargaining of this kind – place union officials at a disadvantage in the negotiating process (for a discussion of these issues see Willman, 1987b: 147–9; Legge, 1989b: 45). This picture of little consultation and less (and, from a union point of view, ineffective) negotiation suggests that personnel specialists are in a cleft stick just as much as the unions. If there are no negotiations, the major role for a contracts manager type of personnel department in relation to new technology is eliminated. If, however, there is a substitute stress on consultation, communications, training and the development of a multi-skilled committed workforce, a human resource management approach, as will be discussed below, can result in line management again being identified as the key actor of *a* personnel function if not *the* personnel *department*.

The Informal Challenge If most employees welcome IT investment, and if, in the minority of cases where negotiations take place, the unions' position is far from strong, does any confrontation occur which might conceivably demand the involvement of personnel specialists? Clearly, in situations where employees perceive IT as accompanied by deskilling, enhancement of management control and labour intensification, negative attitudes are likely to develop. These may not be expressed in formal opposition owing to the union weaknesses already discussed. In this volume Collinson's chapter on the introduction of on-line processing in the insurance industry paints a vivid picture of clerical workers' informal resistance, through work avoidance and data manipulation, to the work intensification that accompanied such changes. But informal resistance cannot be totally discounted; in particular, where the risks/costs of error are high and where there is unpredictability in the task, employees are likely to have some room for manoeuvre in informally challenging managerial task definition and controls. Indeed, case studies by Wilkinson (1983) and Wilson (1988) of CNC operators provide illustrations of just such challenges.

The point about such forms of resistance, though, is that, even where they occur, they are unlikely to require the involvement of personnel specialists. There are several reasons for this. First, it is not clear that such challenges will be defined by management as 'resistance' and hence as an industrial relations problem. This is because the very situations that allow room for operators to reassert control in the face of deskilling are those of task unpredictability and high cost of error, where (a) management are likely to opt formally for some skill retention, or even enhancement – thus obviating the need for such 'challenges', or (b) failing that, to collude with operators' skill retention activities, such as informal programming and other adjustments, in order to manage uncertainties at the point of production. As Price (1988: 257) points out, where there is a tradition of cooperative industrial relations, managements will prefer to incorporate employee preferences, other things being equal, in order to 'take the workforce along with them'.

Secondly, even where such challenges are not obviated or condoned by management actions, employees' opposition may be taken lightly by management owing to perceptions of its inconsistency and fragmentation. Collinson's clerical workers coped with work intensification by unpaid overtime and working evenings and Saturdays, as well as engaging in work avoidance and data manipulation (see Chapter 8). Wilson's example (1988) neatly typifies a problem for workforces in developing a coherent strategy of opposition. In order to gain new skills and maintain a 'skilled' designation, it may be in the interests of employees to welcome 'flexible specialization'. But, in doing so, they may perceive an increase in labour intensification and hence a worsening of the effort–reward bargain. To maintain skills may involve taking initiatives that are not being paid for, as refusing to take initiatives and act flexibly may decrease the opportunities for skill acquisition and hence undermine the case for improving pay in the future. If, as a result, employees' challenges are inconsistent and frag-mented, line management may define each challenge as a separate incident and a problem of routine work flow administration rather than as a concerted workforce strategy requiring the assistance of the personnel department.

Plus ça change?

The analysis of personnel specialists' lack of involvement in the management of technical change, presented earlier, rests largely on research conducted in the early and mid-1980s, before HRM had become the flavour of the month and the notion of 'competitive advantage' had achieved the clichéd status that it enjoys today. But in the light of such developments, along with the 'boom–bust' climate of the late 1980s and early 1990s, has their involvement decreased, remained much the same or increased in recent years? Is it likely to change in different ways during the next decade? If there has been a change, how do we account for it?

It should be said at the outset that the data we have to answer these questions and develop speculations about future possibilities rest on three major sources: WIRS 3 (Millward et al, 1992) and studies by the Warwick Industrial Relations Research Unit (Storey, 1992a) and the Warwick Centre for Corporate Strategy and Change (see, for example, the chapter by Hendry in this volume). Other useful insights are appearing in case study based doctoral theses (e.g. Newell, 1991). But what is notable about much of the empirical research conducted in the late 1980s (see, for example, the majority of case study research published in the journal *New Technology, Work and Employment*) is a concern with the relationships between technological change and *outcomes* in areas such as flexible specialization, up/down skilling, employee commitment and employment levels (e.g. Burnes, 1988a; Davis, 1988; Shenkar, 1988; Phillimore, 1989; Lloyd, 1989; Wiedemeyer, 1989) rather than with the *processes* of initiation and implementation. Perhaps this is yet one more reflection of the values of the enterprise culture! That said, two findings emerge. First, while the evidence for the UK would suggest that personnel specialists are still marginalized in the management of hardware investment decisions and implementation, organizational changes, heavily dependent on IT software investment, have become explicitly imbued with HRM *considerations*. I refer here to the search for enhanced flexibilities in the interests of market responsiveness and cost-cutting, whether via teamwork, core–periphery strategies, delayering or JIT/TQM. Secondly, because such initiatives tend to be the projects of a revitalized and legitimized line management, they further marginalize personnel specialists.

The evidence for these assertions (from the WIRS series, see Chapter 3, this volume) is as follows. First, there has been no slackening in the pace of either organizational or technical change in 1990 as compared to 1984. Secondly, as already discussed, only a minority of establishments, even allowing a very forgiving definition, possess specialist personnel managers, and that only in the largest establishments. In the majority of workplaces, as in 1984, employee relations matters are dealt with on a local basis by general and line managers. To quote Daniel and Millward, 'on-site specialist personnel managers for dealing with the planning, implementation and aftermath of technical change are not at all widespread' (this volume, p. 67). This raises a real problem for personnel specialists' contribution at strategic level. In what sense can personnel specialists act strategically if other functions hold the operational reins? (These issues are discussed further in Chapters 4 and 8, this volume). Thirdly, the WIRS 3 survey evidence suggests that employee relations generally have increasingly become the province of line managers, while such personnel specialists as exist at establishment level have tended to become involved in a narrower range of concerns within this field, with their preoccupations moving away from trade union relations towards employment law. Sewell and Wilkinson's chapter in this volume paints a similar picture – of many of the traditional functions of personnel specialists being devolved to the line, while the remaining responsibilities become deskilled and subject to external control (see Chapter 7). Millward et al (1992) conclude that there were no differences between workplaces involved in technical change and those that were not, in terms of the presence of personnel specialists. (This contrasted sharply with the case of organizational change, for which there was a substantially greater chance of the presence of personnel specialists.) Finally, although informal discussions with employees about technical change appeared more widespread in 1990 than in 1984, an even smaller proportion of managers in 1990 than 1984 reported that technical change had been introduced in workplaces with recognized unions with the agreement of union representatives. Significantly, this represents a fall in the number of workplaces with any form of union representation between 1984 and 1990. The 1990 results also show that negotiation about the introduction of change was virtually confined to workplaces where support for the union(s) (as indicated by level of membership) was extremely high (Millward et al, 1992).

Storey's case study data (1992a) are highly consistent with the WIRS 3 findings and add additional flesh to the starkness of survey data. This research, conducted between 1986 and 1988, comprised a core of fifteen case studies of large, multi-site, multi-divisional private sector manufacturing (such as Ford, Whitbread, Smith and Nephew, Plessey) and key public sector organizations (for example, National Health Service and British Rail). Additionally, the research was informed by visits to 'panel' organizations where significant new management initiatives were reportedly taking place (for example, Birds Eye Walls – team working; Metal Box – strategic business units). With regard to the 'core' case studies, Storey (1992a: 20) aimed to examine organizations 'typical of the mainstream of British employment', rather than companies representing 'the exceptional, greenfield site, Japanese-owned, late arrivals'. With the aim of examining 'developments in the way the contemporary employment relationship is managed', he conducted interviews with 'vertical slices' of senior, middle and first-line line managers, supplemented by interviews with personnel specialists of equivalent levels (1992a: 19). His analysis, discussed below, derives from all these sources and so interestingly contains both personnel specialists' and line managers' views of their respective involvements in the management of change.

It is perhaps significant that Storey's respondents (and Storey himself, judging by the published text) have little to say specifically about personnel specialists' involvement with *technical* change. However, inferences can be made on the basis of comparing WIRS' and Storey's findings about personnel specialists' involvement with *organizational* change. In other words, if we accept from both sets of WIRS data that personnel specialists' involvement in organizational change was higher than their involvement in technical change, and if Storey (1992a: 164) finds personnel specialists' involvement with organizational change to be largely reactive, with 'few instances where personnel were apparently at the leading edge of change . . . even in those companies . . . moving ahead with major initiatives', then it is reasonable to infer that such managers' involvement in technical change has probably *not* become more central in the late 1980s.

Indeed, within his 'core' companies, Storey found four styles of personnel management prevailing – often with more than one style evident in a company. Using the dimensions of interventionary/non-interventionary and strategic/technical, he identified four styles: **advisers** (strategic/non-interventionary); **handmaidens** (tactical/non-interventionary); **regulators** (tactical/interventionary) and **change-makers** (strategic/interventionary). In general terms 'advisers' were those specialists who had withdrawn their physical presence from the day-to-day employee–management interface and concentrated, as internal consultants, on conjuring a climate that might facilitate employee relations directions envisaged by the line. 'Handmaidens' survived by providing services – often of a routine administrative/welfare nature at the behest of the line. In both these cases, although Storey does not provide specific examples, one cannot envisage anything more than a highly marginalized role for such specialists in relation to technical change.

The 'interventionist' roles Storey identifies offer more possibilities. The 'regulators', while interventionist, represent the classic 'contracts' type manager (Tyson and Fell, 1986), engaged as tacticians in devising, negotiating and defending the procedural and substantive rules which govern employment relationships, but rarely involved with issues of wider business strategy. Relating this to the WIRS 3 findings, it might be suggested that such personnel specialists' best chance of involvement with technical change might lie at the implementation stage in a negotiating role, *if* they are located in an organization where levels of union membership are high. We have already seen, however, that WIRS 3 found even less negotiation of technical change in 1990 than in 1984. Finally, there is the 'change-maker' role, of which Storey identifies two variants:

the 'hard' version, in which the personnel specialist subsumes personnel within the dominant business culture, and the 'softer' version that highlights the distinctive nature of personnel's input into the management team (cf. the early 'conformist' and 'deviant' innovator distinctions of Legge, 1978). In adopting such a posture, potentially a highly proactive, interventionary role could be envisaged for personnel specialists, with involvement in technical change from initiation onwards. Interestingly, though, Storey found that only two of his fifteen companies (Ford of Europe and Jaguar) had personnel specialist teams which approximate to the 'change-maker' style and these adopted the 'hard' rather than the more distinctively personnel 'soft' version (1992a: 182–6). From the HRM initiatives described in both companies (for example, employee involvement in Ford; extensive training, communications, new supervisory roles, TQM and quality circles in Jaguar), technical change might have been implicit in, but was not to the forefront of, personnel specialists' initiatives. Given the lack of negotiation over technical change, reported by WIRS 3, the fact that 'in most mainstream companies personnel had found it "safer" and more attractive to remain attached to the proceduralist symbolic realm' (1992a: 187) is not suggestive of any radically different posture on the part of personnel specialists in general than in the early to mid-1980s. Indeed, this judgement is reinforced when it is remembered that Storey's research focuses on just those organizations that have long been recognized as possessing strong specialist personnel/IR departments.

Plus c'est la même chose

In retrospect, it is easy to account for personnel specialists' continued marginalization in the management of technical change. First, the explanations in relation to the early to mid-1980s not only still hold, but have been reinforced by the return of severe recession and the continuing decay of unions' power and their marginalization in industrial and social life. New realism in industrial relations has lost its novelty and become a taken-for-granted fact of life after a decade of uninterrupted Conservative government. Secondly, the fact that personnel specialists may have retreated to non-interventionist roles (adviser, handmaiden), or stuck with a symbiotic relationship in which the host partner (unions) continues to grow weaker, is hardly a stance for developing a proactive role *vis-à-vis* technical change.

Around 1987/8 it might have been possible to propose a different scenario if (as presumably many of the electorate did) one had believed in the reality and stability of the Thatcher 'economic miracle'. It could have been argued that since July 1986, in response to growth, the levels of unemployment had fallen from their mid-1980s highs and were claimed to be below two million. Even allowing for a slow-down in the economy following the rise in interest rates from late 1988, it could have been argued that, assuming no major recession (who in those days could have anticipated German reunification and wild currency fluctuations and interest rate variations in leading capitalist countries?), the labour market was likely to tighten further in the 1990s owing to demographic trends and possible implications of the Single European Market. Indeed, it was noticeable, even as late as 1989, how lamentations about unemployment had given way to alarmist warnings from government and employers about impending skills shortages. In 1989, too, it may be remembered that Atkinson published his paper entitled 'Four stages of adjustment to the demographic downturn'. At that time an argument was presented (see Legge, 1989b: 50) that if tight labour markets re-emerged, in a context where the over-capacity of the 1970s (and hence threat of plant closure) was considered to have been largely eliminated, then it might have been expected that unions would have been in a position to adopt a more militant bargaining posture. And, as Legge continued in 1989:

> If inflation continues to grow at a time when employers attempt to combat high interest rates by a vigilant control of costs, employees may well find for the first time since 1982 that real incomes are no longer rising. In this combination of circumstances memberships may be supportive of their unions' adoption of a strong negotiating stance and employers may find their erstwhile ability to avoid negotiating technical change undermined. In other words, if the labour supply situation becomes problematical, unions and 'contract manager' personnel specialists at plant or divisional level may be in a position to resume a modified version of their symbiotic relationship of the 1970s. It may be remembered that the Warwick Company Level survey found negotiation over new technology to be more common where plants were operating at full capacity (Martin, in Marginson et al, 1988: 181). If the economy escapes recession, a combination of inflation, high interest rates and tightening labour market could well increase the levels of involvement of a 'contracts manager' style personnel specialist at the implementation stage of IT. (1989b: 50)

As we all know, the economy did *not* escape recession and, from an employers' point of view, the only problematic issue in relation to the *numerical* labour supply has been plant closures and business failure. Whether there is any likelihood that the relationshps posited in the 1989 quotation are likely to re-emerge in the 1990s will depend on two factors. First, that there occurs an economic up-turn that is relatively enduring. This is highly problematic in the UK given the size of its manufacturing base and consequent structural deficit, not to mention the uncertainties embedded in the global economy and the geo-political order, such as the transition of non-market to market economies in Eastern Europe, German reunification, foreign debt etc. Secondly, that union institutions regain their vitality and centrality. Although Storey (1992a: 258–9) suggests that, on the basis of his research, there was

> little evidence of any forthright move to abandon pluralism in favour of a wholehearted commitment to an individualistically based human resource programme [and that] . . . some adopted a stance which, in effect, was designed to safeguard at least a modicum of trade union representation and collective negotiation from the more rampant aspirations of their line and general manager colleagues,

the smart money is definitely elsewhere. Storey went on:

But an alternative position was taken by at least an equal, if not indeed a greater proportion of the personnel and IR specialists interviewed. This was to profess prime interest in the new initiatives and markedly to downplay the significance and even the legitimacy of trade union representation and collective relations. They argued that competitive pressures had made unavoidable an approach which valued flexibility, leanness, learning and commitment. Personnel was seen as central to bringing about this profile and this was to be achieved through initiatives on training, selection, appraisal, new reward systems and the like. Some went so far as to state that when measured against this agenda the 'old obsessions' with unions and contracts and grievance procedures were essentially 'irrelevant'. (1992a: 259)

Such evidence, as Storey (1992a: 258) suggests, points to 'a downplaying of [trade unions'] status and significance' rather than a resurgence. Furthermore, those specialists that maintained a 'contracts manager' or 'regulator' type role were often labelled as 'the custodians of procedure' and *'their vested interests were made suspect'* (1992a: 259, emphasis added). (Significantly, the Warwick Company Level Survey of 1985 found a negative relationship between the influence of personnel considerations on strategic decision-making and union recognition, although the latter correlated strongly with the existence of large specialist personnel departments at corporate or divisional level.) An increasing emphasis on devolved management and the creation of strategic business units further undermines proceduralism through the 'loosening of uniform control rules' and the 'dismantling of company-level bargaining machinery' (1992a: 195–6). At the same time it calls into question the rationale for large corporate or divisional personnel departments whose prime function has traditionally been to act as gatekeepers to union advances and manage the institutional framework of industrial relations (Purcell, in Marginson et al, 1988: 79).

Enter HRM?

While personnel *specialists* may continue to play a marginal role in relation to technical change, this is not the end of the story. There is a growing body of evidence from the mid-1980s onward, chiefly emerging from case studies originating in the Warwick Centre for Corporate Strategy and Change and the Industrial Relations Research Unit, that personnel – or HRM – *considerations* are increasingly recognized in the initiation and implementation of organizational changes that are rooted in technical change. Investment in IT lies at the heart of initiatives redolent of the buzz words of the enterprise culture: quality, flexibility and customer responsiveness. Initiatives have taken two major forms: those in operational management (such as TQM, MRP, JIT and CAM) and those in organizational design (not just the development of new team-based work systems, consequent on the operations management changes, but strategic initiatives such as decentralization to single business units and the 'delayering' of swathes of middle management 'support' staff, redefined as 'overhead'). Both types of change are designed to serve similar if potentially incompatible ends: cost-cutting, quality enhancement and increased flexibility and customer awareness both inside and outside increasingly permeable organizational boundaries.

By way of exemplar, the relationship between decentralization, 'downsizing' (cuts in staff numbers at all levels), 'delayering' (reducing the number of levels in the hierarchy), technical change and HRM considerations may be explored further. As many commentators (e.g. Drucker, 1988) have pointed out, IT, through its information capture, storage, manipulation and distribution capacities, allows the number of management levels and numbers of managers, erstwhile largely engaged in manually serving the information requirements of large centralized bureaucracies, to be cut drastically. The impetus for such 'downsizing' has been provided by the perceived need to cut costs (for example, in banking, see Cressey and Scott, 1992); for delayering, to achieve greater customer responsiveness (for example, in BP and BT). Usually the two pressures go hand in hand. A corollary is often devolved accountability, with the creation of Strategic Business Units, target-setting, introduction of multi-faceted performance indicators and devolved budgeting – aspects of the tight–loose control advocated by such gurus of excellence as Peters and Waterman (1982) – all reliant on sophisticated data bases and flows facilitated by IT.

The HRM implications of decentralization, downsizing and delayering are massive. First, there is the task of managing redundancy and potential morale problems during restructuring. Secondly (as will be discussed further below), devolved accountability to operational line managers is likely to necessitate new training and development initiatives to equip them to perform wider, team-based, more generalized and commercially orientated roles. Evidence would suggest that for the *surviving* middle managers, at least in the short term, job enrichment is more likely (see Dopson and Stewart, 1990) than the grim predictions of truncated career patterns due to flatter structures (Drucker, 1988). Nevertheless, decentralization, downsizing and delayering, in theory at least, raise a third issue: the re-examination of a host of interrelated personnel policies, ranging from career paths and issues of succession to development, appraisal, performance-related pay and so on. This underlines a more general point: that HRM considerations are likely to permeate technically based organization changes if the latter are considered (a) to be part of a general business strategy rather than an ad hoc development, (b) to involve staff deployment issues critical to delivering the business objectives of the business strategy.

The findings that have emerged from the research programmes of Pettigrew's and Hendry's teams on strategic change and on changing patterns of human resource management in banking, retail, computer supply and manufacturing sectors (see Hendry and Pettigrew, 1987; Hendry and Pettigrew, 1988; Hendry et al, 1988; Pettigrew et al, 1988; Hendry, 1991) and in merchant banking, life insurance, motor manufacture and book publishing (Pettigrew and Whipp, 1991) suggest that IT investment goes hand in hand with new concepts of service provision or work organization that demand new skills, knowledge and capability from shopfloor, supervisory and managerial staff. While acknowledging the still unresolved debate as to whether HRM really differs from personnel -management (see Legge, 1989a), *if* it is accepted that, in theory at least, HRM involves an integration of personnel policies and activities with business decisions, one might expect HRM considerations to weigh heavily in IT investment decisions, assuming such investment is regarded as an important tool in achieving competitive advantage. Indeed, in three of the case studies for which we have reports – TSB, Halfords and GKN Hardy Spicer – IT investment was crucial in the updating of process technology and, in further cases of computing suppliers, their very business was IT.

The evidence presented by Hendry, Pettigrew and their colleagues serves, if anything, to reinforce the picture and interpretations that emerge from the earlier Warwick Company Level Survey. Clearly human resource considerations are raised at the initiation stage when changes in IT products and investment in IT processes are mooted as part of business strategy – the GKN Hardy Spicer case in particular illustrates this – but the extent to which traditional personnel specialists are involved in such policy-making is questionable. The research team's observations all point to HRM, particularly at policy-making levels, becoming the province of managers with a high degree of business credibility – a credibility not always found in personnel departments. Significantly, they state:

> For personnel functions there is not just an issue of developing skills in new areas but also one of needing to link together business, technical and HRM skills. Our research suggests that there is unfortunately a shortage of people with such skills and competencies within firms. The problem, however, is not just the shortage of people with sufficient skills and competencies: it is also one of recognizing the legitimacy of HRM. Putting capable personnel professionals into punishing environments is not a successful strategy. *For this reason, the trend detectable in some firms towards putting line managers into the most senior positions to oversee the personnel function, may represent a breakthrough in the acceptance of HRM issues at the highest level.* (Hendry et al, 1988: 41, emphasis added)

More recent evidence from Storey's research (1992a) confirms this picture. First, in his 'core' companies HRM was becoming increasingly vested in senior and middle line management, not just as a delivery mechanism for new approaches in employee relations, but as 'the designers and drivers of the new ways' (1992a: 194). In Smith and Nephew, Ford, Bradford City Council and Peugeot–Talbot, senior management were increasingly giving HRM issues a high profile in their general deliberations on business strategy, while, at the same time, maintaining that personnel policy itself had been taken over by the executive (1992a: 172, 204). As a director of manufacturing at Peugeot–Talbot UK stated:

> The central personnel function is now basically a co-ordinating activity. The personnel director leads for us in the formal negotiations with the trade unions. But on the major policy shifts in areas such as communications, management,

quality, team building, problem-solving teams and the like, these are matters for the executive.

Secondly, the major initiatives undertaken to achieve competitive advantage were often rooted in technical change generally and in IT specifically (TQM, MRP, JIT, organizational designs which place operatives in teams or created 'cells', computer-aided manufacture). Thirdly, the prime movers in both initiating and managing such change were manufacturing managers rather than the 'notably reticent' 'foot-dragging' personnel specialists (1992a: 194). Indeed, there was a general recognition by both personnel specialists and line managers of this state of affairs. Just as the personnel director of a manufacturing company acknowledged:

> I have to admit that TQM and the Top Management Workshops represent two of the main thrusts in our management development strategy and, to be perfectly honest with you, they are now the major planks in our human resource strategy as a whole. You are correct in saying that neither of them was launched by us. We sort of inherited them . . .

so, in one of the process companies, a manufacturing manager, referring to issues surrounding the introduction of TQM, MRP II and the achievement of enhanced flexibility stated: 'I don't see that personnel helped us in this!' (1992a: 183, 201). The vesting in line management of HRM initiatives rooted in technical change, Storey argues (1992a: 196), reflects the 'crucial fusion' of devolved management and the non-proceduralized approach of HRM, with its emphasis on direct communications with employees, participation and involvement, hands-on management style, on-the-job coaching and development.

On the one hand, the creation of cost and profit centres (SBUs) at lower levels within organizations, as suggested earlier, has given line management both a broader remit and enhanced legitimacy as the key contributor to the 'bottom line'. In many of Storey's case study organizations, the old-style, technically orientated, reactive 'progress chasing' production manager has been transformed into a proactive (albeit technically orientated) 'manufacturing manager' 'actively seek[ing] to find new ways of reducing costs, or improving quality and of deploying labour, materials and plant in new configurations which will add value to the processes in hand' (1992a: 198). In some cases this transformation has gone one step further, with the manufacturing manager evolving into a proactive, but commercially orientated 'business manager', aware of the total organization and its interface with the wider environment of customers and suppliers, 'competent in SWOT analysis, planning, target-setting, finance, marketing and the management of change' (1992a: 198). In both cases, line managers have increasingly become generalists, directing a team of support functions towards the achievement of business goals. As Storey quotes the director of manufacturing at Peugeot–Talbot: 'Manufacturing manager is king' (1992a: 202).

This transformation, in itself, has given line management the responsibility for a wider mix of employees and for the management of change.

This in turn brings human resource issues higher up line management's agenda as the IT-dependent new initiatives in operations management and organizational design, already referred to, have implications for a whole host of HRM issues such as recruitment, selection, training and achieving attitudes and behaviours that deliver the required quality and flexibilities. As Storey points out, line management is both the object of HRM-inspired initiatives in such areas as well as the designer and deliverer of its repercussions to the shopfloor.

Conclusions

The evidence appears incontrovertible that, as a general rule, in the 1980s and early 1990s the role of personnel specialists in relation to technical change has been marginal. It would also suggest that this state of affairs is likely to persist. The reasons are not hard to find and may be summarized as follows:

At the **initiation** stage:

- When IT investment is perceived as strategic it tends to be within a decision-making perspective that prioritizes concerns of the product market over those of labour supply. The 'contracts manager' style of personnel specialist, characteristic of large corporate personnel departments, is seen as pre-eminently concerned with issues that by this logic are at the end of the decision-making chain. Hence involvement at the initiation stage is seen – often by personnel specialists themselves – as inappropriate or unnecessary.
- Where IT investment is regarded as routine, personnel specialists have no 'natural' involvement in what are taken-for-granted operating decisions of line management.

This delays any potential involvement of personnel specialists until the implementation stage.

At the **implementation** stage:

- Many employees have welcomed rather than resisted IT, regarding its benefits as far outweighing its potential costs.
- For this reason unions' potential bargaining position over the introduction and implementation of IT is undermined. It is further weakened by a range of socio-political, market and institutional factors.
- As a result, negotiating over IT has been the exception rather than the rule, again excluding the 'contracts manager' style of personnel specialist.
- Where informal resistance has occurred to the way in which IT has been implemented, it is suggested that this may readily be defined as a workflow systems problem and thus the responsibility of line management rather than personnel specialists.

- Where managements have sought through consultation, team-building and training to develop employee commitment and optimal utilization of new technologies, this has often been in the context of devolved management and the revitalization and legitimization of line management, transformed into 'manufacturing' or 'business' managers eager to experiment with non-proceduralized approaches to managing change (Storey, 1992a). In these circumstances HRM *considerations* in relation to technical change – albeit rarely as systematically as the prescriptive texts might advocate (1992a: 188, 315) – are increasingly important, but as *an executive and line management rather than personnel specialist concern*. Furthermore, Storey's research (1992a: 185) would suggest that where non-proceduralized HRM approaches are adopted, any residual role for personnel specialists may be under threat from specialists perceived by the line as possessing more relevant expertise, such as the public relations department or external consultants.

Some qualifications must be made to these broad conclusions. Clearly there *are* exemplar cases where personnel specialists are centrally involved in the management of the organizational aspects of technical change. Hendry's chapter on GKN Hardy Spicer, Preece's on Venture Pressings, and Clark's on Pirelli Aberdare (Chapters 4, 5 and 6, this volume) show what 'change-maker' personnel specialists can contribute. (Equally, though, McLoughlin's research described in Chapter 9, and Bessant's in Chapter 10, suggest that these are the exceptions rather than the rule.) There is also some evidence that the contribution of personnel specialists may be underestimated. While they may not be involved in the decision to invest, the recruitment and training standards already achieved and the existing employee relations climate may be taken account of implicitly in investment decisions without any overt participation of the personnel department (see Chapter 4). Furthermore, personnel specialists in the interests of achieving line cooperation in and ownership of organizational changes that accompany technical change, and to secure their place as 'one of the business team', may deliberately downplay their functional contribution while highlighting that played by the manufacturing managers (see Chapters 4 and 5). Certainly there is plenty of research evidence, quite apart from chapters in this volume (see especially Clark's discussion of Pirelli Aberdare, Chapter 6, and Bessant's of Factory 2000, Chapter 10) to suggest that personnel or HRM *considerations* in technical change are being taken very seriously indeed. In a sense this is inevitable as the 'software' aspects of technical change become increasingly prominent in the search for competitive advantage.

How far these conclusions can be generalized is debatable. Storey's Warwick-based research probably exaggerates the extent to which both personnel specialists and HRM considerations are involved in technical change in the UK, dealing as it does with large sophisticated 'household name' companies. Whether the findings can be generalized to similar organizations in Europe and the United States is even more questionable, given their differing personnel management/IR traditions and institutions. Exemplar Scandinavian case studies of the 1970s and US 'excellence' stories of the 1980s are no basis for generalization. Unfortunately, given the prevalent focus of European and US (as well as UK) studies of technical change on outcomes rather than processes, there is not as yet the empirical evidence to draw meaningful conclusions, let alone comparisons.

PART II

HUMAN RESOURCE MANAGEMENT AND TECHNICAL CHANGE IN PRACTICE

3

Findings from the Workplace Industrial Relations Surveys

W.W. Daniel and Neil Millward

This chapter is based on data from three large-scale surveys of around 2000 British workplaces undertaken in 1980, 1984 and 1990.[1] When the Workplace Industrial Relations Survey (WIRS) series was planned, we had two main purposes in mind. The first was to establish an empirical basis for measuring and analysing change in workplace industrial relations over time. In each of the surveys in the series core questions were asked about such matters as trade union representation, membership and recognition; pay bargaining; communication and consultation; and about management organization for industrial relations. We now have the answers for each of the first three surveys (Millward et al, 1992).

The second purpose was to provide a framework within which new substantive issues could be introduced in each of the surveys. The theme adopted for the 1984 survey was the use and introduction of what was then the still relatively new microelectronics technology. The questions on new technology in the 1984 survey were the subject of separate analysis and resulted in a companion volume published alongside the main source book (Daniel, 1987). The expectation in 1984 was that we would drop the new technology module and move on to other themes in the next and subsequent surveys. But when we came to design the 1990 survey we decided to retain a limited number of the questions on technical change from 1984, for two reasons. First, a number of members of the social and economic research community found the data interesting and useful and there were requests from those sources for key questions to be repeated. Secondly, we found the section on technical change particularly valuable as an anchor for our data on consultation and participation. We had included in each of the surveys a number of general questions on forms of consultation and communication used at workplaces. But we found that the answers to particular questions on the types of consultation used in the event of specific changes, and the extent of joint regulation of such changes, served as invaluable complements to answers to the general questions.

Because the questioning on technical change was more full in the 1984 WIRS, the bulk of the analysis in this chapter is based on the results of that survey. We draw on the results of the 1990 survey to supplement the basic analysis in two ways; first, to update the findings of the 1984 survey on such matters as the extent of different kinds of change; and secondly, to see whether, where that was possible, relationships and associations that emerged in the earlier analyses continued to apply.

The Nature of the Questions

Each of the surveys in the WIRS series consists of a set of face-to-face interviews in a nationally representative sample of workplaces across virtually all sectors of the British economy. The main respondent in each workplace is the senior manager responsible for personnel or industrial relations matters, but where appropriate there are also interviews with employee representatives, usually from trade unions. Only very small workplaces (with less than 25 employees) are excluded from the series.

For the design of our questions on new technology in the 1984 WIRS we drew heavily upon the work of Jim Northcott and his colleagues at the Policy Studies Institute (PSI). In the early 1980s he established a series of surveys on the adoption of microelectronics technology in UK manufacturing industry which provided the principal source of information on the microelectronic revolution in that sector.[2]

In addition, we decided that if we were going to analyse different aspects of a particular form of technical change, we needed also to look at other types of change. We therefore distinguished between three forms of change. For ease of reference, we retrospectively attached the labels advanced technical change, conventional technical change and organizational change to the three different forms when discussing them in our analysis.[3] The labels were not used in the interviews with managers – only the descriptions on a card with a different letter to identify each type of change. The three distinct forms of change affecting manual workers were described as follows:

A **Advanced technical change**
    The introduction of new plant machinery or equipment that includes microelectronic technology (including computer-controlled plant, machinery or equipment)
B **Conventional technical change**
    The introduction of new plant, machinery or equipment, not including microelectronics (excluding routine replacement)
C **Organizational change**
    Substantial changes in work organization or working practices not involving new plant, machinery or equipment.

Our initial question to managers was whether any of these forms of change had occurred at their establishment in the preceding three years. If this was so we asked further questions about the most recent change, prioritized as above. When we identified a particular change episode we asked a series of questions about that episode. The questions were designed to establish levels of management decision-making about the change; the extent of consultation with workers and their representatives; the impact of the change upon earnings, staffing and job content; and the reactions of different groups to the change (Daniel, 1987). Similar questions were asked about changes affecting office workers (clerical, secretarial, administrative and typing staff).

When we decided to include questioning on different types of change in the survey, we expected that we would be using the results to put the microelectronic revolution into perspective. We did not expect that the form of change would make any intrinsic difference to, for instance, the reactions of the workers affected or of trade union representatives to the change. Previous research and writing on technical and other forms of exchange led us to expect that reactions would be chiefly shaped by two sets of influence. The first concerned the content of the change, especially its implications for levels of pay and earnings; for the number of people employed in the section or sections affected, but also at the workplace generally; and for the nature of jobs in terms of both the physical conditions of working and the levels of skill, autonomy and responsibility provided by jobs. Secondly, we expected that the methods adopted to introduce the change would be important. Here we were thinking principally of the forms and extent of communication and consultation and the extent to which change was introduced through agreement. We conceived of the form of the change, whether it took the form of an advanced technical change, a conventional technical change or an organizational change, as essentially its *packaging*. The packaging might influence initial reactions owing to preconceptions, but such first impressions were likely to be superficial and of little importance relative to the more substantive issues. In short, we expected to conclude our analysis by showing that microelectronic change was intrinsically no different from other forms of change that had been endemic in industry for the previous 20 years or more. In so far as we did find differences in relation to the form of change, we expected those to be a consequence of the differential implications of the change for earnings, employment and job content or of the different strategies adopted by managers to introduce different forms of change.

In the event, our expectation that the form of change would have no intrinsic impact could not have been more misplaced. One of the major findings of the technical change analysis was that there were marked differences in reactions to different types of change that were independent of any other features of the change. Indeed, the form of change emerged as a principal source of independent variation in the analysis. Reactions to technical change emerged as consistently and substantially more favour-

Table 3.1 The extent of major change affecting manual workers in the previous three years, 1984 and 1990

	All sectors (%)			Private manufacturing industry (%)		
	1984		1990	1984		1990
	All workplaces	Workplaces with 25+ manual workers	Workplaces with 25+ manual workers	All workplaces	Workplaces with 25+ manual workers	Workplaces with 25+ manual workers
Any of the three forms of change						
Proportion of workplaces experiencing change	37	47	53	65	69	66
Proportion of manual workers employed at workplaces experiencing change	57	60	63	78	79	77
Advanced technical change						
Proportion of workplaces experiencing change	15	22	23	31	36	41
Proportion of manual workers employed at workplaces experiencing change	32	35	35	53	55	56
Base: establishments employing manual workers as specified in column headings (n)						
Unweighted	1,853	1,423	1,401	580	538	575
Weighted	1,749	985	954	412	321	345

able than reactions to organizational change, independently of the content of the respective changes.

The Rate of Change for Manual and Non-manual Workers: 1984 and 1990 Compared

The 1984 WIRS demonstrated just how far change had become a feature of workplaces and part of the working lives of employees across all sectors of employment. Office workers in service industries were affected as much as manual workers in manufacturing industry. Each of the three types of change that we identified was common, and workplaces often experienced a combination of all three. The 1990 survey confirmed that the overall rate of change was maintained in the intervening years though the balance between the different types of change altered slightly.

Table 3.1 summarizes the results for manual workers from the 1984 and 1990 surveys. In each case the figures refer to technical or organizational changes that took place in the previous three years. The most appropriate basis for the comparative analysis is workplaces with 25 or more manual workers.[4] The proportion of such workplaces experiencing any of the three forms of change rose from 47 to 53 per cent. As would be expected, changes were more common in larger workplaces and the proportion of manual workers employed at workplaces introducing any of the three forms of change rose from 60 to 63 per cent. The rate of advanced technical change was similar at each of the two points in time, about a quarter of workplaces being affected by it.

Change affecting manual workers was most common in private manufacturing industry, which employs manual workers most frequently. In that sector, the overall rate of change remained about the same while the rate of advanced technical change increased slightly. Indeed, in larger manufacturing plants – those with 100 or more employees – advanced technical change affecting manual workers was the norm, involving 55 per cent of plants in 1990; three-quarters of large manufacturing plants had experienced one or other of the two types of technical change. Thus the manufacturing case studies in Chapters 4, 5, 6 and 7 illustrate a normal situation in these sorts of plant, not an atypical one.

The broad picture of a constant or slightly increasing rate of change also emerged from our analysis of non-manual workers (see Table 3.2). There did appear, however, to be differences in the patterns between the public and the private sectors. In 1984 the rate of change affecting office workers was higher in the private than the public sector and that was particularly true for change involving computers or word processors. But in the intervening years the rate of change increased quite sharply in the public sector while it slackened slightly in the private sector. These differences may, of course, have been a result of a time lag in the adoption of personal computers and word processors in the public sector. The overall effect was to produce a slight increase in the rate of change for non-manual workers.

Table 3.2 *The extent of major change affecting non-manual workers in the previous three years, 1984 and 1990*

	All sectors (%)			Private sector (%)		
	1984		1990	1984		1990
	All workplaces	Workplaces with 25+ non-manual workers	Workplaces with 25+ non-manual workers	All workplaces	Workplaces with 25+ non-manual workers	Workplaces with 25+ non-manual workers
Any of the three forms of change						
Proportion of workplaces experiencing change	49	63	67	53	67	64
Proportion of manual workers employed at workplaces experiencing change	71	74	73	72	77	70
Advanced technical change[1]						
Proportion of workplaces experiencing change	35	49	52	41	57	52
Proportion of non-manual workers employed at workplaces experiencing change	61	65	60	66	71	58
Base: establishments employing non-manual workers as specified in column headings (n)						
Unweighted	2,010	1,547	1,581	1,185	878	1,048
Weighted	1,985	1,012	1,004	1,260	614	665

[1] Involving word processing or computing.

Table 3.3   *Types of change introduced in the previous three years affecting manual and non-manual workers, 1984 and 1990*

	Manual workers (%)		Non-manual workers (%)	
	1984	1990	1984	1990
Advanced technical change	22	23	49	52
Conventional technical change	24	—[1]	20	—
Technical change of either kind	37	40	57	55
Organizational change	23	29	20[2]	41[3]
No change	53	47	37	33
Base: establishments employing 25 or more workers of the type specified (*n*)				
Unweighted	1,423	1,401	1,547	1,581
Weighted	985	954	1,012	1,004

[1] Not asked separately in 1990.
[2] Question asked only in relation to 'office workers'.
[3] Question asked in relation to all non-manual workers.

Table 3.3 provides a little more detail on the extent of the different types of change recorded by the two surveys. Although separate questioning about conventional technical change was dropped in 1990,[5] the figures suggest that both types of technical change affected manual workers in similar proportions over both periods. For non-manual workers, the pace of technical change remained the same, but the figures suggest that technical change increasingly involved computers or word processors. Organizational changes became more common for both manual and non-manual workers. The increase looks particularly marked for non-manual workers. This is partly explained by the way in which the group referred to was confined to 'office workers' in 1984 but expanded to include all non-manual workers in 1990. But there is no doubt that an increase did occur and that it was particularly marked in the public sector.

Perhaps the most striking feature shown by Table 3.3 is the extent to which, by 1990, change was more common among non-manual than manual workers. Traditionally. technical change was conceived of as a phenomenon that principally affected manual workers. Now it more frequently affects non-manual workers. In 1990, 55 per cent of workplaces experienced technical change among non-manual workers compared with 40 per cent of workplaces with technical change affecting manual workers.

Types of Workplace Involved in Major Technical Change

A broad picture of the types of private sector workplace most commonly affected by major technical change is given in Table 3.4. Technical change (of either of our two types) affected 50 per cent of all workplaces in the period 1987–90. It affected 66 per cent of manufacturing plants, over 75 per

Table 3.4 *Proportion of workplaces experiencing (a) microelectronics-related technical change and (b) any major technical change, in 1987–90 by various characteristics of workplaces*

	Microelectronic technical change (%)	Any major technical change (%)
All workplaces	41	50
Private sector	41	51
Manufacturing	50	66
Manufacturing plants employing 100 or more	69	78
Services	36	45
'High tech' industry	55	60
Not 'high tech'	39	51
Ownership		
Independent establishment	25	40
Branch of larger organization	45	55
Head office	50	51
Foreign-owned	43	54
UK-owned	40	51
Size of workplace		
25–99 employees	34	46
100–499	59	67
500 or more	75	79
Size of enterprise		
25–500 employees	32	46
500–4,999	44	53
5,000 or more	50	60
Union recognized	46	59
No recognized union	36	46
Workforce composition		
Percentage of workforce manual		
70+	22	38
31–70	52	62
0–30	55	58

cent of those with 100 or more employees and 60 per cent of workplaces in 'high technology' industries (Butchart, 1987). Larger workplaces and workplaces belonging to larger enterprises were affected in a clear majority of cases and, partly because they tend to be larger plants, so were the majority of unionized plants. Plants belonging to foreign-owned companies were slightly more affected than UK-owned plants. Those employing a high proportion of manual workers were substantially less likely to be affected by technical change.

Within this broad picture, it is clear that the plant-based case studies reported in later chapters are ones that have characteristics that make them especially likely to have experienced technical change. Although they each have their particular characteristics and histories, they fit into the dominant pattern of technical change, rather than being maverick examples that have little relevance to the broad sweep of industry and commerce.

Worker Support for Technical Change

As explained above, after we had identified particular technical change episodes in our WIRS interviews with both managers and worker representatives, we asked them a series of questions about the episode. At the end of the sequence we asked what the reactions of different categories at the workplace had been, including the workers directly affected by the change, their first-line managers, their shop stewards, if any, and full-time union officers if they became involved.

Figure 3.1 shows managers' accounts of the reactions of the workers involved to technical changes, both advanced and conventional. It is immediately apparent that support was reported in the large majority of cases of all types of technical change. In many cases the support was described as *strong*. For instance, support from the manual workers directly affected was reported for 85 per cent of conventional technical changes affecting manual workers, this support being described as strong in the majority of the cases. Slightly less support was reported for advanced technical changes, but it remained the case that reactions were described as favourable in nearly 80 per cent of cases. Managers' accounts of the reactions of office workers to technical change revealed even higher levels of support. Accounts of strong resistance to technical changes were very rare.

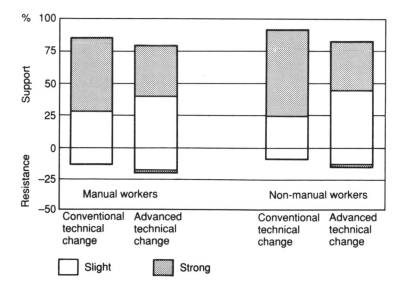

Figure 3.1 *Worker reactions to technical change* (all figures in this chapter are based on 1984 survey data)

Comparisons of managers' accounts of the reactions of different categories of employee to technical change were initially slightly misleading. For instance management respondents' reports of the reactions of the four different employee groups to advanced technical changes affecting manual workers are given in Figure 3.2(a). It shows that support was most wholehearted among first-line managers, as would be expected, although it is noteworthy that there were nearly as many among this group with reservations as among the affected manual workers themselves. Thereafter, Figure 3.2(a) gives the impression that there was less support among shop stewards and even less among full-time union officers, *where they became involved.* But our further analysis revealed that this qualification was critical. The further analysis showed that both full-time officers and shop stewards were more likely to become involved in the more problematic cases. When we confined our comparison of the reported reactions of the different groups to the cases in which union officers became involved, we found the picture revealed in Figures 3.2(b) and (c). It is apparent that, even according to the accounts of managers, the general level of support from shop stewards was similar to that from the workers affected and the support from full-time officers was greater than that from the workers. The picture was completed with the help of our interviews with shop stewards., They reported a higher level of personal support for particular technical changes than the support received from the workers affected (see Figure 3.7 below).

Overall, the balance of our evidence pointed to widespread support for technical changes, including advanced technical changes, among both manual and non-manual workers – and even stronger support from their trade union representatives.

In the light of different reactions to our evidence on the extent of worker support for technical change, we need to emphasize a number of points at this stage. First, as will have been clear from our account of the structure of questioning, the results are not based upon attitudinal data. The results are based upon accounts of particular, identified events. In most instances, we had the reports of two independent observers, that of our principal management respondent and that of the relevant union representative. In some instances we had the separate reports of three observers. As we explain later, in larger manufacturing workplaces we tended to have the reports of works managers as well as of personnel managers and union representatives. There was a high degree of consistency and congruence between the independent reports. Our conclusions on the level of support for technical change would have been similar whichever account we had taken. The fact that all three accounts pointed to similar conclusions gave added weight to them. In addition, our findings were not confined to a particular type of worker or sector of the economy: we found similar levels of support for technical change on the shopfloor and in the office, and in public and private services as well as in manufacturing industry.

Secondly, all the behavioural data that we covered in the survey were

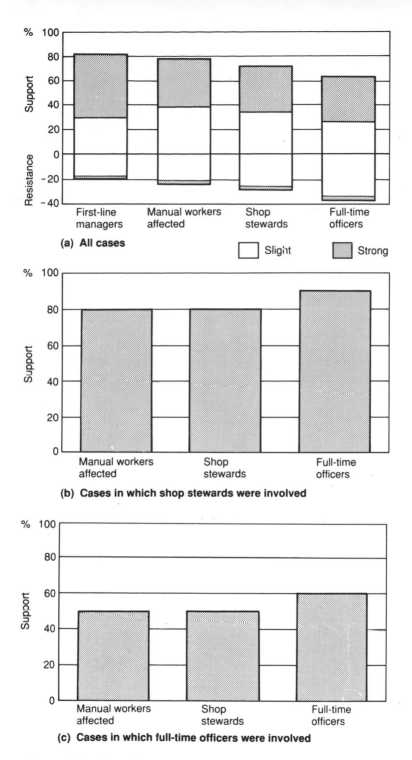

Figure 3.2 *Reactions of different categories of personnel to advanced technical change affecting manual workers*

consistent with the different reports of reactions to particular change episodes. The supporting behavioural data included our evidence on the high rate of technical change affecting office workers as well as manual workers across all sectors of employment in Britain; the low level of formal disputes or industrial action associated with technical change; and the absence of any evidence that the strength of trade union organization at workplaces served as any obstacle to the adoption of new technology. Indeed, in so far as we found any association at all between levels of trade union organization and strength and the use and introduction of new technology, we found that trade union recognition and high levels of membership density were favourable to technical change.[6]

Thirdly, of course, the sharp contrast between the accounts we received of reactions to organizational changes compared with technical changes clearly demonstrated that the evidence we found on the level of support for technical change was not simply a consequence of our method of enquiry. That takes us on to a further consideration of those contrasts.

Support for Technical Change Compared with Resistance to Organizational Change

As outlined in the introductory section to this chapter, we built into our survey design the potential for analysing the implications of different forms of change. We distinguished between conventional technical change, advanced technical change and organizational change. The account of worker support for technical change, given above, shows that support was stronger for conventional technical change. From case studies subsequently carried out to explore the reasons for the contrasts, we found that the greater appeal of conventional technical change arose from the fact that conventional new technology tended to be familiar, to pose few threats to people's capacity to cope, and to be self-evidently an improvement upon the technology it replaced; it tended to be quicker, more productive, safer, cleaner and to produce improved quality. Advanced technical change raised slightly more apprehensions, owing to the greater uncertainties associated with its unfamiliarity, but it was still generally supported.

As Figure 3.3 shows, however, organizational change provoked much more mixed reactions. Organizational change was resisted more often than it was supported among manual workers. Reactions to organizational change among office workers were fairly evenly balanced between the favourable and the unfavourable, but they were much less supportive than they were towards technical change. Indeed, the relative levels of support for the three different types of change were remarkably consistent as between manual workers and non-manual workers. For both, cases of

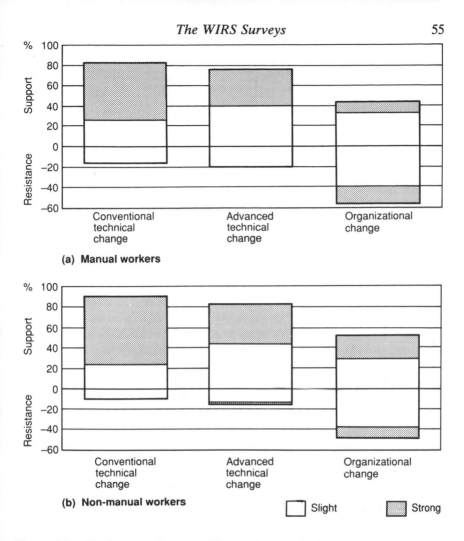

Figure 3.3 *Worker reactions to different forms of change among (a) manual workers and (b) non-manual workers*

strong resistance to change were heavily concentrated in the organizational change category.

The contrasts between reactions to technical change and organizational change revealed by Figure 3.3 are striking. But we have immediately to correct one misconception about the contrasts. Some commentators have wrongly inferred that the pattern in Figure 3.3 shows that workers like new technology, but they do not like the changes in working practice and organization required by technical change (Roberts, 1987). That is certainly not what the analysis shows and in order to demonstrate why that is the case we need further to emphasize certain features of our survey design. In the interviews we identified specific change episodes with respondents. We then asked detailed questions about a specific episode.

These included questions about the implications of the change for the pay of workers in the section affected; for the level of staffing in the section; and for the degree of skill, responsibility, interest, variety and supervision involved for the jobs of workers. The questions on the reactions of workers and others to the change were asked at the end of the series. It was clear from the sequence of questioning, the form of the questions and the position of the questions that they addressed all aspects of the change. If support for the change was reported, that represented support for the change *as a whole*, including in the case of a technical change its associated organizational change. Indeed, the balance of our evidence, overall, was that, far from it being the case that workers liked new technology but disliked consequent organizational changes, the introduction of new technology smoothed the path of changes in working practice that were less readily accepted in its absence.

Part of the reason why commentators found it so difficult to accommodate the contrasts between reactions to different forms of change is that they were so unexpected. We certainly did not expect them. We had not foreseen that the form of change would have any intrinsic implications for reactions to changes. Accordingly, when the differences first emerged our initial reaction was that they were interesting but that we would almost certainly find that they were readily accounted for by the differential content of the different forms of change. We immediately set about exploring the implications of the different changes in our analysis for levels of staffing in the section affected; for total employment at the workplace; for rates of pay and earnings; and for levels of skill, responsibility and autonomy provided by jobs. We also looked at the extent to which the different forms of change were introduced through different means and whether, for instance, there were higher levels of employee participation, consultation or joint regulation in cases of technical change which might also have contributed to the greater support enjoyed by such change.

We certainly found that technical change was more likely than organizational change to be associated with higher earnings and enriched job content and less likely to be associated with job loss. We thought we had found the answer to our contrasts. But we had not. The contrasts persisted independently of variations in the content of changes. The pattern may be illustrated by the results in relation to job loss.

Figure 3.4 compares levels of support among manual workers for the three different forms of change in relation to changes in the level of employment at the workplace over the previous year. We distinguished between workplaces where managers reported job losses in the previous year and workplaces where no such losses were reported. We analysed reactions to the three different forms of change in the two different circumstances. Responses to the question ranged from strong support to strong resistance. The maximum score was +200 which would have been achieved if all respondents had said there was strong support. A score of

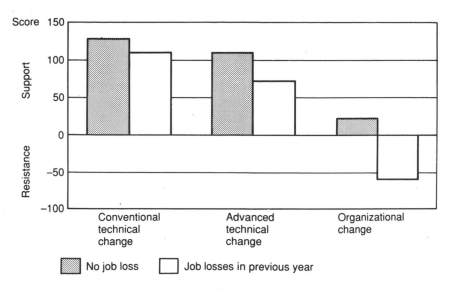

The scores were calculated by giving an arbitrary value of +200 to strong support, +100 to slight support, −100 to slight resistance and −200 to strong resistance and dividing the sum by the proportion who expressed views. The result was then rounded to the nearest ten to provide a mean score.

Figure 3.4 *Reactions of manual workers to different forms of change in relation to job loss*

100+ represented the equivalent of all respondents saying there was slight support.

Figure 3.4 shows, first, as would be expected, that support for change was reduced (or resistance was heightened) in circumstances where there were job losses. But, secondly, and more surprisingly, support for technical changes was reduced much less than might have been expected and remained strong even in the face of job losses. But, thirdly, and most remarkably, so favourably were workers disposed to technical change compared with organizational change, that *technical change in circumstances of job losses was supported substantially more strongly than organizational change in circumstances where the level of employment was stable or growing.* That pattern typifies the robustness of comparative reactions to the three different forms of change, independently of the content or circumstances of the change.

Similarly, just as we found no way of accounting for the contrasts through differences in the content of changes, so we could not explain away the contrasts through variations in the means through which they were introduced. Indeed, as already indicated, technical changes tended to be accompanied by lower levels of consultation and negotiation, while organizational changes were associated with higher levels.

Supplementary Evidence from Works Managers

We were able to take our preliminary analysis of the contrasts between organizational and technical change a little further through additional data gathered in the 1984 survey on manufacturing industry. A feature of the WIRS design is that it is based upon multiple interviewing at workplaces. This chiefly involves both manual and non-manual worker representatives as well as principal management respondents. But in both the 1984 and 1990 surveys it also involved an additional specialist manager at the workplace. In 1984, because of our special interest in technical change, we included an interview with a works manager in selected cases. We sought interviews with works managers in those manufacturing establishments where our main respondent was a personnel specialist. In practice, this meant that we spoke to works managers in the larger manufacturing plants: their average size was around 350 employees.

The interviews with works managers added two main strengths to the survey. First, the results provided useful corroboration of the information provided by our interviews with personnel managers. Secondly, we were able in our interviews with works managers to explore certain aspects of both technical and organizational changes in more detail than was possible in our main management interviews. In particular, we asked questions about different types of managerial initiative to bring about greater flexibility in the working practices of manual workers, as well as more detailed questions about the change episodes that we identified.

Through this extra questioning we were quickly able to infer that many of the organizational changes identified in larger manufacturing plants were productivity agreements; they sought changes in working practice, including the creation of multi-skilled craftsmen and enhanced craftsmen and the more flexible use of production workers, and they provided increased rates of pay. The reactions of workers and their representatives were similar to those that have generally characterized responses to productivity deals. The agreements were initially resisted, but attitudes softened once the changes were implemented (Daniel and McIntosh, 1972).

When, however, we compared the extent to which larger manufacturing workplaces that had introduced any (or none) of the forms of change had adopted more flexible working practices, we found a marked difference between those that reported organizational changes and advanced technical changes, on the one hand, and those that had introduced conventional technical changes or no changes, on the other (see Figures 3.5, 3.6). Advanced technical changes, like organizational changes, tended to be associated with the relaxation of demarcations between production and maintenance workers, the introduction of multi-skilled craftsmen and, especially, the introduction of enhanced craftsmen.

But, once again, the main difference between the organizational changes and the advanced technical changes lay in the reactions of the manual

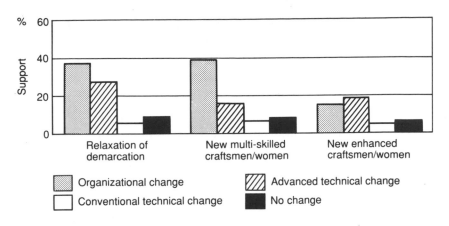

Figure 3.5 *Forms of flexibility associated with different forms of change in manufacturing industry*

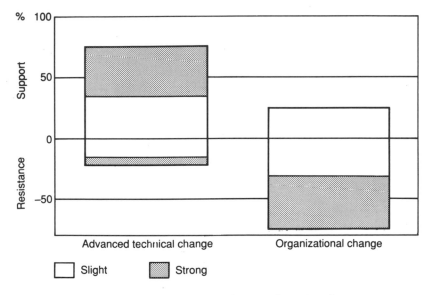

Figure 3.6 *Works managers' accounts of manual workers' reactions to change in manufacturing industry*

workers involved. That is shown in Figure 3.6. It is apparent that the support for the technical changes compared with the resistance to the organizational changes was particularly marked in these manufacturing industry cases.

It was the evidence of support for technical change in circumstances of job loss and more flexible working practices that fundamentally shaped our view of the role of technical change as it emerged from our analysis. Overall, new technology emerged as positively attractive to workers and their representatives to the extent that it sugared the pill of other less palatable changes. We discuss some of the reasons for the contrasts later in the chapter.

Qualifications to the Picture of Support for Technical Change

Two main qualifications need to be made about the general picture of worker support for technical change revealed by our results. First, we have emphasized that our evidence was not attitudinal and was firmly anchored in the multiple reporting of particular events. But the evidence was cross-sectional. We were asking managers and shop stewards retrospectively about reactions to events at a particular point in the process of change, at the time when many workers would have been in the frame of mind most favourable to the change; a time when initial doubts might have been stilled and uncertainties resolved; when they were experiencing any benefits in increased earnings and job enrichment; and before they had become habituated to such benefits. Previous PSI research on productivity agreements, which represented a particular form of major organizational change, showed that there were substantial variations in the reactions of workers and shop stewards to changes at different stages of their introduction (Daniel and McIntosh, 1972). Proposals for change tended to be resisted initially. Agreements on change tended to be reached only after hard bargaining over increases in rates of pay in relation to the nature of changes in working practice. Subsequently, after implementation, the changes were welcomed and they were welcomed more because they made work more interesting and satisfying than because of the improvements in terms of employment. Not only did feelings about the change vary at different stages, but different features of the change were salient at different stages.

The present study was cross-sectional, so we were not able to explore patterns of variation in reactions over time. But we did make some attempt to take account of our previous results, in two ways. We phrased our question to the main management respondent about reactions at the time *'when you were bringing in the change'*. More substantially, in the interviews with both works managers and shop stewards, where there was less pressure on the length of the interview schedule, we distinguished between reactions at two different stages; first, when news of the proposed change was initially mooted and, secondly, later, at the time of the interview. Figure 3.7 shows the accounts of manual shop stewards of their own reactions (and of those of the manual workers affected) to the three different forms of change at the two different points in time. It demonstrates three findings. First, it illustrates the point made earlier that manual shop stewards consistently reported that their own reactions were more favourable to change than those of the manual workers affected. Secondly, in relation to each type of change and for both stewards and workers there was a marked shift in favour of the change between initial reactions and

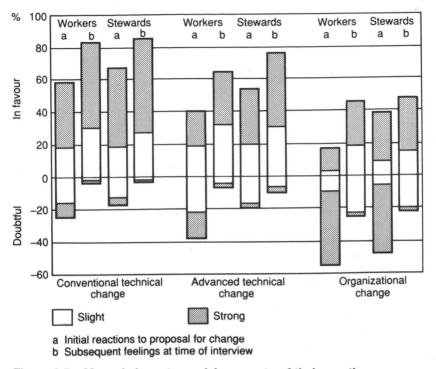

Figure 3.7 *Manual shop stewards' accounts of their reactions, and those of the manual workers affected, to different forms of change*

subsequent feelings. Thirdly, however, it remained the case that, so far as technical changes were concerned, initial reactions were reported as favourable, on balance, and doubts were largely dissipated at the subsequent stage. Nevertheless, as feelings about change tend to be more favourable later in the process, the reports we received of reactions to change are likely to have been, if anything, more favourable than they would have been had we been asking at an earlier stage in the process.

The second qualification we have to make to the general pattern of worker and shop steward support for technical change is that there were pockets of resistance. There were cases where strong resistance was reported even at the later stage. Those cases tended to be concentrated in particular types of workplace, especially larger workplaces and those belonging to nationalized industries (Daniel, 1987). There was agreement in the independent reports of managers and shop stewards that there was less support for technical change affecting manual workers in places employing 500 or more manual workers and, regardless of workplace size, there was less support for technical change in the nationalized industries than in any other sector. As the nationalized industries emerged as the sector characterized by the highest level of centralization, it was tempting to speculate that less favourable reactions at workplace level owed something to that degree of centralization. Accordingly, we should emphasize that our analysis is confined to the reactions of workers and union representatives to changes at workplace level. We collected no information about the stances of union representatives in circumstances where decisions about new technology were jointly regulated at levels above that of the workplace.

Understanding Worker Support for Technical Change – and Why it has been Neglected

The survey findings on both the extent of worker support for technical change and the contrasts with reactions to organizational change were so unexpected that we quickly decided that they required further investigation. We therefore undertook a number of follow-up case studies based upon workplaces included in the survey. The aim was to explore reactions to different forms of change in more detail and depth than is possible through form surveys. We focused upon advanced technical changes and organizational changes.

The reasons why technical change was intrinsically more attractive than organizational change quickly and readily became apparent as soon as we posed the question in those terms. In summary, new technology represented progress and advance; the benefits of new and improved machines were concrete, manifest and demonstrable; they represented competitive advantage – the modernity of its technology symbolized the standing of a manufacturing workshop to all who knew the industry, both internal and external; investment in new technology represented confidence in the future and hence improved longer-term job prospects and security; many features of new technology were familiar to workers and valued in their domestic and leisure lives; and, finally, the introduction of new technology tended to be an incremental and continuous process. Overall, the introduction of new technology tended to be associated with success.

In contrast, organizational change that was introduced independently of new equipment tended to be more frequently associated with failure. It was often seen as an admission of poor or unproductive organization in the past. It was more likely to be viewed with suspicion or challenged, principally because the benefits derived from different forms of organization tended to be seen more as a matter of judgement and were by no means self-evident. A proposed new form of organization tended to be an abstraction developed in the minds of a small section of management, sometimes, initially, only one person, often outside the culture of the workplace, even located elsewhere. There was the problem of communicating the idea of the change before it could be 'sold'. Organizational change tended to be seen as a management solution arising out of management failures. The chief implications of such change identified by workers tended to be work intensification and possible job loss which were to be evaluated in terms of the wage–work bargain. Any other benefits were considered or recognized only after the change.

That summary may be amplified a little under the following headings.

Technical Change is Seen as Progress

The idea that technical change represented progress was implicit and often explicit in the reactions of all parties. At best, this meant that there was a predisposition to welcome and support the adoption of new machines for that reason. At worst, it was assumed that progress was inevitable and irresistible, so that even if it was not welcomed it had to be endured. Reorganization, independently of any new machines, in contrast, had no such positive qualities and was certainly not regarded as irresistible. New forms of organization tended more frequently to be seen as quite legitimately challengeable and certainly modifiable if not stoppable.

New Machines have a Concrete Form and Products

New machines had a concrete form and generally had a concrete output. Their superiority over older machines was often immediately apparent from their appearance. Even where it was not, it was generally easy to demonstrate that superiority in terms of the quality or quantity of the output from the machine. The implications and benefits of new technology were quickly communicated to workers through these means. New forms of organization, in contrast, started as an abstraction, an idea in the minds of management. The benefits, if any, became apparent only after implementation.

The Newer the Machines, the Better the Workplace

Workers and union representatives were generally knowledgeable about the systems of production in their industry. Talking to other people and visiting other workplaces quickly enabled them to establish how advanced and modern was the technology at their own workplace compared with that in other parts of their own organization and that used by their competitors. They attached importance to being among the leading group because it was intrinsically satisfying and gave them competitive advantage. Different forms of organization in other enterprises, however, were much less visible; workers were much less aware of them and had little intrinsic interest in them.

Investment in the Future and Improved Job Security

A major reason for welcoming technical change among both union representatives and the workforce was that it represented investment in the establishment which was interpreted as signifying that the workplace had a medium-term future. Important here was the background of the early 1980s when there had been widespread closures and job losses in manufacturing industry generally. Many of the workplaces that we studied had suffered heavy redundancies during that period. In that context, any signs that the workplace was judged to have a future and that there were good prospects of job security were especially welcome. Even in workplaces that had suffered no recent redundancies, new technology was still seen as a symbol of increased job security. This pattern represents a striking reversal of many of the initial forecasts from commentators when the microelectronics revolution was first heralded. Many saw the new technology as resulting in widespread job losses and being resisted because of its threat to jobs. But by the end of the 1980s, on our evidence, new technology was being welcomed because it represented increased job security.

In contrast, organizational change did tend to be more associated with job loss in the minds of workers. First, they were much more conscious of the possibility of short-term job loss arising out of organizational change. Such changes were more frequently associated in the minds of workers with decline and contraction than with investment in the future and with growth. Secondly, they rarely had confidence that organizational changes were likely to make more secure the future of the workplace and of jobs within it.

New Technology is Familiar and Valued in Non-work Contexts

Workers tended to be familiar with applications of microelectronic technology in many of the consumer goods that they valued at home. The personal computer, the word processor, the video recorder and video games were common in the homes of many. Through them they had learned both some of the basic concepts involved in microcomputer processing and VDUs and the power and benefit to be derived from the technology.

Technical Change Tends to be Incremental and Continuous

Technical change in established manufacturing workshops tended to be incremental. Existing processes were modified, refined, developed or extended. Each step in the process tended to involve an extension of what was already familiar. If a completely new system of production was being introduced then it was likely that new technology would be introduced into new premises or at least a new unit. In setting up such greenfield operations, managements tended to seek all the benefits of greenfield sites. They sought to introduce new working practices and forms of organization (see Preece, this volume). Staff for the new units tended to be selected, or were self-selected, on the basis of their keenness to operate the new technology and the new working practices that it required. When and if the new systems were extended to the remainder of the workforce, then the new working practices had become established and they tended spontaneously to accommodate them.

Changes in working practice also tended to be continuous and incremental. Informal changes took place all the time on the job to adjust to different circumstances and other changes. But when they took that form they were not seen as organizational change. Indeed, an essential characteristic of the idea of organizational change appeared to be that it was discontinuous. It involved a conscious decision to stop doing things the way that they had been done and to do them differently. It represented a choice to make a change in direction rather than to make incremental improvements.

Personnel Managers

In a number of areas the WIRS series has highlighted the extent to which general practice in British work organizations falls short of conventional ideas of good management, implicit in management writing, teaching and public policy. That has been particularly the case in relation to personnel/human resource management, defined in the broadest terms. We approached the first survey in the series with the expectation that professional personnel management had been spreading widely in Britain as part of the codification and formalization of industrial relations during the 1970s, encouraged by the growth of employment legislation and also as a result of increased resources being put into management education and training. In the event, we were struck by the pervasive amateurism revealed by our results. In most workplaces personnel work was done by managers who in no sense of the word could be called specialists. Only about a half of the managers who spent a major part of their time on personnel matters had job titles that identified them as personnel managers in the broadest definition of the term. Furthermore, only a half of personnel specialists had any formal qualifications for the job. In general, personnel management was done by general managers or specialists in other functions for whom personnel management was only a small part of their work. It was only when the size of workplaces was over 200 or even 500 employees that it became normal for personnel specialists to be employed.

The 1990 survey showed that little of substance had changed in the decade following our initial findings and it is useful to summarize the position we found in the latest survey. We do this by examining the characteristics and responsibilities of our primary management respondents in the 1990 WIRS interviews, managers who were selected for interview as being the senior person at the establishment responsible for industrial relations, employee relations or personnel matters. For this purpose we limit our attention to cases – in fact, the vast majority – where the respondent was actually based at the workplace in question, rather than at the company headquarters or a similar higher-level administrative centre in a multi-establishment organization. We deemed our workplace respondents to be 'employee relations managers' if they spent 25 per cent or more of their time on personnel or employee relations matters.[7] Just under a half (46 per cent) of workplaces with 25 of more employees had an 'employee relations manager' so defined. Among larger manufacturing plants (with 100 or more employees), 59 per cent had one.

A stricter definition of an 'employee relations manager' would naturally have given us a lower figure for their prevalence. Those spending a half or more of their time on employee relations matters were present in about 25 per cent of workplaces; those spending 90 per cent or more were to be found in 10 per cent. Whatever definition we chose, employee relations managers were much more common in larger workplaces than in smaller ones – so much so that it was mainly in workplaces with fewer than 500 employees that other characteristics of workplaces were clearly associated with the employment of personnel specialists. In these smaller and medium-sized workplaces the likelihood of having an employee relations manager was greater if the establishment was in the service sector rather than manufacturing, employed predominantly women rather than men, was part of a larger organization rather than being an independent firm, and was foreign-owned rather than British. There was also a positive association with the presence of recognized trade unions.

But staying with our broadest definition – those spending 25 per cent or more of their time on employee relations matters – it is clear that only a minority of such managers had a job title which denoted them as a personnel or similar specialist. In fact, only 30 per cent of them had the term 'personnel' in their job title, 2 per cent had a title that included 'industrial, employee or staff relations' and almost none were known as 'human resource' managers. Again, specialist personnel job titles were much more common among respondents in large workplaces and in the types of workplace mentioned earlier, where employee relations management was evident as a specialist activity. Yet even in larger manufacturing plants (with 100 or more employees) only half of employee relations managers had specialist job titles.

Overall, then, it was only a minority of 'employee relations managers' on our broad definition that had a specialist personnel or similar job title. Most of the majority were general managers. In fact, more of the majority had job titles that indicated overall responsibility for the workplace or a similar general management position than any other type of managerial job. Moreover, the 54 per cent of respondents who were not 'employee relations managers', but were nevertheless the senior person responsible for employee relations at their workplace, were also very commonly general managers.

We could elaborate this picture by discussing the survey findings on the qualifications and experience of those engaged in employee relations management. Or we could discuss the presence of specialist staff to assist in such activities. But our broad conclusion would be the same. This is that there is a substantial personnel function only in the largest workplaces, while in the majority of workplaces employee relations matters are dealt with on a local basis by general managers and line managers with much wider responsibilities. Thus *on-site* specialist personnel managers for dealing with the planning, implementation and consequences of technical change are not at all widespread.[8]

As already indicated, this picture differs little from that revealed by earlier surveys in the series. Indeed, our evidence suggests that employee relations matters have increasingly become the province of line managers. Personnel specialists have tended, over the period, to become involved in a narrower range of concerns within the general field of employee relations; and, judging by their increasing use of external legal advice as well as other evidence, their preoccupations are moving away from trade union relations towards employment law. However, such tendencies have not fundamentally altered the picture of personnel management in Britain during the course of the past ten years and our findings from the mid-1980s on the role of management, including personnel management, in technical change are still highly relevant now.

Personnel Managers and Technical Change

The first and main finding to emerge from our analysis relating to personnel management and technical change was that, in most workplaces, there were no professional personnel managers to play any part in technical change. Beyond that, we had two other sets of relevant information. The first was analysis of the extent to which workplaces that were more inclined to introduce technical change were also more inclined to have professional personnel functions. The second was some direct questioning on the roles of personnel managers in larger manufacturing plants.

On the first question we found no evidence that the existence of a professional personnel function made it more likely that workplaces would introduce technical change; or that workplaces with a high rate of technical change were more likely to develop specialist personnel departments. In terms of the presence of an 'employee relations manager' (however we specified their level of activity on employee relations matters), the presence of a manager with a 'personnel' title, and the existence of local specialist staff to assist in the work of the personnel function, there were no differences between workplaces involved in technical change and those that were not. This pattern contrasted sharply with the case of organizational change. In places that experienced organizational change there was a substantially greater chance of there being a more developed specialist function. In the case of technical change, then, the implication is that any initiatives intended to have any impact on the way managements handle the employee relations aspects of such changes must target managers as a whole and not just personnel specialists.

Our second set of information on the role of personnel managers reinforced the picture of a surprisingly low level of involvement in technical changes but a higher profile in cases of organizational change. The information was derived from our supplementary interviews in 1984 with works managers in manufacturing industry. As explained earlier, we sought such interviews in manufacturing plants where our principal management respondent was a personnel specialist. The information therefore is based on those larger manufacturing plants where the specialist personnel function was more highly developed than normal. In view of that, the picture that emerged of the role of personnel managers in major changes was very modest indeed. Table 3.5 shows that, according to works managers, personnel managers were involved in the introduction of major changes in less than half of the cases identified. Even in the instances where the personnel department was involved, it was rare for it to be fully involved from the start. In only 14 per cent of cases did works managers report that personnel management was involved in the initial decision to make the change. The most common pattern, where the personnel department was involved, was for it to be brought in after the decision to make the change had been taken when its role was to deal with the personnel implications of the change. In only one-third of all cases, however, was the personnel department involved either from the start (14 per cent) or immediately after the decision to make the change was taken (20 per cent).

The most striking and illuminating source of variation in the involvement

Table 3.5 *Works managers' accounts of the role of the personnel department in the introduction of major change, 1984*

	Any major change (%)	Advanced technical change (%)	Conventional technical change (%)	Organizational change (%)
Personnel department involved	46	50	(13)	(80)
Personnel department not involved	52	46	(87)	(20)
Not stated	2	4	(1)	—
Stage of involvement				
Decision to change	14	15	(1)	(30)
Immediately after decision to change	20	19	(2)	(50)
After decision to tell workers	6	9	(2)	—
Later stage	6	7	(8)	—
Base: works managers who reported a major change in the previous three years (*n*)				
Unweighted	241	176	40	25
Weighted	56	37	12	7

The percentages in brackets should be treated with caution, as the unweighted base is 20 or more but fewer than 50.

of personnel managers was provided by the three different forms of major change identified (see Table 3.5). The personnel department was most heavily involved in organizational change, introduced independently of new plant or machinery. It was involved in the large majority of such cases, and where it was involved it was invariably brought in at an early stage. By contrast, personnel managers were very much less frequently involved in the introduction of advanced technical change, and where they were it was often at a much later stage. Perhaps most striking of all was the infrequency with which the personnel department was at all involved in the introduction of conventional technical change. In only 13 per cent of such changes did works managers report any involvement and in most of those instances personnel managers were not brought in until a comparatively late stage in the proceedings. In terms of broad conclusions on the role of personnel management in the introduction of technical change, it appears that in the mid-1980s at least technical change was largely seen as a technical matter within which there was no established role or function for personnel management (Daniel, 1987).

Finally, it did appear that where personnel managers were involved in advanced technical changes, and especially where they were involved at an early stage, their involvement was associated with a stronger level of worker support for the change. That was particularly notable in the framework of a general picture where the involvement of personnel managers, full-time trade union officers and the use of higher levels of consultation and negotiation tended to emerge as responses to initial reluctance to accept change.

Involvement of Employees and their Representatives in Technical Change

If conventional wisdom assumes that professional personnel managers are among the main agents managing the human side of technical change, then it equally assumes that communication, consultation, involvement and negotiation are the principal means for bringing about the acceptance of change. In that context, four main findings emerged from our 1984 analysis. First, the general levels of discussion, consultation and nego-tiation over technical changes were remarkably low. Secondly, managers generally tended to consult and negotiate when they were required to do so, either because there was initial resistance to the proposed changes or because of the existence of appropriate institutions and established procedures. Thirdly, discussion and consultations and negotiations of all types, including the informal, were more common where trade unions were present and were recognized by management for collective bargaining. Fourthly, the levels of consultation and negotiation were one set of issues

Table 3.6 *Extent and form of consultations over the introduction of technical change affecting manual workers in relation to trade union recognition*

	1984 (%)			1990 (%)		
	All establishments	Manual union recognized	No recognized union	All establishments	Manual union recognized	No recognized union
One or more of the forms of consultation	82	88	69	85	89	81
No consultation	16	10	30	14	10	18
Not stated	2	2	1	1	1	1
Formal – union channels						
Discussed with shop stewards	35	50	*	27	48	*
Discussed with full-time officers	13	18	—	14	24	1
Formal – non-union channels						
Discussed in established JCC	14	18	4	20	27	11
Discussed in specially constituted committee	10	12	4	10	12	7
Informal						
Discussions with individual workers	60	60	62	59	57	63
Meetings with groups of workers	36	41	24	50	51	49
Base: establishments with 25 or more manual workers and experiencing technical change (n)						
Unweighted	680	585	95	762	598	164
Weighted	364	253	111	396	219	177

* Fewer than 0.5 per cent.

from which substantially different pictures emerged from the accounts of worker representatives compared with managers.

In our 1984 survey, managers in 16 per cent of workplaces had no consultations with manual workers or their representatives about major technical changes, according to the accounts of managers themselves.[9] The proportion of workplaces where there was no consultation rose to 30 per cent in workplaces without recognized unions for manual workers compared with 10 per cent in places with unions. A feature of the findings was the extent to which consultation through formal non-union channels was also much lower in non-union workplaces than in unionized workplaces. It was only in relation to the highly informal category of *'discussions with individual workers'* that levels of consultation reported by managers in places where unions were not recognized matched those where they were. In consequence, the biggest contrast between union and non-union shops lay in the *number of different channels* of involvement used. In union shops the number was much greater and included union and formal non-union channels as well as less formal discussions.

The results from our 1990 survey largely reflected the picture revealed in 1984, although the comparison between the two surveys revealed evidence of interesting changes (see Table 3.6). There was a slight reduction over the period in the proportion of cases affecting manual workers where managers reported no consultation, yet that was largely a consequence of a reported increase in informal discussions with groups of workers. A reduction in reported discussions with shop stewards (perhaps largely arising from the decline in the proportion of workplaces with shop stewards) was matched by an increase in the use of established joint consultative committees.

Consultation over changes affecting non-manual workers had been greater than over changes affecting manual grades in 1984, largely because of a higher reported incidence of informal discussion, and for non-manual workers there was less change in the overall level of consultation between 1984 and 1990 (see Table 3.7). The chief changes appeared to be an increase in the use of joint consultative committees, either established or ad hoc, at the expense of a decline in consultations with shop stewards; and an increase in meetings with groups of workers at the expense of a decline in discussions with individual workers. The bulk of these changes appeared to have occurred in the unionized sector.

Overall, the findings do suggest that there was some increase in levels of consultation with employees over technical change between 1984 and 1990. Perhaps the principal measure of that increase is the smaller part that the most informal and problematic form of consultation (*'discussions with individual workers'*) played in the 1990 accounts. In view of the widespread agreement that it is desirable for workers to be involved in discussions of important changes affecting them, the apparent increase in consultation is to be welcomed. There are two major qualifications, however, that need to be made to that picture.

Table 3.7 Extent and form of consultations over the introduction of technical change affecting office workers in relation to trade union recognition

	1984 (%)			1990 (%)		
	All establish-ments	Non-manual union recognized	No recognized union	All establish-ments	Non-manual union recognized	No recognized union
One or more of the forms of consultation	91	94	86	92	95	89
No consultation	9	6	14	8	5	11
Not stated	*	*	—	*	*	—
Formal – union channels						
Discussed with shop stewards	20	33	*	19	32	1
Discussed with full-time officers	9	15	—	15	25	1
Formal – non-union channels						
Discussed in established JCC	13	18	5	22	35	4
Discussed in specially constituted committee	13	15	10	18	23	10
Informal						
Discussions with individual workers	77	74	80	62	52	75
Meetings with groups of workers	44	44	43	57	54	60
Base: establishments with 25 or more non-manual workers and experiencing technical change (n)						
Unweighted	1,047	803	244	963	676	287
Weighted	569	335	235	524	305	219

* Fewer than 0.5 per cent.

Worker Representatives' Accounts of Levels of Consultation and Negotiation

A feature of the WIRS design is that we include interviews with shop stewards or worker representatives as well as with managers. That feature provides the series with a number of strengths. One of them is that it provides two perspectives upon questions in the grey area between the straightforwardly factual and the judgemental or perceptual. Questions about consultation and negotiation clearly fall into that grey area. There can be genuinely different views, when discussions have taken place, as to the nature of what occurred; whether, for instance, it was communication, joint consultation or negotiation. Similarly, there can be genuinely different views over the extent to which contacts were sufficiently substantial to justify being described as '*discussions about the change*'.

Not surprisingly, therefore, we received a different picture of the level of different types of consultation from our interviews with worker representatives than from our interviews with management respondents.[10] When we confined analysis to workplaces where we interviewed both managers and worker representatives, we found that worker representatives consistently reported less consultation than managers. These were, of course, necessarily the workplaces where unions were represented and consultation was generally higher. But while managers' accounts suggested that there were no consultations in only 4 per cent of such cases, worker representative accounts suggested that there were none in 17 per cent of cases. Worker representatives consistently reported a lower level of consultation for all the types listed, other than, interestingly, discussion in a *specially constituted joint consultative committee*. Clearly there is less scope for differences of perspective over whether or not such a new committee was established than over whether discussions that warrant being described as such were held through normal or existing channels. In general, worker representative accounts suggested a level of consultation 25 per cent lower than that reported by managers through each of the other channels. Two conclusions follow from these findings, one particular and one more general.

First, our figures on absolute levels of consultation derived from management interviews need to be qualified by the accounts of worker representatives. The actual levels were likely to be somewhere between the two accounts. The pattern of variation in levels of consultation emerged as much the same whichever account was analysed. Second, and more generally, in surveys of organizations it can never be sufficient to rely upon the accounts of just one party to answer questions that require judgement or allow for substantial interpretation.

Negotiation over Change

A second qualification to our findings on change in levels of consultation between 1984 and 1990 arises from the results of our questioning on negotiations over technical change. In both surveys we asked managers in workplaces with recognized trade unions whether changes had been *negotiated with union representatives and dependent upon their agreement* or *discussed with union representatives in a way that took their views into account but left management free to make the decisions* or *not discussed with union representatives*. In the 1990 survey, 6 per cent of managers in workplaces with recognized trade unions reported that technical changes were introduced with the agreement of trade unions. This is a slightly smaller proportion than the equivalent figure in 1984, but in overall terms it represents an even greater decline in the amount of change introduced with trade union agreement because fewer workplaces had any form of union representation in 1990 than earlier. The 1990 results also show that negotiations over change were largely confined to workplaces where union organization was particularly strong, as measured by trade union density.

Our analysis produces three clear findings relevant to trade union representation, worker involvement and technical change. First, trade union organization generally provided a framework favourable to the introduction of technical change. Secondly, managers in workplaces where unions were recognized were substantially more inclined to consult and involve workers in technical change, through non-union as well as through union channels. Thirdly, although there may have been a decline in the proportion of workplaces where there were no consultations over technical change, there has also been a decline in the more substantial forms of consultation that occur when managers have to come to terms with institutions representing workers' interests. Overall, the fall in trade union representation during the 1980s, unaccompanied by the development of any other institutions that require or encourage managers to consult or negotiate (Millward et al, 1992), represents a loss of worker influence and involvement in change at the workplace.

Conclusion

Drawing upon the most authoritative, large-scale research evidence available, it is clear that technical change was, and remains, widespread throughout the British economy. A feature of the pervasiveness of technical change is the extent to which non-manual workers, in general, and office workers, in particular, are subject to change resulting from new technology. Traditionally, it has been manual workers in manufacturing industry who have mainly been affected by advances in methods and systems of production. But the development of the personal computer, the personal word processor and systems of office automation resulting from the microprocessor mean that office workers are affected by technical change more frequently than manual workers.

Workers affected by technical change generally support its introduction, often strongly so, while trade union representatives and full-time officers are usually even more supportive.[11] By contrast, worker reactions to organizational change – involving changes in work organization or working methods, but without changes in technology – are much more mixed; organizational change more frequently meets with resistance. Workers tend to feel that proposals for organizational change are associated with past failures and the advantages of the change are less visible and concrete than is the case with new technology. Technical change, furthermore, represents progress and advance, competitive advantage and managerial confidence in the future. The attractions of new technology are such that its introduction can act as a lubricant for less popular change in organization and working practices.

Professional personnel or employee relations managers generally play little or no part in the planning and implementation of technical change. This is principally because the majority of workplaces still do not have such specialists. But even in the larger workplaces, where personnel managers are more common, they tend to be brought into the process as fire-fighters, rather than as key players in a management team engaged in designing and planning a major change and its implementation. General managers and line managers, even other functional specialists, generally play more central roles than personnel people. The lessons to be drawn from the material in this volume are thus of relevance to managers across the board, not just to personnel and related specialists.[12]

This is not to say that personnel managers play no role in technical change. When personnel managers are involved in advanced technical change, and especially when they are involved at an early stage, the level of worker support for the change tends to be stronger. That finding is particularly notable as, generally, the involvement both of personnel managers and that of trade union officials is a response to initial reluctance on the part of workers to accept change. That tendency is part of a characteristic style of British managers which can be termed *reactive* and *opportunistic*. Further evidence of the style is provided by the uses of consultation and negotiation. First, the level of employee involvement, either directly or through representatives, is remarkably low. Secondly, this is partly because technical change is generally so readily accepted. It is also because managers tend to engage in consultation or negotiation over change only when they are required to do so, either because there is initial resistance or because of the existence of de facto rights embodied in representative institutions, usually based on a trade union framework. In so far as the coverage of trade union representation has fallen sharply over the past decade, there has been a corresponding decline in the institutional framework for worker involvement in technical and other changes.

Acknowledgement

The research reported in this chapter was made possible by generous support from the Leverhulme Trust.

Notes

1. The ED/ESRC/PSI/ACAS Workplace Industrial Relations Survey series is sponsored by the Employment Department, the Economic and Social Research Council, the Policy Studies Institute (with funds from the Leverhulme Trust) and the Advisory, Conciliation and Arbitration Service. It entails interviews with managers and employee representatives in a nationally representative sample of workplaces with 25 or more employees in virtually all sectors of the economy. For further details see Daniel and Millward, 1983; Millward and Stevens, 1986; Millward et al, 1992.

2. The publications from the series of surveys are listed fully in Northcott and Walling, 1988: 300–4.

3. It is, of course, not possible to make absolute distinctions between technical change and organizational change. Most technical changes will require changes in working practice and organization. Organizational changes take place in a particular technical context and may be a consequence of previous technical changes or a preparation for prospective technical changes. In practice, however, our respondents were readily able to distinguish between changes that fitted the three different descriptions provided. Moreover, and more importantly, the three different types of change identified provided major and consistent sources of variation in the analysis.

4. The questions about technical and organizational change were asked in the 1990 survey only in cases where there were at least 25 employees of the relevant category (manual/non-manual). All comparisons between the 1990 and 1984 results are made with this restriction.

5. In the 1984 survey managers were asked about the three types of change separately. In 1990, as a minor economy, they were asked about technical change and organizational change and then those reporting technical change were asked whether it included microelectronics technology.

6. These conclusions are supported by independent analysis of the survey data using multivariate statistical methods (Latreille, 1992).

7. The previous question in the interview had indicated what we meant by this term by asking whether items like recruitment, training, systems of payment, grievance procedures, discipline and terms and conditions of employment were part of their job responsibilities.

8. It might be argued that our concentration on *on-site* personnel specialist resources seriously understates their availability to workplaces involved in technical change because in multi-establishment organizations such resources are available at divisional and head offices. We have two responses, one theoretical, one empirical. The theoretical argument is that the most sustained and effective input from personnel specialists is likely to be made where they are on site throughout the course of the change, rather than only on an occasional basis. The empirical response is that the availability of specialists at higher organizational levels is by no means universal and certainly does not provide an alternative to an on-site specialist in the majority of cases.

We substantiate this by using results of a question asking our workplace-level management respondents who were in multi-establishment organizations whether there was a specialist personnel or industrial relations manager or director at a higher level with whom they had contact. Again our definition of a specialist was a broad one. In manufacturing industry they were not widespread. In plants that had experienced technical change an *on-site* specialist was present in 30 per cent of cases; yet only 50 per cent had an *on-site specialist or one at a higher level in the organization*. However, in the private non-manufacturing sector the pattern was different. Here the availability of personnel specialists at a higher level in the organization more than doubled the availability of specialized personnel resources to workplaces involved in technical change (from 24 per cent with only an on-site specialist to 63 per cent with either type). Even so, nearly 40 per cent of establishments in this sector had *neither* an on-site specialist nor access to one at a higher level in the organization.

9. Note that the 1984 figures for manual workers have been based on workplaces which had either form of technical change, advanced or technical, in order to make them more comparable with the 1990 figures. The 1984 figures confined to advanced technical changes

revealed a more marked contrast between union and non-union workplaces (Daniel 1987: Table VI.4, p. 120).

10. See Daniel, 1987: Table VI.7, p. 126, for a comparison of managers' and manual shop stewards' accounts of the extent and form of consultation over the introduction of advanced technical change.

11. It might be argued that the high level of worker and trade union support for technical change revealed by WIRS was a product of the period of buoyant economic growth experienced in Britain in the 1980s. This is hardly so. The changes that were the focus of our detailed questioning in 1984 had actually occurred in the period 1981–4, when the recession of the early 1980s was still going on. Moreover, the feeling among employees that investment in new technology shows managerial confidence in the future and helps to strengthen competitiveness and increase the security of jobs rather than weaken it seems as likely in the current recession as in the earlier one.

12. Broadly speaking, the human and organizational aspects of technical change are only likely to receive as much management attention as the technical features of the change if their importance is appreciated and acted upon by managers in general, not just personnel specialists.

4

Personnel Leadership in Technical and Human Resource Change

Chris Hendry

The 1984 Workplace Industrial Relations Survey (Daniel and Millward, this volume), identified a low level of personnel involvement in technical change. In contrast, the Hardy Spicer case provides fairly compelling evidence of the close involvement that personnel specialists can have in introducing new technology and the advantages of this for successful implementation. This contribution was recognized in 1988 when the company won the first IPM/Daily Telegraph national award for 'excellence in personnel management'. The early period of plant modernization has been documented in Hendry and Pettigrew (1988) and Hendry (1991).

Hardy Spicer is hardly a representative case, however, in terms of the WIRS sample. In 1983 it had just over 2,000 employees on one site, a full-time professional personnel function, headed by a personnnel director with an industrial relations manager and training manager, and a strong manual union that influenced terms and conditions across the company. It was also part of a manufacturing group (GKN) with a highly unionized culture (although the company had successfully maintained a decentralized approach in its industrial relations). All these factors put Hardy Spicer among a minority of companies in WIRS, while also presenting a number of conditions that tend to be associated with a more prominent role for the personnel function in organizational and technical change.

In this respect, the single case cannot gainsay the weight of evidence from a survey. What it can do is offer breadth as against focus (Pettigrew, 1990). It can reveal processes of involvement over a period of time, which a narrow focus on a decision event (such as the decision to introduce technical change) may conceal. This includes the period that precedes a decision and what follows, as well as fuller exposure of the immediate decision process. The theory of strategic management has long since taken this on board in moving progressively away from the decisionist model of the 1960s to a more 'emergent' view of strategy (Mintzberg, 1978). This includes relaxing the dichotomy between strategy formulation and implementation and a greater appreciation of 'ad hocism' in strategic management (Morris and Wood, 1991).

Thus, the role of personnel/human resource management should not be conceived narrowly in relation to a 'decision' to introduce technical change. It can begin in changes in, for example, recruitment and training standards which anticipate the need for higher levels of skill, and in the development of sound traditions of employee relations and skills over a number of years. These factors may be taken account of implicitly in technical decisions without any apparent participation of the personnel function. The organization with a personnel function is more likely to make these preparations than one without and in consequence to manage technical change more effectively – in contrast to the organization that attempts to create these conditions overnight from a low base. By the same token, the pay-off from building new traditions consistently, for example in skills, creates subsequent opportunities for further technical enhancement. In other words, technical change should not be seen as a once-and-for-all event simply involving the adoption of a piece of hardware (Winner, 1977). These processes are illustrated in the ten years of change at Hardy Spicer.

This incremental, processual view of change has specific relevance to HRM. I have criticized elsewhere the sometimes naive pretensions of 'strategic human resource management' (Hendry and Pettigrew, 1990) in embracing ideas of 'planned change'. At issue is not the ends, but the means. The ideal of greater integration (Guest, 1987) between business objectives and personnel policies is an ideal worth striving for. Where it may go wrong, and where HRM in practice may fall short of normative models, is in the implication that an organization can be designed according to a top-down model of what it should look like. To use Jones' phrase, 'management cannot construct, "de novo", the conditions under which labour is to function' (1982: 199). The question is not 'should systematic change be attempted?' but whether HRM as an ideology encourages an approach to change over and beyond this which is untenable or unsustainable. It is possible at Hardy Spicer to detect an explicit shift in language and ideology from personnel management to HRM across two eras of technical and organizational change, although it is impossible as yet to make comparisons in terms of outcomes or even in terms of substantive differences in style of implementation.

One of the characteristics of HRM, of course, is its attempt to address organizational change in a comprehensive fashion. Equally, technical change has often neglected the need for accompanying organizational change, leading to suboptimization of systems and failed implementations (Bessant, 1991). While the first era of technical change at Hardy Spicer certainly included organizational change, the second era has begun to do so in an even more comprehensive way. This raises the question, 'how far is such organizational change a necessary adjunct to technical change, and how far is it driven by management philosophy?' In each case, we can trace specific effects from technology, as the company has moved from a highly engineered flow-line philosophy to arguably a lower level of engineering involved in cellular manufacture. However, in the second era it seems that management philosophy has begun to assume a more independent and decisive role.

This raises the interesting prospect (developed more fully in John Bessant's chapter in this volume) that certain models of technology currently being adopted in advanced factories allow greater scope for management choice in the social and organizational arrangements; encourage more comprehensive design of these; and encourage a greater role to be given to the human element in the operation of these systems. This suggests a happy conjunction between new systems of technology and HRM, as a form of social engineering and as a philosophy that implies greater employee involvement and fuller use of human potential. In other words, the opportunities provided by a paradigm shift in the design and use of technology may be fundamental to the realization of HRM itself as a paradigm shift in the management of people.

This chapter explores three key themes: (i) the evolution of personnel's involvement in technical change, including the role played by others; (ii) the extent to which there is evidence of a shift towards a new paradigm of human resource management; (iii) the nature and extent of organizational change in relation to specific forms of technology. The presentation of these themes necessarily addresses two other substantive topics which have featured widely in the technical change and HRM literatures during recent years. The first concerns the role of trade unions, including the decision to invest on a 'brownfield' site; the second concerns employee flexibility, especially the development of flexible skills.

System and Employment Change at Hardy Spicer

Hardy Spicer is a subsidiary of GKN, acquired in 1966 along with a number of other companies as part of GKN's diversification into automotive components.[1] At that time, its main product was in conventional propeller ('prop') shafts for rear-wheel drive vehicles. In addition, however, it had developed a special joint – the constant velocity (CV) joint – for use in front-wheel drive cars, and in 1959 had begun to supply the Mini as the first production model to adopt front-wheel drive on a large scale. During the 1960s and 1970s, its CV joint production grew as car manufacturers increasingly switched to front-wheel drive, and CV joints became one of GKN's most profitable businesses.

In the early 1970s, GKN acquired further subsidiaries in Germany and France (the Uni-Cardan Group) in order to gain control of other patents and production facilities relating to constant velocity joints, and in 1978 and 1981 put down plants in the United States in North Carolina. Joint venture deals in various non-European countries and the acquisition of two plants in Spain in the 1980s completed a network of plants which enabled GKN to supply the world's car manufacturers on a pan-European and global basis. While Hardy Spicer is the only manufacturer of CV joints in the UK, it is thus just one of a number of such companies within the GKN Group. The result is that its own performance is constantly measured against facilities in France, Germany, Italy, Spain and the United States, both by GKN and its customers. This is a continuing feature, from the early 1980s, when Hardy's cost structure began to deteriorate relative to the newer plants, to the present time. In addition, some car manufacturers, such as Peugeot, produced CV joints in-house, although only General Motors in the United States and Europe was a direct competitor, while two Japanese firms (NTN and NSK) supplied the Japanese market through licences from Hardy Spicer and Citroën respectively.

The ensuing process of technical change at Hardy Spicer was stimulated by three factors: (i) the pressure for lower prices and higher quality around 1980 from customers themselves under increasing threat from Japanese car manufacturers; (ii) the looming expiry of its patents in 1988, with the loss of significant royalty income and the threat of open competition from Japanese CV joint manufacturers; and (iii) the collapse during the recession of 1979–82 of the UK truck and agricultural vehicle markets which cut profits and sales from its other major product line, propeller shafts.

The immediate financial problem led to the closure of three peripheral plants, the transfer of 'prop' shafts to another company within the Group, and a concentration on CV joints at the main Birmingham site. During this rationalization, between 1979 and 1983, employee numbers were reduced from nearly 3,700 to just over 2,000. These actions produced a significant recovery in profitability. Table 4.1 shows the early recovery. (The renewed decline in the late 1980s was partly the effect of falling royalty income, plus the introduction of divisional charges and exceptional redundancy costs in 1990.)

The company was still at serious risk, however, of losing one or more of its three principal customers, and only avoided this by agreeing a series of five-year sales contracts at lower prices. This forced the issue of plant modernization to reduce operating costs and secure more reliable quality. At around the same time, in 1981–3, the divisional managing director for the automotive businesses took the managing directors and senior production engineers from the Group's CV joint companies on successive visits to

Table 4.1 *Hardy Spicer profit/loss (£m), 1980–1991*

1980	(0.7)	1986	11.7
1981	0.7	1987	8.6
1982	(2.4)	1988	6.7
1983	8.2	1989	(0.6)
1984	10.3	1990	(7.5)
1985	11.6	1991	1.6

Losses appear in parentheses.

Japan to observe manufacturing systems there. As a result, each company was instructed to develop an engineering strategy to take them into the 1990s.

Accordingly, Hardy Spicer engaged consultants in late 1983 with a brief to improve productivity against specific targets for return on sales (at least 10 per cent) and capital (at least 20 per cent). These implied a reduction of 16 per cent in manufacturing costs and an overall cut in the labour force of around 40 per cent – approximately 50 per cent in direct and line-related indirect labour (setters, inspectors, labourers) and 25 per cent in other indirect employees (tooling, maintenance supervision and quality control). Table 4.2 shows the projected impact on employment of the system design adopted in 1984, and what had actually transpired by 1992 as plans were modified.

A second problem was the age and diversity of the machine stock, which contributed to inefficiency, quality problems and material waste. The existing plant comprised nearly 1,400 machines – half more than 15 years old and a third more than 20 years old, ranging from 'stand-alone', manually loaded and operated machines, to modern CNC machine tools with some automation of materials transfer. Modernization aimed, therefore, at a substantial reduction in the machine population and improved layout, making use of the latest in CNC technology and robotics, which was seen by then as having reached a level of maturity and reliability. As the consultants argued, 'the basis for achieving the substantial cost reduction required is a significant investment in flexible automation, including "state of the art" machine tool and materials handling technology'. However, as they also noted, this would require a 'step-change in people policies' – a point emphasized in the devotion of one volume of

Table 4.2 *Changes in occupational categories in manufacturing at GKN Hardy Spicer, 1984–1992*

	1984 Actual	1989/90 Projected	1992 Actual	
Supervisors	2	24	18	
Production foremen	30	0	0	
Chargehands	2	218	142	Technical operatives
Setter-operators/toolsetters	220	21	79	
Direct operators	837	182	390	
Labourers	91	24	16	
Others	6	49	58	Apprentices/research
Inspectors	101	37	43	
Mechanical maintenance	71	56 ⎫	55	
Electrical maintenance	28	28 ⎭		
Maintenance labourers	28	0	1	
			20	New tech. maintenance
Toolroom	63	51	32	
			63	Stores and drivers
	1,479	690	917	

their report (alongside a volume each on the technical and financial aspects) to the human resource implications.

New Technology

With these objectives in view, the question was whether to go for a flexible manufacturing system (FMS) or a 'just-in-time' (JIT) approach. In the event, cutting direct and indirect manning and reducing work-in-progress, in conjunction with relatively high product volumes (thirty-three types of CV joint, three major customers and a projected annual output of around six million joints), led Hardy Spicer to adopt a form of 'just-in-time' manufacture which they termed an 'integrated flexible flow-line'.

This approach was applied to the five components of the CV joint – bells, bar shafts, tulips, cages and inners. New lines had, in fact, been laid down for 'tulips' around 1980, but for each of the other components a substantial investment in new facilities was required. The centrepiece was the 'bell' line. This comprised seven CNC cells carrying out various machining operations, plus induction hardening, and a 'crack detection' facility providing final inspection before the 'bells' went for assembly with the other parts. Each cell was linked by a moving conveyor, with robot arms transferring components to and from machine operations along the 100 metre line. Three shorter lines produced the bar shafts, cages and inner races.

The original plan was for three sets of such lines, entirely replacing old technology for all but rework and short runs, with a total investment of £28m, spread over three phases. Included in this were also radical improvements in manufacturing support services (quality control, plant maintenance, tooling and materials handling), and improved design and development through the purchase of CAD/CAM. Certain of these enhancements were incorporated in the manufacturing technology, through automatic on-line inspection systems and the elimination of handling through automation; other areas, like maintenance and tooling, benefited from new standardized machines and controls. Most support functions, nevertheless, had also to raise their levels of expertise and standards, and develop a new sense of their role involving tighter disciplines and management control. Among these, the consultants' report pointed to the urgent need to strengthen production engineering as the critical function in managing the technical side of implementation. As a result, a new engineering director was recruited and during 1984–6 he recruited fifteen new graduate/professional engineers (out of a department of fifty), while five staff with skills limited to 'tool-proving' activities were redeployed into production supervision, setting and maintenance.

The biggest rethinking of roles and skills, however, concerned direct production employees. Two factors were critical – reduced numbers of production employees (illustrated by Table 4.2), and the need to maintain continuous running of the integrated lines. This meant operators taking all 'first level' decisions at the point of production to keep the line running – including basic fault-finding and maintenance, and validating and editing of programs to set up machines for production (in the absence of hard-wired DNC links). Secondly, to provide flexibility with reduced manning it meant they should operate as a team (backed by a small 'central resource' of specialist maintenance engineers).

These technological 'imperatives' clearly signalled to the company the need to develop multi-skilled 'technical operatives' with a knowledge of machining, programming, hydraulics, electrics and electronics. At the same time, electrical and mechanical maintenance staff were also to become multi-skilled, with the elimination of formal demarcations. The original plans also considered replacing foremen with 'team leaders' in the team, but this was not finally implemented until 1990.

The plans approved in July 1984 envisaged installation of the new lines in three phases over five years. The first set of lines were installed from autumn 1985 onwards and in production by March 1986; the second entered production in November 1987; and the CAD/CAM system was introduced in July 1986. In the event, plans for a third set of flow-lines were abandoned in favour of a series of manufacturing cells. There were a number of reasons for this. In the first place, the introduction of a night shift in August 1986 (subsequently replaced in November 1987 by a continental-style, 12-hour double-day shift system) gave round-the-clock production and went a long way towards creating the capacity which a third line would have provided. Secondly, a third flow-line, with new machining centres, robots and conveyor systems, was extremely expensive. And thirdly, cells gave greater flexibility better adapted to a changed commercial climate and order book.

As a result, GKN approved further investment of £9.5m to set up six machining cells, plus assembly cells and a third bar shaft line, to be installed in two phases through 1991–3 (following the setting up of a prototype cell (Cell 1) in 1989). In this way, cells will account for all assembly work and around a third of bell production. Each cell contains the full range of operations (like a flow-line) but produces the component for a particular customer (or in some cases two). This contrasts with 'tulips' where machines are organized on a group manufacturing principle with all similar machines together. Thus, Cell 1 serves Rover and Ford; Cell 2 Volvo and Chrysler; Cell 3 Nissan; and Cell 4 Landrover.

Managing Technical Change in a Unionized Environment

The way Hardy Spicer went about introducing technical change in 1984 stood out against two well-publicized trends of the time – the move to locate major new investment on greenfield sites and the suggestion that management should limit the role of trade unions. When they put up their investment proposals in 1984, everyone in the company was aware of the recent precedent of another West Midlands car components firm, Lucas, going to a greenfield site at Telford. The supposed advantages of greenfield sites have dwelt on the opportunities to introduce new values and employment practices (see Preece's summary in Chapter 5, this volume). On the other hand, relocating in this way may insufficiently consider the availability of an appropriate skill base at a greenfield site elsewhere, and underestimate the value of building on an existing skill base.

Although the new flow-lines would not use machining skills directly, such skills and know-how have been shown to be indispensable to CNC operation (Jones, 1982; Scott, 1985), and there are obviously then economies in developing the skills of an existing workforce. Hardy Spicer reflected this argument through the strong commitment of its managing director, David Mackin, to training, especially apprentice training, his belief in the ability of the workforce to raise their level of skills, and in the recent raising of training and recruitment standards in anticipation of new technology. The high pay culture was also felt to give the company a highly motivated workforce. In retrospect, therefore, David Mackin believed that it had actually been easier to manage the process as a 'brownfield' development. (However, he and others would also have been aware that GKN had recently built a greenfield factory for CV joints in North Carolina without a local engineering tradition or skill base.)

The major factor in favour of development on the 'brownfield' site, however – certainly in the eyes of the GKN board – was the history of cooperation between management and workforce in adopting new technology and in already achieving big reductions in employment. In effect, the company already operated as a 'single union' site. One union, the Metal Mechanics (then part of TASS) represented 70 per cent of the workforce and dominated the company, with the then AEU having 20 per cent and the EETPU and TGWU a handful each. Moreover, while the bulk of the Metal Mechanics' membership were machine operators, union representation did not split strictly along job and skill lines, and the ten shop stewards on the joint industrial council (JIC) were a highly cohesive group under the leadership of a well-respected convenor. Joint consultation was well developed and the relationship between management and the unions was open, cooperative and pragmatic. As one union member put it, 'Everything gets sorted out here. The industrial relations are brilliant – basically because we don't have inter-union problems, and because of the JIC. We don't stop work while we're sorting a problem out.' Similarly, according to personnel director Brian Clamp:

> We discuss everything and anything. The style is to make a lot of noise, and settle. Graham Gould [the convenor] is essentially looking for solutions to problems. The biggest rows are not about pay issues, but where he feels a lack of consultation that puts him on the spot when he hasn't a ready answer to his members.

This positive industrial relations climate and the pragmatism of the unions was likewise recognized by the consultants in their 'audit' of human resource issues, although they also noted that 'the scale of technological and cultural changes envisaged in the next five years will put severe demands on management to maintain a receptive environment'.

With this tradition of consultation, the unions were brought into the picture as soon as the company engaged consultants to carry out the technical study. As the outlines of the new lines then began to firm up during early 1984, a scale model was built and presentations were made to the JIC, and then jointly by managers and shop stewards in a series of meetings with all employees. As Brian Clamp put it:

> We talked and talked about the concept of the new line. We showed them the model. And we said, the alternative is that we don't do it here. In our conversations, the union really said: 'You've got a free hand, we don't want you saying that the union blocked you. So you tell us what you want, and we will see if we can help you deliver it'. It became increasingly clear to them that we were in a survival situation. We had to invest, and if we invested, it would have a dramatic effect on all their existing agreements.

As a colleague observed, 'Brian was sowing seeds furiously with the convenor over that period'. At the same time, the convenor readily identified the extent of job losses, but saw the positive side of new technology very much along the lines which Daniel and Millward identify in Chapter 3 – as a commitment to the future of the company and a way of saving some jobs in the face of losing them all (probably to one of GKN's other companies).

One of the distinctive aspects of technical change at Hardy Spicer at the outset was therefore the active involvement of the trade unions in the process, and the role of the personnel director and industrial relations manager in maintaining consultation. This belies a unitaristic model of HRM in which management attempts to squeeze out trade unionists. Indeed, the company tacitly rejected the consultants' suggestion that there should be less reliance on the union and convenor as a channel for communication with the workforce, and preferred to continue working closely with its unions. This remained a continuing feature in the industrial relations style throughout the period and a consistent theme into the 1990s. As Brian Clamp put it in 1987:

> We've got a very participative style of operating. The convenor plays a very influential part in the way this company operates, and we're happy to work that way because it's successful. We determine objectives, and then we discuss collectively how we're going to achieve them. He delivers the goods and we achieve what we want to achieve. It works because the workforce trust him to act in their best interests.

That said, the union stance up to 1990 was essentially reactive, responding to proposals the company initiated, and governed by the tight rein on which the convenor held his shop stewards. Thus, from the personnel department's view: 'If the convenor is with you, it's marvellous; if he's against you, it's hell'. With the retirement of the convenor in 1990, however, managers saw the union stance becoming more actively constructive (at the same time as a change in managing director provided a more suitable participatory environment).

Towards the Flexible Factory

'Flexibility' has supposedly been a prime objective of management in recent years (Atkinson and Meager, 1986; Pollert, 1991b), intrinsic also to HRM (Guest, 1987) and certainly an objective at Hardy Spicer. It was not pursued, however, because it gave management a freer rein to exercise control, nor to intensify work (the piecework system already sustained a high level of effort), nor was it pursued independently of other objectives such as the maintenance of equity. Jobs and work organization were modelled on ideas of 'responsible autonomy', with minimal specification of tasks and a minimum of supervision. As the managing director put it: 'We wrote all the nice words in the plan about the Japanese style of management and operator involvement, while trying to get away from the idea of "operators"'. On the other hand, but to the same end, the personnel director, Brian Clamp, saw the actual design as a logical and pragmatic result of the type of technology they had opted for – 'The start point was, "we're going to have few people on the new lines . . . What are we going to do? . . . they've got to be multi-skilled . . . they've got to be flexible"'.

While flexibility was a goal, then, it was pursued not as an end in itself, for productivity reasons, or as an humanistic ideal, but to make the technology work. On top of this it was, from the beginning, also bound up with the idea of employee commitment – maintaining commitment in the way new technology was introduced; developing commitment through new skills and participative forms of working; and fostering commitment through opportunities for additional learning and personal development. Consequently, flexibility was not pursued primarily through a bargaining process, as some kind of 'negotiated flexibility' (as in the example of Pirelli described by Clark in Chapter 6). There were never, for instance, any written job descriptions. The process of evolving skills through training was more important.

Through the 1980s, however, flexibility as an objective was largely confined to the shopfloor. While the first era of technical change sought to address wider organizational relationships, changes in these relationships were slow to come about until the second era of technical change tackled them more directly. Progress towards flexibility can therefore be described in terms of three periods – first, the negotiation of formal agreements, the definition of skills, selection, and training in the immediate period 1984–6; secondly, the struggle towards efficiency and the gradual acceptance of fundamental changes in the concept of supervision between 1986 and 1990; and thirdly, the wider cultural and organizational change post-1990, associated with changes in senior management and cell manufacture but made possible also by the progressive investment in skills over a number of years.

New Terms and Conditions

During the first half of 1984, new terms and conditions were agreed relating to 'new tech'. The key elements covered selection for the new jobs; gradings and pay; a training rate; shifts; flexibility between maintenance crafts; and arrangements and terms for voluntary redundancy. Traditionally, access to the most highly paid jobs under piecework was governed by length of service, with the Metal Mechanics exercising considerable leverage over the allocation of jobs. However, the company was clear that, in the words of Brian Clamp, 'we had to break all those links'. Equally, the union side was concerned that selection to 'new tech' should not be open to management favouritism. The result was an agreement to select through tests open to all employees, despite the absence of a testing tradition other than for apprentices, and despite the Metal Mechanics' traditional opposition. This allowed an element of self-selection into 'new tech'. As Brian Clamp put it, 'I was absolutely floored that we did that, because we'd never used a selection test of any sort, and here we were going from a nil situation to psychometrics'.

The second major departure was over pay. Machine operators enjoyed high status, and piecework enabled them to earn relatively high wages of around £220 per week with bonuses – that is, up to £20 more than setters, electricians, fitters, foremen and toolroom on the skilled rate, and more than some on the bottom of the scale for production engineers. Their status was reflected in the oft-repeated phrase, 'the pieceworker is king', and the prevailing view, accepted by the managing director, that 'the pieceworkers are your motivated people – your skilled, your indirects, are less motivated'. Piecework, however, was not appropriate to machine-paced lines, and a single, basic rate 'technical operative' grade was introduced. However, views continued to differ as to how important some form of incentive bonus payment was to production. In 1984, no provision was made for paying a production bonus, although the convenor remained convinced that incentives were essential to keep men motivated.

The union was also concerned about the rate for working on 'new tech'. As the personnel director commented:

> We feel they are worth more. But the union doesn't, because, they say, 'You spent some of our money (meaning the company as a whole) in training these people. So while you've been training them, we've all had to work harder to support them. So it's wrong if they come out with a better package than what we've got. You mustn't be divisive, so pay them the skilled rate'.

When the first lines came on stream in 1985, therefore, technical operatives' pay, at the skilled rate, remained below what top pieceworkers could earn, and only achieved parity after a couple of years. By the same token, the union sought a training rate £40 (around 20 per cent) less than the top pieceworker could earn, and supported a 'trainee clawback' of training costs from any trainee leaving within an unreasonable period, which the company wrote into trainees' contracts. With these agreements applying to new technololgy, the old and new were symbolically separated by putting a fence round the area of the factory cleared for the new lines (the 'slab').

Skills, Selection and Training

The definition of tasks, jobs, skills, the people needed and the design of training followed the classic lines of systematic training needs analysis. When the lines were first conceived during 1983 and early 1984, an outline picture was formed and the details firmed up during autumn 1984. Reduced numbers of directs and indirects in production and the need to maintain continuous running of flow-lines suggested that operators would need to be multi-skilled 'technical operatives'. To give flexibility with fewer people, technical operatives would also need to function as a team. Significantly, the company rejected the consultants' view that there should be 'clear rules, discipline and strong line management/supervision over the control of work', and put the emphasis on personal responsibility and self-regulating groups, with team leaders within the group performing many traditional functions of the foreman.

In addition to numerical and manual aptitude tests for selection, therefore, the 16PF personality test was used to identify qualities of teamworker orientation and self-reliance. Supervisors' reports were also used to identify any significant problems of bad timekeeping or discipline. Some 800 employees, or half the workforce, opted to take the tests. Care was taken, however, not to demotivate those not selected for the first phase by 'failing' them, since continuing commitment on 'old tech' remained necessary. Instead, employees were told if there were particular weaknesses in education or attitude which they could remedy.

Although it was difficult in 1984–5 to predict staffing levels on the lines accurately, Brian Clamp and his training manager, Paul Trenberth, decided to go for a first training cohort of forty. At the heart of the whole implementation process, then, was the training programme which began in March 1985. This consisted of 6 months' off-the-job training covering team-building, drawing and measurement, basic machining, cutting tools, CNC programming and operation, and hydraulics, electrics and electronics for fault-finding and maintenance. Machining and programming were covered in the company's own training school and by assignments to existing CNC equipment in the factory, but modules for the other areas had to be built up in collaboration with external training providers. Trainees followed these various modules in groups of eight. Smaller numbers of maintenance staff from both the electrical and mechanical side (nine in the first phase) also followed individual programmes to fill gaps in their background and experience.

In addition to the formal programme of training, to develop 'ownership' of the new lines technical operatives also visited the machine suppliers (mostly abroad) to receive some training directly from them, participated in the 'signing off' procedures for the equipment along with quality and production engineers, and carried out the installation. This theme of ownership subsequently carried over into the working week, with the half-shift on Saturdays carrying out maintenance duties. While Hardy Spicer retained strong traditions of training, and was one of the few West Midlands companies to continue taking apprentices during the 1979–82 recession, 'new tech' training raised its commitment to training to a new level and transformed it. The immediate impact was to double overall spending on training between 1984 and 1985–6 to some 1.5 per cent of sales or 6.3 per cent of wages and salaries, with spending remaining high prior to the commissioning of new lines in 1985–7, 1989 and 1992. Up to 1990, some 160 technical operatives had been trained, with another 40 undergoing training during 1992, and a further 20 central service maintenance staff retrained.

The second impact of the new emphasis on training was to give many established employees their first taste of training, in conjunction with shopfloor training in 'statistical process control' (SPC), which began in 1984. Moreover, 'new tech' introduced principles of adult training into the company, with the participative style in which it was carried out important both for motivation and in setting the tone for self-reliance and teamwork later on the job. Third, it laid the basis for a flexibly skilled workforce in the longer term. Despite the fact that there was some rethinking in the second phase about how much knowledge of electronics shopfloor trainees could really achieve – and despite differences of view between the managing director and production managers on the one hand, and the personnel director and training manager on the other, about the value of extended off-the-job training – 'new tech' created a climate for training and education which has continued to grow. This is reflected in a trebling of fees paid by the company between 1991 and 1992 for external courses being taken by shopfloor employees in their own time. As training manager Paul Trenberth saw it, this represented a shift beyond training towards continuing education and personal development.

The Evolution of Jobs and Skills

'New tech' training aimed to develop an understanding of basic principles so that trainees could continue to build specific knowledge and skills subsequently on the job. To that extent, the company knowingly over-trained. The hope was that eventually technical operatives would be flexible between all machines on the line, and even between lines. In fact, this has been tempered for similar reasons to those Clark describes in Chapter 6 of this volume – recognizing 'horses for courses', specialist knowledge and ownership of work areas in particular. As a result, variation has developed in the extent to which individuals are truly multi-skilled. As Brian Clamp commented:

> Bill never goes anywhere but lathes, and he will concentrate on lathes on bell lines 1 and 2, because that's what he's best at, and they know he is, and he's

happy to do that. On the other hand, I've got people who are happy to go anywhere. I think it's good that people can still develop individual interests, and we benefit from that, but it's not structured and orderly.

At the same time, we should be careful how we interpret multi-skilling. First, there is the question 'what do technical operatives actually do?' And secondly, the discipline or job background 'multi-skilled' people come from can colour their views significantly. 'Multi-skilling' is not necessarily the same as upskilling (Lee, 1981; Kern and Schumann, 1984; Hendry, 1990). Thus, in the selection for the first phase, 'skilled' grades initially predominated (including many who had come through the apprenticeship system), with only about a third having been machine operators. In the second and later phases, however, as the apprentice source was exhausted, the ratio of formerly skilled/unskilled grades was more even. The result was, on occasion, a considerable difference in job satisfaction between former machinists and former apprentices ('at the end of the day, I didn't expect to be a glorified pieceworker') – especially when the work involved a large degree of machine-minding when lines were running properly. One way out of this, which allows skills to continue to evolve, has been in the opening up of career paths from the technical operative role into factory management and production engineering.

As I have described in detail elsewhere (Hendry, 1990, 1991), multi-skilling of production workers has also impacted on a number of other skill groups, providing fertile ground for 'contest' and 'negotiation' (Wilkinson, 1983). The background to this was the deliberate avoidance of written job descriptions. As a technical operative put it, 'There is no limit to the job we've got. There's nothing laid down in writing about what the job is. The job is whatever needs to be done'. For those like maintenance and production engineers whose own skills have been increasingly stretched and upgraded, this has provoked no great conflict. The ability of production management and supervision to adjust, however, has been slower.

Accommodating and managing these complex adjustments in role, motivation and careers over time is one of the more subtle tasks of personnel management undertaken by both personnel and line managers. Internally, it focused on the abolition of foremen and adoption of team leaders (see below). Externally, it focused on the need to stem the loss of engineers with increasing experience on leading-edge technology, who were being tempted away by higher salaries elsewhere. To combat this and support the need for rising standards, a new pay and grading structure was introduced in 1987, geared more to external market rates and emphasizing professional qualifications and responsibilities.

Achieving Efficiency: 1986–1990

Nine months on from start-up, by late 1986, the new lines in phase 1 had reached only 30 per cent efficiency (measured, albeit unrealistically, against maximum output over 24 hours' continuous operation). The production manager attributed the number and length of shutdowns to the high proportion (75 per cent) of ex-'indirect' employees selected for the first phase, while the managing director blamed it on their training:

> I wouldn't take shopfloor people off for 6–9 months' training again. They've lost the work ethic. We've trained them in everything else except achievement and there is no impatience to get things done. They switch the line off for hours, and have lost sight of what it is all about. You can almost hear them saying, 'break down, break down, I want to use the skills I've got'. I've actually got the convenor saying to me, 'We've got to watch this multi-skill thing, because it's too interesting for them'.

To correct this, a more directive style of supervision was introduced, retreating further from the team leader concept which the 'new tech' teams had themselves so far been unwilling to adopt. A traditional foreman was put in charge of 'new tech', with more technically orientated, non-production supervisors working closely with the line to overcome technical problems. To technical operatives and maintenance staff, however, the problem was managers' not appreciating the difficulties of making the new plant work. As one technical operative put it, 'Where they went completely wrong was they educated us, then they said, "we'll get you a couple of managers". If I'm going to change my attitudes, then they've got to change theirs, and they should be part of a team'. Figures for training days in 1986 reveal this very starkly – 'management and supervisory training' accounting for only 251 days out of a total of 31,159.

While the question of supervision, along with that of incentive pay, rumbled on through the late 1980s, the company decided it needed to run the existing lines round the clock. Since this proposal for a night shift in August 1986 went back on the original 'new tech' agreements, it was resented – especially since most technical operatives and maintenance staff, not having been machine operators before, had not had to work night shifts on 'old tech'. For a period of 12 months the union agreed to provide a voluntary rota while a more permanent solution was worked out. In November 1987 a proposal for a continental-style, 12-hour double-day shift was approved by ballot, and phase 2 came into operation in 1987 on this basis. The increased capacity from this reduced the need for a third set of lines. Equally, it shows the company continuing to deal with industrial relations issues in a problem-solving, rather than autocratic manner.

Problems persisted, however, in achieving expected levels of efficiency. In phase 1, there were problems with particular pieces of equipment on cages, bells and shafts, while the switch to UK machines (with the lack of standardization) for phase 2 produced a host of new problems. Gradually these were overcome. Modifications were made to the bell line to reduce bottlenecks, including additional turning capacity off-line, and automatic inspection was replaced by visual checking and manual loading off the line. People became more familiar with the equipment. Scheduling improved to reduce downtime. Product design was changed slightly to improve machinability. And eventually, after much argument, a group bonus scheme was introduced in July 1990 which paid up to a quarter of total pay. The cumulative impact was to double output over a couple of months to 70–80 per cent of the design maximum of 240 parts an hour.

Technical and Organizational Change

Despite these improvements, however, Hardy Spicer was failing to meet corporate targets and in 1990 faced renewed financial losses (albeit aggravated by additional divisional and exceptional redundancy charges). In part this was due to the problems of achieving better productivity under renewed price pressure and reliable quality, in part it was the result of a loss of control in other areas – in planning and in top-level customer liaison. The replacement of the managing director in 1990 in the face of these pressures, including that of continually having to meet pan-European productivity standards within GKN, if nothing else proved the point of the chairman in 1982 when he had said, 'a company can only take so much change'. From 1990, under new leadership, there were three developments which then began to hasten the progress of organizational change:

1   the accumulated benefits from the way the company had approached technical change in the first place, including the emergence of a learning culture as former 'new tech' trainees pursued further education in their own time;
2   a more participative style coming from the top, a rethinking of organizational structures across the company (including the introduction of team-based working on the factory floor), and culture change in the form of greater employee involvement being embraced as a declared aim; and
3   the introduction of cell manufacture, which is in the process of consolidating the team-based system of working and for the first time addressing the systematic training needs of 'old tech' employees.

Goodwill and a Learning Culture

Two factors contributed perhaps more than anything else to the continuing commitment of employees to technical change – the phasing of redundancy which allowed employees to manage the onset of retirement, and the extent of training. On top of this, organizational change, then and subsequently, was seen as continuous with beneficial technical changes.

Because it lacked the engineering expertise in 1984 and because of the human costs involved, the company recognized it could not manage all the investment in one go. The fact that the age profile of the workforce was heavily skewed meant then that it was able to phase the loss of jobs over a 5-year period through natural wastage and early retirement. At the same time, intensive training demonstrated a continuing commitment to the workforce. As Brian Clamp, the personnel director, reflected:

When we started, we said we would take responsibility for training our workforce to cope with change – we won't buy people in with those skills, we will train our existing workforce. I think that meant a lot to them because it gave them fairly good security. They knew, because we had this long-established practice of dealing with problems by voluntary redundancy, that people could plan their retirement. You could leave the company when you chose almost, with a bit of money. And I suppose that gave them warm feelings towards the whole philosophy of new technology and change.

As long as you recognize you have an obligation to all the people who work in the company, and not just to a handful of picked people, then I think you get the sort of response we got. Because we talked about what we were going to do with individuals, they recognized we knew we had a responsibility. I think that pays off in all sorts of ways, and it allows us to be flexible. Similarly, if you put time and effort into training, then a lot of the problems you hear elsewhere we never had. We never paid for SPC; we don't pay average earnings for training. We have a set rate we pay them when they train, and they all accept it.

Indicative of how this has paid off in the longer term, many 'new tech' trainees have gone on after their initial training to take further courses under BTEC and City and Guilds, and progressed into jobs in engineering and production. Meanwhile, the company has laid on literacy and numeracy courses from time to time as less advantaged groups in the workforce have requested them, and since 1990, as the training function has taken over the budget for management development, supervisors and managers have increasingly been drawn into this 'learning culture'.

Organizational and Cultural Change – Towards Teamworking

Flow-line manufacture was modelled on principles of teamwork. The 'custodians' of this ideal, however, tended to be in personnel. At the same time, departmental barriers largely persisted, despite attempts to break them down (in, for example, joint SPC training for shopfloor, production engineers and quality engineers from 1984). In 1990, however, a new managing director, Tom Wood, and a new manufacturing director, Geoff Pearce, combining responsibilities for production and production engineering, created the basis for a stronger teamwork orientation throughout the company by introducing a different philosophy of management.

From 1986 to 1990, the idea of team leaders on 'new tech' was in effect deferred. Factory management were suspicious of something which would entail a shift in role from foremen acting as 'gofers' to the factory manager to team leaders acting more independently. Technical operatives were also reluctant to take on something which meant no pay for additional responsibilities, while they also objected that it went against the idea they had been taught of personal responsibility and independence. Personnel managers and line managers meanwhile had other problems on their hands in getting the new plant fully up and running efficiently.

In 1988–9, BRD, a local sister company of Hardy Spicer, implemented the team leader concept under its managing director, Tom Wood. In 1990, Tom Wood took over as managing director of Hardy Spicer. Unlike his more autocratic predecessor, he had a strong belief in delegation and that if you gave people ownership, it would release more of their potential. Foremen blocked that energy. BRD had, therefore, got rid of foremen. As a result, in October 1990, Hardy Spicer followed suit, appointing team leaders and abolishing foremen across the whole factory.

Thus, the team leader principle, originally conceived in 1983–4 in relation specifically to 'new tech', has now been adopted wholesale. To make this happen two other things were necessary. First, teams had to be formed. The flow-lines had defined teams from the beginning. On 'old tech', however, some reorganization had to take place to define work areas more clearly. Of the twenty-five to thirty teams per shift thus formed (in addition to the eight teams per shift on 'new tech') some are still felt to be too large, with teams ranging from five to twenty workers. Secondly, piecework had to be abolished and replaced by a system of team bonuses. Thus, the adoption of team bonuses in 'new tech' in 1990 was part of this much wider process.

The team leader concept put in place had certain precise characteristics which we should note. First, it was agreed at a special management–union conference that team leaders should not be appointed by management, but be elected or nominated by the team, with management simply having the power of veto. Initially also it was agreed they should not be offered more pay, since the convenor took the view that people should take the job because they wanted to, not because of the carrot of more money. However, they later received a small allowance of just £10 a week. On the management side, however, there is some dissatisfaction at the overall quality of team leaders. Secondly, the team leader is an active working member of the team, responsible for improving team efficiency and liaising with other departments and sections, but with no disciplinary supervisory role. They are also without the burdensome administrative functions which were felt to be giving difficulties at the Rover car factory nearby, where team leaders had also been created. Thirdly, the role was implemented at a lower hierarchical level than at BRD, where they are called 'facilitators'. The higher the level, the more potential there is for conflict between a trade union role and a 'supervisory' role. Even so, there have been some conflicts of role where a team leader is also a shop steward. This has been complicated by the concurrent changes involving the abolition of piece-work and the reorganization of teams where a shop steward may have to put the team's case against the assignment to the group of a particular individual.

Alongside these changes at shopfloor level, there have been two other reorganizations that touch the higher echelons of the company, and strike at functional boundaries which had more or less remained intact through the 1980s. Towards the end of 1990, Hardy Spicer adopted the philosophy of 'concept-to-customer' to provide better coordination of functions in product design and development. Five product engineering teams (PETs) of four to seven people, depending on the scale of work for particular customers, were formed, with staff from applications engineering, production engineering, quality engineering, sales and purchasing working closely with customers and manufacturing. A lot of work was done on team-building with these groups, and this has now been linked to accreditation under the national programme to promote management education in the UK known as the Management Charter Initiative (MCI). Against the background of a general dearth in management training before (as the figures for 1986 illustrated), this also represents an important broadening of the whole training effort in the company.

While some production engineers have been assigned to commercial engineering in this way, the remainder have been assigned to a reorganized factory system and located in new offices on the factory floor. Since autumn 1990 manufacturing has been progressively reorganized into five separate factories (for the five components of the CV joint), each with its own group of decentralized production engineers and maintenance engineers under a factory manager and two shift deputies. In this way, the philosophy of giving people a greater sense of ownership is being implemented through the 'small factory concept'.

However, as Tony O'Leary, the new human resources director appointed from Venture Pressings (see Chapter 5), notes, 'new ways of working require new ways of managing'. Despite one or two new appointments and in-house GKN management development programmes, there still remain perennial weaknesses in leadership skills and the level of technical competence, although these are not unique to Hardy Spicer within British industry. On the other hand, Hardy Spicer is now much more closely linked into GKN's graduate engineering scheme (while continuing with its own sponsorship of apprentices on to degree programmes, which has somewhat different aims) than it was five years ago, and two graduates have recently been appointed from this into the new factory manager jobs.

In addition to specific reorganizations, a major 'activity-based costing' consultancy exercise took place in 1991 aimed at reducing costs. This has resulted in the formation of cross-functional project teams (currently around ten) to work on specific problems of performance in different parts of the company. Finally, Hardy Spicer began to engage with TQM by participating in NEDO's 'Strategies for Success' scheme with a major customer, Nissan. With the example of the Rover company's 'Rover 2000' vision and mission statement nearby, Hardy Spicer have sought to crystallize these various organizational initiatives into a vision statement of their own – 'Hardy Spicer 2000' – with business-focused mission objectives developed for each function. In this way, the need for 'new ways of managing' is being framed within a cultural statement focused on customer need. As such, this originates as much from general and line management as from the personnel function.

Cellular Manufacture

Since 1991, the adoption of cell manufacture, with its associated principles of teamworking, has sharpened up the whole system of teamworking and acted as a stimulant to systematic training to underpin it. Cells consist of a group of activities, arranged in a 'U'-shape, producing a whole component for a particular customer, or assembling it. They contain the same sequence of processes and range of machines as, for instance, on the 'bell' line. The difference is there is no automation of material flow (that is, no robots and no moving conveyors), although the just-in-time principle still applies. In some respects, therefore, it involves a lower level of technology. Technically, the changes consist of new machines and refurbishment of existing ones, with restructuring to improve process flow, while cellular manufacture in the assembly factory is modelled on the system in Hardy Spicer's sister company in Spain.

Employees have greater control of the process and a greater sense of ownership, however: they produce a complete component; they are closer to the quality problems and can intervene more quickly; and they have the motivation to do so because the six or so people in each cell (one of whom is also the team leader) are physically closer together and get a common bonus. This is a major change from 'old tech', especially for assembly workers, whom 'new tech' entirely passed by. To support the introduction of cells (and teams generally) there has been an unparalleled effort to assess individual training needs, beginning with basic numeracy, literacy and the ability to read technical drawings; detailed training manuals have been written; some ninety or so trainers/team leaders have been appointed to cover all sections in every shift; employees are undertaking a 6-week full-time training programme prior to the setting up of each cell; and novel use is being made of video by trainees to analyse their work processes. In these ways, a systematic effort is being made to raise work standards all round.

Because there is no moving line, however, there are not the same technological imperatives for multi-skilled 'technical operatives' which automation of the 'transfer' process (Bell, 1972) under JIT occasioned. Although cell manufacture means operators managing a number of machines and, for some, learning to operate CNC for the first time, such changes belong to an earlier period of automation. As a result, it remains an open question whether the 'old tech' system of setters and operators should be retained or whether the company should go, nevertheless, for multi-skilled setter-operators. The desire to flatten the organizational structure certainly points to the latter. As such, it raises the interesting thought that management are being guided by a belief in people's potential as much as by engineering considerations. Thus, there is a retreat from automation, partly influenced by capital considerations and increased product complexity, but based also on a belief that people are more flexible than machines. As Geoff Pearce, the manufacturing director, argues:

> Even the Japanese moved far too quickly. In the mid-1980s, the rate at which they introduced automation was phenomenal. I think they're now feeling the pain of that, because I don't believe they fully explored and utilized the flexibility of the human being on the line. I'm of the opinion we don't fully explore that here when we introduce automation. You can over-engineer a job. In most cases we don't need an all-singing-all-dancing automated system.

Conclusion: Change and the Role of Personnel

One of the problems in evaluating organizational change of any kind is disentangling the claims of different individuals to have been the prime mover in the process. As we have seen, a major impetus to the whole process came from outside Hardy Spicer, from Trevor Bonner, the divisional managing director. Even the critical sales agreement with Ford which secured Hardy Spicer's immediate future in 1982 was concluded at divisional level. Bonner also appointed a new chairman to Hardy Spicer in 1982, and in 1990 replaced the managing director when the company made renewed losses. The role of a higher corporate authority in these kinds of decisions is hardly surprising.

At company level, Hardy Spicer's personnel director, Brian Clamp, was always at pains to emphasize that the changes were a team effort, and made a point of sharing the presentation ceremony for the 'excellence in personnel management' award at the 1988 IPM conference with the union convenor and industrial relations manager. New appointments during the 1980s also contributed significant technical and personnel leadership:

a new production engineering director in May 1984;
a quality manager in early 1984;
a training manager (Paul Trenberth) to run SPC training and subsequently the training of technical operatives in which he introduced an entirely new style of training to the company; and
a new production director in April 1987 (promoted to another GKN company in 1990).

In the 1990s, further changes included a new managing director (1990), a new manufacturing director experienced in cell manufacture (1990) and a 'human resources director' also with experience in cell manufacture (1992) who replaced 'personnel director' Brian Clamp. In 1990, the union convenor, Graham Gould, also retired. While these changes emphasize the contribution of many individuals, through the 1980s continuity and leadership was provided by the managing director, personnel director and union convenor.

The account of technical change clearly shows the leading role played by personnel in conceiving the necessary changes relating to people and steering them through, and that technical change ought not to be seen as a once-and-for-all event. This involvement began with the establishment of sound industrial relations structures; the raising of apprentice recruitment and training standards in 1982–3; and then contributed significant input to the consultants' proposals in 1984 in the volume devoted to the human resource implications of technical change and its design. The complex unsettling of skills and role relationships which flow-line technology induced meant that the personnel function had a continuing part to play in managing these adjustments over a number of years, culminating in the eventual implementation of the team leader concept in 1990 after this was originally defined in the plans drawn up in 1984. Thus, we see genuinely 'strategic' behaviour which combines both planning and adaptation to an evolving situation.

That aside, there is a clear implication that more radical forms of technological change produce a greater involvement on the part of personnel. In this connection, it is the automation of the transfer process, combined with just-in-time principles, which is crucial. The first era of technical change thus supports a relatively determinist view of technology (Clark et al, 1988; McLoughlin and Clark, 1988) albeit with humanistic consequences. The second era, since 1990, however, sees a greater degree of organizational change against a lower level of technical change. Technical change now appears to be framed within organizational change rather than the other way round. One way in which this can come about is that managers' perceptions of what can be expected of employees rise. Technical change and training can itself set a virtuous spiral of this kind in motion (Hendry, 1990). However, although the training of technical operatives has certainly contributed to this at Hardy Spicer, it seems more due to two other factors.

First, a new generation of managers has come in with ideas about human potential drawn from the socio-democratic tradition, and to some extent with specific influences from HRM. In this way, managerial values are as much conditioned by societal values as by what they see of the workforce skills around them. Secondly, however, there is the philosophy of manufacturing itself which allows the human factor a more significant role, while organizing employees into business-related units. Customer influence in this respect is significant. New Japanese customers, Nissan and Toyota, and older customers like Ford and Rover who have been influenced by Japanese practices, have become more and more visible on the shopfloor at Hardy Spicer. The detailed attention they give to the machines that do the work for their products (to the extent that the company cannot change these without their consent), and the training of employees on these, create pressure for teamworking and for employees to take responsibility for quality, delivery and continuous improvement. In turn, these demand a different order of commitment that goes beyond a simple conception of skill. As John Bessant observes in Chapter 10 of this volume, this transition from being manufacturing-led to customer-led (evident at Hardy Spicer in its restructuring of both design and manufacturing) means that personnel or human resource issues are likely to become of strategic importance. More broadly, the conjunction of a paradigm shift in manufacturing and towards HRM, hinted at earlier, fulfils the demand of Hayes and Abernathy (1980) for management to give more primacy to the person over the machine, and Hayes, Wheelwright and Clark's (1988) vision of a dynamic manufacturing system orientated towards continuous learning.

Whether the personnel function retains custody of these is another matter, though. Brian Clamp was always clear that personnel should not be taking responsibility for dealing with factory floor issues. Equally, though, team leaders were frequently at the department's door with problems, and were dealt with on the grounds that factory management were incapable of doing so. Clearly, middle management have been a weak link. What the effect of a human resource proficient/technically competent factory management might be on the personnel role, should it develop, is uncertain. It may well be that leadership passes to manufacturing management (Storey, 1992a) and to a rejuvenated middle management within it.

In this connection, the self-presentation of personnel is also critical. Throughout the period described, Brian Clamp was always adamant that he was doing personnel management, not HRM, and disliked the term 'human resource management'. Yet many of the strategic and systematic qualities HRM lays claim to were well in evidence. What HRM brings is a greater espousal of the language of business, and overt reference to culture change. This may simply reflect, however, a strategy for legitimacy described years before HRM appeared (Legge, 1978). The problem for personnel in espousing HRM is that it requires the personnel practitioner to plan and act strategically while the operational reins pass increasingly to line managers. The position of personnel in HRM may thus be undermined by the attenuation of its functional role (Torrington et al, 1985) which has been observed in practice to be occurring.

Note

1. The initial fieldwork on which this case is based was carried out in April–May 1987, following preliminary interviews with the managing director and personnel director. The main period of interviewing consisted of tape-recorded interviews with the managing director, personnel director, production engineering director, commercial director, works manager, quality manager, training manager, training and development manager, industrial relations manager, a foreman, the convenor, a group of eight technical operatives in training and three technical operatives who had completed theirs, with further interviews on the shopfloor. In addition, interviews were conducted with the company chairman, divisional managing director and Group human resources manager. Use was also made of company documents, including the consultants' report of 1984. From 1987 onwards, regular contact was maintained with the personnel director on in-company developments. A more comprehensive update was carried out in September 1992, through interviews with the manufacturing director, the new human resources director and with the personnel director after he left the company.

5

Human Resource Specialists and Technical Change at Greenfield Sites

David Preece

Greenfield sites allow managers to design human resource policies and practices largely unencumbered by pre-existing structures and approaches. They thus provide a rare opportunity to study what key decision-makers perceive to be desirable policies and practices to underpin the effective utilization of advanced technology. This chapter will begin with a general review of that part of the greenfield site literature which relates to human resource management and technical change, looking particularly at the role of specialist human resource managers and the significance of personnel/HRM issues. It will then go on to present data from a case study of a greenfield site set up in 1988 to manufacture car body panels using a mixture of automated and more conventional press lines and materials-handling equipment. The study will show how human resource specialists played an important role in the design of the new organization and its culture as well as in the implementation and operationalization of HR policies in areas such as work structuring, payment and grading systems, training and employee relations, communications and consultation. The chapter will conclude with some reflections on the importance of greenfield sites as an 'opportunity structure', both in relation to technical change and to human resource management.

Greenfield Sites, HRM and Technical Change

What are greenfield sites? It was somewhat easier to answer this question during the 1970s and early 1980s than has been the case since. The most often quoted overview of the UK literature was published in 1985 and based on data collected in 1984 (Beaumont and Townley, 1985). While the term has continued to remain in currency, not so much attention has been given to the phenomenon in the mainstream literature in recent years, which has tended to concentrate on other developments such as HRM, flexibility, Japanization and 'lean' production. Japanization (incorporating practices such as 'just-in-time', reduced lead times and quality management, see Ackroyd et al, 1988) and lean production (see Womack et al, 1990) are of particular interest here, both because the concepts permeate the greenfield site literature and because they are particularly associated with companies that operate in the motor manufacture and motor components supplier sector (the focus of the case study reported in this chapter).

So what are the defining features of greenfield sites? The essence of the term 'greenfield' is a geographical location where there are no pre-existing buildings. There are at least three main types of greenfield:

- **Company greenfield**, where a new company is established and begins operations for the first time on the new site
- **Replacement greenfield**, where an existing company builds and opens a new plant, and one or more of the company's older plants are closed, with the work and maybe some of the employees transferring to the new site
- **Expansion greenfield**, where a new plant is built and opened by an existing company with other plants. These continue in operation, at least in the short term.

There are, of course, a number of variations on these three basic types. For example, in some cases, new sites may have been set up explicitly to have a 'demonstration effect' on more traditional practices in the rest of the company, in others (particularly multi-divisional companies) new personnel policies may only apply to non-management staff as the company may wish to retain the flexibility to move managers across the divisions. However, in all cases the new geographical location is an 'opportunity structure' giving managers the chance to do something 'new', whether it be in the personnel, technical or other area of operation.

What are the main kinds of human resource strategies and policies which appear to be commonly developed and implemented at such locations? These can be briefly summarized drawing on the existing literature (IDS, 1984, 1990; IRRR, 1984, 1985a, 1985b, 1986a, 1986b, 1987a, 1987b, 1987c, 1988, 1990, 1991; Beaumont and Townley, 1985; Yeandle and Clark, 1989a, 1989b; Oliver and Wilkinson, 1989; Gleave and Oliver, 1990):

- Emphasis on new values and philosophies
- Fewer tiers of management
- 'Open' management style
- Devolution of responsibility and autonomy
- Redefinition of role of the supervisor/first-line manager
- Enhanced downward information flows, especially to groups or teams of employees
- Adoption of an HRM rather than traditional 'personnel management' approach
- Reduction of status differences, often involving single status or harmonization
- Functional labour flexibility (extended task/job range, reduced job demarcations)

- Systematic recruitment procedures, with emphasis on selecting employees with the 'right' or desirable attitudes
- Emphasis on training as a continuous process for all employees
- Either no union recognition, or single-union agreement
- Simple pay and grading system, usually rewarding achievement and the attainment of extra skills
- Joint consultative arrangements, often with elected delegates representing all employees rather than a union-based system.

Of course, many of these can also be found at brownfield sites. However, *it is the combination and integration of a wide range of these policies and practices, driven by an explicit human resource philosophy, which is typical of greenfield sites.* It is therefore important at an analytical level to distinguish between greenfield and brownfield sites, because although there are examples of major HRM innovations on brownfield sites (see, for example, Chapter 4, this volume), the existence of a greenfield site does appear to make a difference in terms of what can be, and has been, aimed for in the human resource management arena. In the words of Beaumont and Townley, the greenfield site 'offers the prospect of a *tabula rasa,* . . . the possibility of establishing work organization, job design, personnel and industrial relations policies afresh rather than attempting to tackle these issues on an ad hoc basis in existing plants. It provides the opportunity to experiment with the development of a coherent "greenfield" philosophy' (1985: 169). What is achieved in practice, of course, is another matter (see for example, Wickens, 1987; Trevor, 1988; Garrahan and Stewart, 1992; and the case study in this chapter and in Chapters 6 and 7, this volume).

In focusing on human resource strategies and policies, of course, there is a danger of overstating their significance in the original location decision compared with what are generally regarded as 'first order' technical or financial considerations (see for example, IDS, 1984; Whitaker, 1986; IRRR, 1990, 1991). However, it is important to recognize that human resource issues are not confined to the objectives and policies to be pursued *within* the plant. The local labour market can figure prominently in terms of wage levels and labour supply, as can perceptions of the general industrial relations climate of a country, particularly for foreign-owned companies contemplating 'inward investment'. Taking all this into account, there is substantial evidence that personnel/HR issues figure prominently on the agenda of companies that have established greenfield sites.

To what extent have human resource specialists been involved in planning and resourcing such sites under conditions of advanced technical change? There are a number of problems in attempting to answer this question. First, the main sources of relevant company-level information in the UK are *Industrial Relations Review and Report* (IRRR) and *Incomes Data Services (IDS) Studies*, both of which tend to reification. Their usual approach is to say 'the company' has decided to do this or that without identifying the actors involved. There is also a problem with what is meant by involvement. Does it mean actually being a party to the decision to adopt new technology, or does it mean involvement in the sense of contributing to the design of organization structures, new jobs, payment systems, employee selection and training, and so on? Different authors may be reporting different degrees of involvement on the basis of different interpretations, thus giving a misleading impression of the nature and degree of change. In addition, while we do know a certain amount about human resource specialists and about technology, when we add in greenfield sites the amount of data becomes very limited (although see also Chapter 6, this volume). However, two preliminary observations can be made.

First, the survey data which have influenced our perception of specialist HR involvement have tended to focus on the formal institutional context and may not have been sensitive enough to some of the nuances and complexities of organizational practice and processes. For example, when the role of HR managers in technical change is studied at close quarters, as in the longitudinal case studies of engineering companies and building societies which I conducted between 1983 and 1987, one finds that their involvement varies widely across different organizations, time periods and types of technology (Preece and Harrison, 1988; Preece, 1989). There were also indications of organizational learning, of an awareness that, with subsequent introductions or modifications of new technology, some of the earlier mistakes could be overcome with the help of specialist HR involvement and advice (Preece, 1989). There was even some evidence that HR specialists themselves may have actually understated their own contribution, either deliberately or unintentionally. For example, in one of the engineering companies, the HR manager deliberately took a 'low key' approach, arguing that new technology was nothing really new. He commented that if the Personnel Department 'was to go in in a high profile way, it would immediately be assumed that something drastic was about to happen' (1989: 214).

The second observation is that specialist HR involvement in technical change is likely to be greater both in foreign-owned companies and on greenfield sites. When the two are put together, then the chances are likely to be even higher. This is because, as Guest has noted, the HR department in foreign-owned companies 'has a higher profile and greater credibility' as an innovator in organizational processes and behaviour (1991: 162). This may be both a result of, as well as a contributory factor in, the features that characterize greenfield sites and play a part in their formation.

Case Study: Venture Pressings Ltd[1]

Background

The case study company was formed in February 1988 and is a £40m joint venture between Jaguar Cars and GKN Sankey. It is the sole supplier to

Jaguar of all its 'outer skin' car body panels. For Jaguar, as we will see, the search for a consistently higher level of panel quality was a key driving force in its involvement in the joint venture and the project work which preceded it. From a very early stage of the project discussions, the adoption of an HRM orientation within the organization was seen as being crucial to the attainment of these quality objectives.

The plant is located on a greenfield site on the outskirts of Telford in Shropshire, some 35 miles away from the nearest Jaguar plant in Birmingham. The factory has been constructed in the shell of what was previously a GKN Sankey tractor factory, and both the building and site have been extensively refurbished and equipped with entirely new services such as telecommunications, drainage and a new high perimeter wall blocking off the factory from other nearby plants. Although work has been transferred from other factories, these are quite separate, formally and legally, from GKN and Jaguar, and so the site (despite its mix of technologies, see below) approximates closest to a 'company greenfield'.

The main building houses fifty-three presses of up to 1,400 tonnes operating capacity. There are nine production lines, including two press lines equipped in total with fourteen materials-handling, programmable Comau robots which transfer body panels between presses without the need for manual intervention. The presses themselves are essentially 'old' presses, having been transferred from two GKN Sankey plants, although they have been substantially refurbished, including the fitting of new electrical systems and the incorporation of computer software facilitating statistical process control through continuous monitoring. The highly advanced Comau interpress robots installed on the two automatic press lines allow flexible handling of a variety of body panels through component interchange for mid-air transfer of panels between presses. There is a main toolroom for all die modifications and refurbishment, and two satellite toolrooms located in the manufacturing cells which support minor service operations. There are also Herwo die carts and quick slide adjustment systems for toolsetting purposes.

The £4m investment in interpress robots enables the production of over 300 panels an hour at maximum output. Overall the plant is capable of producing 80,000 car body panel sets per annum on a three-shift, 5-days-a-week basis. A tool transfer programme was completed in January 1992 with the release of dies from the Swindon factory of the Rover Group and from Karmann in Germany.

A single-union agreement was signed in May 1988 with the GMB. As well as giving sole recognition to the union it provided for a company council to be established as a forum for discussion and consultation, and for negotiating pay and terms and conditions of employment. The agreement commits employees to flexibility and mobility. The total number of employees as of May 1992 was 230. In addition, there were around forty-five manufacturing operative staff engaged on short-term contracts. This was somewhat short of the anticipated number, which was around the 320–330 mark and based on the projection of two-shift working, which, in the event, did not materialize. This was due to the depressed state of demand worldwide in the luxury car market and the entry of Japanese producers into this sector. The result was a downturn in volume at Jaguar (bought by Ford in 1989) to 25,000–30,000 cars a year in 1991–2 from a peak of over 50,000 in 1988–9. Venture Pressings Ltd (VPL) had been gradually building up employee numbers during late 1990/early 1991 in preparation for two-shift working when it became clear that Jaguar's sales were not likely to improve noticeably in the short term. The second shift was cancelled and fifty staff were made redundant in February 1991.

The mission statement expresses the commitment to develop a business 'which will rank alongside the leading manufacturers of automotive body pressings worldwide'. Emphasis is placed upon the achievement of quality products, continuous improvement, and employees as the 'key resource' of the company. A strong HRM orientation is apparent throughout.

Human Resource Management at VPL

Let us now focus on the structure, policies and role of the human resources department, which (as of April 1992) was headed by an HR manager assisted by a personnel administration officer and three specialists, responsible respectively for personnel, training, and health and safety. The HR manager, Anthony O'Leary, was the second appointee to the embryo company in April 1989 after the director and general manager (DGM), who came from GKN Sankey. He was a member of the executive management group and reported to the DGM. He had previously worked for a number of years for Jaguar, latterly at its Birmingham plant as the industrial relations manager.

The HR manager had sole responsibility for appointing his own staff. This was also true for the other executive managers, who had been 'headhunted' by the HR manager and the DGM with the help of an executive recruitment agency and were given a brief to select their own staff with the support of the HR department. All four personnel professionals had previous automobile manufacturing experience, three having previously worked for Jaguar (amongst other auto manufacturers), and the other (the health and safety officer) for Vauxhall, and, prior to joining VPL, Nissan in Sunderland.

The Human Resources Plan for 1990, the first to be developed for a full year of operations, was indicative of the type of organization and culture that its designers, the HR manager and the DGM, were attempting to create. The aims for the HR department were to: 'develop initiatives and strategies that take advantage of the unique opportunity presented by a greenfield site situation to adopt the very best methods of Human Resource Management and thereby support the achievement of VPL business objectives'. This translated into the following HRM objectives:

- The creation of a highly skilled, flexible and quality-conscious work-force
- The expansion of employees' capability to the maximum of their potential
- The development of effective leadership and team-building techniques
- The provision of competitive reward and benefit systems and appropriate occupational care mechanisms.

This plan was underpinned by the single-union agreement. Under 'General Principles' in the 'Working Practices' section of the agreement, it is stated that:

> To ensure maximum utilization of facilities and manpower, the company, employees and the Trade Union agree to complete flexibility and mobility of employees (following appropriate training); the introduction of practices to increase productivity (which could lead to changes in staffing levels and mixes of tasks); and the determination of staffing levels, methods and work arrangements by the Company.

Before examining the implementation of these objectives and principles in the manufacturing area, it is necessary to say something about the structuring of manufacturing work. The core concept is that of cellular manufacturing, or simply, 'cells'. Employees are allocated to a team of between eleven and seventeen people, headed by a team leader. In turn, team leaders report to a cell manager, who is responsible for between two and four teams. The three cell managers report to the production manager. Although cell members develop certain specialist skills, they are expected to take on a range of other tasks according to business requirements; this has included, for example, cell technicians doing production work. When some particular expertise possessed by a worker in one cell is needed by another cell, team leaders negotiate directly between themselves to share this expertise – for example, by a temporary transfer or exchange of staff.

The attempt to achieve functional flexibility and mobility of labour did not just rely on the single-union agreement and management planning. It began with the recruitment and selection of employees, where use was made of a range of diagnostic techniques, such as aptitude tests, psycho-metric profiling, assessment centres and interviews. Indeed, the principal personnel officer was recruited for his expertise and experience in this area, and spent the first 18 months or so of his employment at VPL (from May 1989) developing and setting up the procedures, and then using them to recruit all the staff below executive management level. When interviewed, he commented that he was trying to develop techniques for selecting people who were likely to work 'effectively' in a team environment, that is, working flexibly with a readiness to be mobile and cooperative. However, the DGM and HR manager wanted a balance of skills and experience, as well as labour flexibility, mobility and cooperativeness; hence they aimed for (and achieved) an average age profile of 35. All new employees went on a 4–8-week off-the-job induction programme, where there was again an emphasis on team-building and flexibility. A major vehicle for trying to achieve this was outdoor pursuit training, which took place either in the Shropshire Hills or mid-Wales.

Following the completion of the induction programme, employees entered an on-the-job modular training programme where the emphasis was on skill acquisition. The training took place within the cell, facilitated locally by the team leaders, who had received training as trainers as part of their 8-week induction programme. Once employees are assessed as having completed a skill module satisfactorily, they advance one incremental point up their given salary band (each band has ten incremental points). There were a total of six grades in the company's structure and no job descriptions – as the human resources manager put it, these were seen as being 'unnecessarily inflexible and restrictive'.

Human Resource Specialists, Technical Innovation and Manufacturing Cells

We have already seen that the human resources manager played a key role in the design of the company organization and HR philosophy and other key HR issues such as recruitment and selection procedures, staffing, employee relations and working practices. In the original project plan, which he wrote in 1986, the then Project Director (who was working for GKN Sankey at the time, and was later to become the DGM) had put HRM policies and practices at the forefront as a central element of the type of culture he saw as necessary to achieve the organization's objectives. When it had become clear that the company would come to fruition, he set about making his first appointment, that of the HR manager. Tony O'Leary was 'headhunted' for this post from Jaguar. One of his crucial attributes was that, as the DGM put it, 'he had walked on the coals', that is, he had a good deal of experience of working in an adversarial climate in the auto industry where multi-unionism, conflict and factionalism were the norm. The DGM, Derek Deans, described how his experience of the press-work sector at GKN had been very similar to his new HRM manager's experience of Jaguar, and had taught him how an organization should *not* be structured if you wanted 'to get the best out of people' and achieve an effective and profitable company. Tony O'Leary clearly shared not only similar experiences, but also a similar vision. Interviewed about the range of possibilities for the new company which were explored between 1986 and early 1988, the DGM commented:

> In writing the various projects, certain things were accepted as definite requirements – things like we were not going to have just another pressings factory because we knew we could never encourage the calibre of labour in to make it work . . . We looked at the other end of the spectrum. We wanted young, high quality people who were ambitious, whom we would train, who had loyalty to the company and a commitment to the product and getting the quality and everything which goes with that . . . and . . . we've removed all of the known traditional barriers for both sides, and from that base we expect them to be able to have high levels of productivity and the business should create wealth and everyone should benefit . . . Many of these [requirements] were 'stakes in

the ground' in the original writings, and what Tony O'Leary has done is he's beefed that up and added to these stakes to get where we are now. The company has basically turned out very very close to what we all planned. I say 'close' because we are actually further advanced on the human resource front to what was in the original plan, and we've gone into manufacturing cells and several other areas, all driven, of course, towards this issue of high quality.

Again, then, we see the way in which the search for a high and consistent level of panel quality was a key driving force in the establishment of the company. The following extract also illustrates the importance attached to the achievement of the single-union agreement in the launch of the company:

> One of the main things at the front end was getting the single-union agreement in place – i.e. having the work done for this before we signed the legal agreement, and quickly after forming Venture Pressings we got the single-union agreement, because that agreement was the first building brick of . . . all the other philosophies – of open management, of common employment terms, and pendulum arbitration. From that solid position we were able to move forward in a human resources mode to really put a lot of meat around that. (DGM interview, September 1990)

Other early decisions included: (i) to set wages above those available in the local area in order to draw a large number of applications and facilitate the selectivity exercise; (ii) to have a flat management structure to help achieve effective communication and briefing; (iii) to recruit the executive management team as early as possible, and to then get them to select staff for their departments.

So, some of the key decisions had already been taken before the HR manager joined the company, and he then proceeded to flesh them out, add the detail and implement them. However, this process did still allow him a good deal of influence. A number of key HR decisions were taken, of course, in the early board meetings. (The board consisted, apart from the DGM, of three non-executive directors from each of the two parent companies.) Although the HR manager, along with the other executive managers, was not a member of the board, he attended on a regular basis to make presentations and offer advice, and was normally present when human resource issues were on the agenda. In addition, while the HR manager was not a party to the writing of the project plan for VPL, other personnel specialists were, for Jaguar's human resources department made inputs into the plan, not least through their director, who was subsequently to become one of Jaguar's members on the VPL board.

By the time the human resources manager began to work at VPL, the style and philosophy of the new organization had been set. It is clear, however, that he fully embraced that philosophy and was eager to operationalize it. In his view, if UK companies were to compete in world markets, they would have to at least match Japanese and (western) German methods of operation: 'You've got to look at the best, at other models of excellence – which is basically what we've done'. However, he argued that there were some areas where Japanese practices could not be uncritically transferred across to the UK. He gave the example of supervisors, where he understood that in Japan they receive respect simply because of their post, 'whereas in this country you have to motivate people . . . rather than just expect them to give you their support automatically'. A recognition of these cultural differences may be one of the reasons why Japanese transplants commonly appoint a British personnel/human resource director with some years of previous experience of working in UK companies.

The achievement of this 'best practice' in the press-work sector was interrelated to the decision to establish operations on a greenfield site. While business, operational and financial considerations were to the forefront of the project team's deliberations which preceded the establishment of VPL, human resource issues were also of paramount significance. When the locational decision was in the process of being made, another GKN site was becoming available as well as the Telford one, and it was located *nearer* to Jaguar's plants. However, the management problem was that on this site there was still an extant workforce. As the HR manager put it:

> If the decision had been taken to go there you could still have called it a greenfield site, but it would not have been really because it would have been taking over an established facility, and it would have raised the questions 'well, what about the workforce, what happens to them, do they then get opportunities in the new company?' That would have been a sensitive situation. On the other hand, there was no one at Telford who was automatically going to be thinking that they had a right to be given first consideration. [At the new VPL site, the work previously done by GKN had already been moved to another GKN factory, and people had moved with the work a few hundred yards away, the other side of the wall subsequently built by VPL.]

Thus, the human resources programme and the business plan for VPL originated, and were designed and implemented, in an integrative way – to such an extent that it is difficult on occasions to separate out the two 'elements', for they were never really seen as being separate. This is pointed up in the following comments of the HR manager on the issue of HR values and organization design:

> Derek [Deans] and I set about to develop a company with certain principles and certain values and we sought to find other like-minded people, firstly at the senior level and then subsequently that cascaded through the organization, and it was very, very important that people who we recruited to key jobs shared the vision. So, it was a continuous process. I designed major features of the HRM programme to complement the business that Derek was looking to create, and then the other people who came in responsible for their functions designed their own requirements in a similar way. I wrote all the organization for each department, but when each manager came in, they fine-tuned things . . . when I first arrived, in my first week, Derek said 'you'd better write an organization'. So I did. And that was the beginning of how the thing would be structured as people. (Interview, April 1992)

It is of interest to note that, as senior managers were recruited, not only did they not question the philosophy, but they did not see too much need for 'tinkering' either. For example, the manufacturing manager fully supported the cell concept, the number of cells, and their design and structure.

Let us now, then, focus on the decision-making process concerning the manufacturing cells and the choice of technology. It has already been established that it was the DGM and HR manager who took the key cell decisions, but what were their reasons for adopting cells? According to the HR manager:

> Derek Deans envisaged flexible manufacturing teams, where there would be continuous development of workforce skills, and none of the traditional barriers. I helped him to take that a stage further . . . This was an opportunity to continue along the same line, but without the difficulties that we'd got in Jaguar of breaking down the attitude and overcoming multi-union problems. It was also what Derek had seen worldwide, where he'd looked at manufacturing excellence in lots of different organizations. It was a combination of experiences and concepts, and me developing the structure of the cell manager supported by team leaders who would be team developers and trainers, and each team leader would have an integrated group of maintenance and production people, and then the support service from engineering.

Decisions relating to the manufacturing technology were taken by the DGM and the manufacturing manager. These decisions were driven by the original, formative objectives in setting up the company. As the DGM stated:

> If you take the robotic lines, the technology was put in essentially to improve quality through reducing damage caused by handling – it's also consistent, and there's less risk . . . it was a technically-inspired decision to do with the real reason Venture Pressings was being set up, which was to give Jaguar control of their own supply of high-quality parts. So there is no HRM influence in that sense at all.

There were also financial considerations: if more money had been available, a third line may also have been robotized, in addition to the initial two. However, there was a clear recognition of the crucial importance of labour in achieving effective and efficient cell-working given the choice of technology. As the HR manager commented: 'The HRM influence has been in the thrust of releasing the potential that exists in the workforce, rather than to do with the way the facility was set up'.

There is a limit, of course, to the amount of detail which can be laid down by senior managers in designing the cells and the jobs and working practices within them. This is especially true of a greenfield site, where people are 'starting from scratch' and where there is an emphasis on flexibility – an anti-job-description, anti-bureaucracy culture. This implies that it may well not be seen as appropriate and necessary to have a very detailed work design and organization structure. In any event, what this has meant is that the lacunae in detailed regulations about working practices, particularly in the early months of the existence of the company, have been filled by the employees working in the cells. Comments made by a cell manager, in response to a question about the main challenges in manufacturing, capture this:

> There were no rules, regulations or procedures when I started. You couldn't take anything for granted. For example 'Go and get x from the Stores' – no Stores! The challenge was to establish a working environment, with a lot of 'green' labour. I often put the problem to the skilled men and asked them 'How are we going to do it?', rather than telling them. Effectively, the men themselves have helped to develop most of the procedures.

A team leader commented, on a similar issue:

> People came for a certain way of working, but no one's really sure what it was. I'm not sure what exactly I expected. At the end of the day, I'm going to change it through our work . . . That's taken a lot of people a while to grasp.

Differences in the technology employed across the cells do *in themselves* lead to differences in labour requirements, both quantitatively and qualitatively. The main contrast is between the robotic and non-robotic lines. The former have four technicians. The equivalent 'manual' line has around twenty-two people, the majority of whom are operatives performing a lot of manual handling work (in the robotic cells it is the robots, of course, that move the panels through the presses). However, 'the principles that underpin the cell – teamwork, involvement and development – they're all the same. It's just that the application of those principles inevitably differs because the work composition is not the same' (HR manager).

The more advanced robotic technology cells generate a need, not only for technicians, but also for a manager/supervisor who has the requisite skills to understand the processes – this is in addition to being orientated towards production and having a 'business' sense. As the engineering manager said of the cell managers and team leaders: 'So they've got a complete little business all on their own to run.' And, later: 'He has to have the drive of a production supervisor as well as a technical background and understanding'. Of course, it is not easy to find such people, especially if there is a lack of time in which to train them. This takes us back, inter alia, to the recruitment and selection process and, therefore, the role of personnel specialists.

There are a variety of ways in which the personnel specialists have influenced cellular operations. At the time of the research in 1992, the principal personnel officer (PPO) visited each cell every working day, talking 'informally' to people, getting an impression of what was happening. Every employee also had a briefing session for the last 30 minutes of the Friday shift. This brief was compiled and largely written by the HR manager, with inputs from other staff. Together with the DGM, he then dropped in on all the weekly cell briefings. (The cell members themselves also had a brief from the cell manager/team leader at the beginning of each shift.) Personnel specialists were also involved in cellular operations through personnel administration. A computerized personnel records system has been in place since early 1991, allowing the PPO to monitor absence and attendance. Employees also raise queries on an individual basis with personnel staff. The training and development programme requires regular involvement in order to monitor progress, deal with problems etc. Completion of a skill/training module triggers the reward system. Appraisals are conducted with all employees on the anniversary of their appointment, and while personnel specialists are not usually directly involved, they do check that it happens and that it is recorded etc. The HR manager recognized that the relevant line managers must be involved in, and ideally have 'ownership' of these matters. As he put it:

> So, we're involved at the strategic level in all the planning that takes place, and the actual delivery involves us a great deal, but, clearly, a lot of the most important things that go on out there are between the team leader and individual employee, and we can't be part of that – that's specific to them. We have to hope that the team leader is going about that in the way that our culture and philosophy says that they should. And, if they don't, it's probably some time later that we find out about it. You pick things up that, maybe, there's a relationship problem of some kind etc. That's why I think the role of line management is so important.

Conclusion

The material presented in this chapter has demonstrated how human resource specialists *can* play a central and, indeed, *leading* role in managing technical change given favourable circumstances. One key 'circumstance' is a greenfield site, and this has been the focus in the preceding analysis. At Venture Pressings we saw that the HR function did make important contributions to the design of the organization and its culture, policies and procedures. This contribution can be traced back to the project group which was formed three years or so before the company formally came into existence in 1988. Personnel specialists from Jaguar, as the joint-owner-to-be of VPL, were particularly prominent in those early discussions. It should be emphasized, however, that during the 1980s Jaguar had been one of the oft-quoted examples of a UK company that was adopting elements of human resource management. In this sense, at least, it *may* have been atypical, although Storey has recently argued that rather more in the HRM area appears to have been happening by the late 1980s than was previously realized (Storey, 1992a, 1992b). At Jaguar, human resource management issues *were* considered strategically at board level, and in fact, the company 'adopted and indeed pioneered many of the policies and practices associated with the concept of human resource management' (Goodman, 1989: 611). It would seem likely that these developments had an influence upon the thinking and ideas of Anthony O'Leary and the other two former Jaguar personnel specialists who were to join VPL shortly after its formation. It was also seen that VPL's HR specialists played a key role in the design, implementation and monitoring of the company's structure and culture, and its human resources policies and practices. The HR manager, along with the DGM, 'provided the leap' and rejected the 'logic of incrementalism' (Stopford and Baden-Fuller, 1990), buttressed by the rhetoric and reality of human resource management (cf Keenoy, 1990b).

Present and ex-Jaguar managers, then, have had a formative influence on VPL, not least, but probably by no means exclusively, in human resource management policies and procedures. At the same time, VPL managers have been selective in what they have 'transferred across' from Jaguar, taking advantage of the opportunities provided by the establishment of a greenfield site. But, clearly, influences on VPL's senior managers extended beyond Jaguar (and Ford as owners of Jaguar since 1989). There is the specific GKN Sankey presence. But there is a much wider influence through: (i) the Japanese automobile transplants, especially Nissan, because of its early presence in the UK and the publicity surrounding its new HR practices (the principal health and safety officer referred to some of the documents in use at VPL as being 'Nissan documents with the VPL logo substituted for the Nissan one'); (ii) VPL and Jaguar's knowledge of what the latter's two main German competitors have been doing (BMW and Mercedes); and (iii) the trade, business and management press. Nevertheless, the 'leap in imagination' and innovative nature of what has happened at VPL should not be understated. The designers have created an organization largely on their own terms, yet, of necessity, within the contexts of the UK economy and manufacturing sector in the early 1990s. We also saw that non-HR specialists, as well as the HR specialists, were acting as 'agents of HRM'.

In a very real sense, managers and technical and human resource specialists in greenfield site companies such as Venture Pressings have come full circle: some 'problems', such as 'will we get this past the union or the workforce?' have largely gone, and technical issues have come to the fore. But we may now be at a stage in the process of technical change where people issues have again become central – issues such as workforce skills, training, commitment and mobility. The engineering manager nicely captured the change in contrasting his previous experience in motor manufacturing with what he had found at VPL:

> Within the motor industry the majority of your time is spent on dealing with people problems. Here, the majority of your time is spent on dealing with technical problems, in getting the job done, as opposed to the ramifications of, if you did it, what would be the people problems that you would get by doing it – you don't have to worry about that.

In this case, then, there were a number of circumstances favourable to human resource specialists playing an influential role in organizational management and manufacturing practices, and it could be argued that, between 1988 and 1990, they were even in the ascendancy over financial specialists (cf Armstrong, 1989). How long this will continue at Venture Pressings, and whether the human resource specialists will still drive HRM (or whether it will pass to manufacturing management, for example), given depressed economic conditions and retrenchment, and given also that some of the original 'visionaries', such as the DGM and HR manager, have recently left the company, remains to be seen.

Acknowledgements

The author would like to acknowledge the assistance, advice and unfailing patience of Anthony O'Leary, in particular, and a number of other employees of Venture Pressings Ltd in the preparation of this chapter. Mandy Macartney typed and re-typed successive drafts with good humour, effectiveness and fortitude.

Note

1. The case study material was obtained from company documentation, observation and, in particular, semi-structured tape-recorded interviews. The interviews lasted from 75 to 150 minutes, and were conducted during the period September 1990 to April 1992. In the case of the human resources manager, this involved visiting the same individual on a number of occasions throughout this time period. The following people were interviewed: the director and general manager, human resources manager, engineering manager, quality manager, principal personnel officer, principal health and safety officer, principal training officer, a cell manager and a team leader.

6

Full Flexibility and Self-Supervision in an Automated Factory

Jon Clark

Advanced technical change and greenfield sites provide two of the most favourable conditions for the introduction of new human resource policies and flexible patterns of working (see Daniel, 1987: 166–80; Cross, 1988; Pollert, 1991b: xxiii; Preece, this volume). This chapter examines these issues, drawing on evidence from a longitudinal study of Pirelli Cables' experimental computer-integrated manufacturing (CIM) plant in South Wales.[1] It begins with an examination of the reasons behind Pirelli's decision to invest in the new plant and the importance of different personnel/HR issues in the planning and implementation of change. As we will see, specialist personnel managers collaborated with senior general managers to design a distinctive set of new human resource policies for the new site.

The second part of the chapter concentrates on one central feature of the new arrangements, the contractual requirement on all non-management employees to be 'completely flexible'. Few issues have so absorbed the attention of human resource practitioners and academics in the past decade than flexibility (see Atkinson and Meager, 1986; Daniel, 1987: 166–77; Marginson, 1989; Marsden and Thompson, 1990). Recently, however, Pollert has voiced strong criticisms of the debate so far on three main grounds: first, that many studies have overestimated the significance of changes in flexibility and the commitment of employees to them; secondly, that the term has served to obscure an underlying trend towards the tightening of management control and increased supervision; and thirdly, that many claims about changes in flexibility have rested on speculative theory rather than concrete empirical evidence. In this chapter, detailed evidence from Pirelli's Aberdare factory will be presented which shows that there are cases where there have been significant – although by no means total – changes in functional flexibility and a radical change in supervisory practices involving a much greater decision-making power for employees about the day-to-day conduct of work (see also Chapters 4, 5 and 10 in this volume for similar findings).

The Context: Setting Up and Laying Out a CIM Factory

The Decision to Invest

In September 1985 the board of Pirelli General (PG), the UK cable-making arm of the Italian multinational Pirelli Group,[2] took the decision to replace its Southampton plastic cables factory with a new automated manufacturing plant at a projected cost of around £18m. The plastic cables division, which produced mainly 'low tech' building wires for house wiring, plugs, electrical appliances etc., had been losing money since the early 1980s, and the factory, which had been built in 1912, was in need of major repair. The lay-out was inefficient and cumbersome, the machinery needed a major overhaul, management structure was top-heavy, labour costs were high, and industrial relations were highly formalized and bureaucratic. Moreover, the site was close to the city centre and ripe for inner-city development. For all these reasons, PG senior managers drew up a 5-year Strategic Plan in mid-1984 proposing that they should establish a new advanced technology building wires factory somewhere in the UK.

At this very time, the Milan-based managing director of the Pirelli cable sector worldwide was expressing concern that the Group had failed to keep up with advanced production techniques in its building wires factories, and was keen to involve one of the national companies in an experimental use of CIM systems. It was the coming together of the national requirements of PG in the UK and the multinational interest of the Pirelli Group worldwide that provided the impetus for the decision to invest. Three main features of the 1985 UK board decision are important for our purposes:

1   UK management was expressly required to be experimental and 'state of the art' (also in its human resource policies).
2   Full use was to be made of the most up-to-date electronic aids.
3   Costs (labour and material costs, work-in-progress, completed stocks) were to be reduced to a minimum in order to achieve maximum profitability.

However, while there was strong Group involvement in the board's investment decision, much of the detailed planning and implementation was left to corporate and divisional managers of the national company.

The first major implementation issue was where to locate the new factory. One senior member of PG's accounts department was seconded to cost the alternatives, and after spending nearly a year exploring a number of options in England and Wales (including Deeside, Telford, Aberdare and South Hampshire), the company opted for a site in Aberdare in the Welsh valleys. This site had previously housed Pirelli's 'special cables' operation, which had transferred to Hampshire between 1982 and 1985. By the time the new factory opened in 1987, the old buildings had been razed to the ground, and a completely new one erected on the same site.

The availability of the site and of various local subsidies and development grants clearly weighed significantly in the decision to locate at Aberdare. However, human resource considerations were also extremely important: locating 150 miles from their other sites in South Hampshire meant that the company could break more easily with its existing industrial relations arrangements; labour costs in South Wales were around 25 per cent lower than in South Hampshire; unemployment in the valleys was high; there was a large pool of mainly semi-skilled employees (including some who had worked in the old factory) who would be available and willing to work; and finally, the company had taken soundings with the Wales TUC and had concluded that it would be able to secure a new-style single-union agreement for the site on condition that it was open and fair about the procedure for selecting the union.

Designing a High Tech System to Manufacture Low Tech Cables

Between 1985 and 1987 a number of detailed choices had to be made about the computer-integrated system for the new plant and the factory lay-out. It should be remembered that at this time such systems were very much in their infancy. Indeed, when in 1985 Ingersoll Consultants initiated a study on CIM in British plants, they had to abort it when their researchers reported: 'we can't find any' (quoted from Jones, 1988: 458). Space does not allow a detailed description of how Pirelli managers and technical specialists assembled the CIM system and designed the factory lay-out. What follows is an outline of the process of manufacturing building wires and the production system and lay-out of the new factory.

Manufacturing building wires consists of four main processes: metallurgy (breaking down a rod of solid copper into a series of fine wires of different sizes), laying-up or assembly (twisting and bunching the fine wires into the requisite form), extrusion (insulating and sheathing the laid-up cables), and rewind and packing (cutting up the completed cable into the required lengths and rewinding it on to different size drums or putting it in boxes for despatch and sale). The architecture of the new CIM system was based on two general principles: a hierarchy of three software-driven operating systems and the goal of full integration within and between them. At the top of this hierarchy is the **business system**, embracing commercial, administrative and finance functions; in the centre is the **manufacturing system**, embracing the complete sequence to be followed from metallurgy to packing for a particular product to be manufactured and prepared for despatch; and at the bottom is the **process-control system**, encompassing the programmable logic controllers (in the form of computer screens) attached to each of the separate pieces of manufacturing equipment, together with the automatic guided vehicles (AGVs) which transport the reels of cable (bobbins) from one stage of the manufacturing process to the next.

The three systems are configured so that orders input into the business system can be used by planners to generate a production schedule, which can then be downloaded into the manufacturing system to provide direct instructions to the individual machines via the process-control systems. Many of the operations previously carried out by separate machines (with separate staffing) are now tandemized, that is, linked together in one continuous machine process. The lay-out is modular and sequential so that movement of cable from one manufacturing stage to the next is over as short a distance as possible. The lay-out, as planned in 1985–7, is still virtually identical in 1993.

Human Resource Issues and Specialist Personnel Involvement

There was no specialist personnel involvement in the decision to invest in the new factory or in its design and lay-out. However, the encouragement from Group headquarters to develop experimental arrangements in all aspects of factory management provided an important cultural impetus for the design of the new human resource policies. In what follows, these will be analysed in three separate sections corresponding to different stages in the process of change. As we will see, each of these stages and issues involved different combinations of corporate and divisional managers and different degrees and levels of specialist personnel involvement.

Organization Design and the Appointment of the Divisional Management Team

Already in late 1984, in anticipation of the board decision to invest, the company had appointed the person who was to be overall project manager for the new site and its designated first divisional manager. Unusually for Pirelli, which tends to promote its senior managers from within, he was appointed from outside as it was concluded that there was no internal candidate with the appropriate experience to manage the new plant. The new appointee had nearly 30 years' experience in the cable-making industry, and was a charismatic, commercially successful and self-confessed maverick personality who was attracted by the opportunity to be involved in the experiment from the beginning. It was this man, together with three people who appointed him – the then UK managing director of Pirelli General, the senior corporate personnel manager (henceforth personnel director), and the then divisional manager of the Southampton Plastic Cables plant (which the new plant was to replace) – who formed the corporate project team which in 1985 and 1986, took critical decisions about the organization structure for the new factory and its senior management team.

Already in the spring of 1985, the personnel director, who had been a founder member of the PG personnel department in 1960 and had a wide network of contacts in personnel and industrial relations circles, approached the ACAS Work Research Unit in London and commissioned from them a paper – based on an outline of the CIM operating principles applicable to the new site – which presented a range of options for the new plant based on current best practice (on the role of the WRU, see Tynan, 1986). While the major part of the 29-page report completed in July 1985 contained proposals in areas such as greenfield/brownfield options, job structure, work organization, employee representation, employee involvement, payment systems and management style, it also reviewed current UK practice on organization design which helped convince the project team to go for a flat and lean organization structure.

There were to be only three levels of management: the divisional manager; three senior functional managers (operations, commercial, and administration); and eight middle/junior managers (three shift managers, plus one each in production planning, systems engineering, maintenance, accounts, and training and recruitment). From interviews about this decision, it is clear that two main factors shaped the outcome: the assumption that the majority of traditional management functions would be built into the CIM system, and the need to reduce costs (including labour costs). For the purposes of this chapter, it is important to note that (a) personnel, although not in the job title, was seen as one of the three senior functions on site (the first administration manager was a divisional personnel manager at another Pirelli site with some experience in finance) and (b) a middle/junior personnel management position was created with special responsibility for recruitment and training. Indeed, the high priority given to human resource issues at this stage was reflected in the high status of the new administration manager, whose post was graded at a higher level than any of the other divisional personnel managers in the company.

Although all four members of the corporate project team were convinced that personnel would be a crucial function in the planning and initial operation of the new plant, the involvement of the corporate personnel director in discussions about organization design was a vital factor in establishing the high status of the personnel function. Subsequently, in 1990, once the plant had settled down, the site personnel function was downgraded to the same level as at other Pirelli sites, and the site accountant replaced personnel on the senior management team.

Establishment of a 'Best Practice' Human Resource Philosophy and Policies

By early 1986 the operations manager and commercial manager for the new factory had also been appointed, both from within the company. The divisional management team was now in place and, together with the UK managing director, took over day-to-day responsibility for managing the project from the corporate project team. In the meantime three working groups were established to give detailed consideration to the main areas where innovation was both expected and required: (i) information systems and software; (ii) machinery/equipment; and (iii) personnel. While the first two included technical specialists from Pirelli Group HQ in Milan, the personnel working group, which was established in 1986, was composed only of UK managers – the prospective divisional manager, the newly appointed plant administration manager, and both the personnel director and employee relations manager from the corporate personnel department in Southampton. The early involvement of corporate and divisional personnel specialists in the design of human resource policies for the new unit enabled the company to develop an integrated HRM strategy well in advance of project implementation.

From interviews with members of the personnel working group, it is clear that there were two basic reference points for its work: the need to devise work structuring and industrial relations arrangements which would be appropriate to the operational requirements of the CIM system, and the need to keep down labour costs. In addition, however, it was soon agreed within the group that human resource practices in the new plant should, *where possible*, be progressive and forward-looking, building on current best practice in the UK. As we have seen, a paper had already been commissioned from the ACAS Work Research Unit in 1985 outlining a range of state-of-the-art human resource policies for the new plant. Following the establishment of the personnel sub-group in 1986, ACAS arranged for members of the group to visit a number of UK-based companies regarded as leaders in the fields of work design and industrial relations, including Black and Decker, Carreras Rothmans, Cummins Engineering, Kodak and Nissan UK. Out of all these deliberations and visits, an HRM strategy was elaborated which included a participative management style, integrated payment systems, single status, full functional flexibility, skills-based training, dispute and grievance procedures with conventional arbitration as the final stage, elaborate employee involvement mechanisms and union recognition arrangements.

On this latter issue the personnel director had already made a separate approach in 1985 to ACAS Wales and the Wales TUC, which both had a successful track record in advising on procedures for the conclusion of recognition agreements on greenfield sites involving inward investors. This is not the place to tell the story of why Pirelli decided to go for a single-union agreement, nor how it arrived at the particular substantive terms (on this see Yeandle and Clark, 1989a, 1989b). Suffice it to say that in May 1987 it signed an agreement with the Managerial, Administrative and Technical Staff Association (the white-collar section of the GMB) giving the union sole recognition rights for the plant.

Consistent with many other agreements of the time (see Bassett, 1986), it included a whole range of matters which would not have been found in more traditional recognition arrangements. In particular, its provisions on flexibility were both radical and wide-ranging. Under the agreement, the union accepted that employees would be 'completely flexible', undertake 'any tasks which are within their capability' (following, if necessary, 'any appropriate training'), and vary shifts and patterns of work 'to meet operational needs'. In addition it was agreed that management had 'the right and responsibility of managing the Unit's operations on a day-to-day basis . . . and that accordingly no restrictions or delays shall be applied by the union or any employee to the fully effective implementation of the Unit's operational requirements'. These terms were subsequently incorporated in every employee's contract of employment, so that although all non-management employees were hired under one of three generic job titles – producer, maintainer, administrator – they could contractually be required to carry out any function within their capability.

The agreement as a whole, which also included provisions on employee communication, training and involvement, reads like a manifesto for a 'human resource management' approach to personnel management (see Chapter 1, this volume), albeit with a significant role for the workplace union and its representatives. It was the product of a personnel working group which included three personnel specialists and the new divisional manager. This combination ensured that, although the context for the new strategy was guided by the need to be appropriate to the new CIM system and to reduce labour costs, the eventual outcomes were also strongly personnel-driven. Most importantly, the participation in the sub-group of the senior general manager-designate of the new plant ensured that he was in accord with, and came to 'own', the strategy and the policies as they were elaborated and implemented.

Implementation of New HR Policies in the Initial Stages of Factory Operation

Greenfield sites allow organizations considering the introduction of advanced technical change to design, lay out and equip a site according to current and future business requirements rather than within the constraints of existing buildings and machinery. As far as human resource issues are concerned, the parallel degree of freedom is the 'opportunity structure' (see Blau, 1990: 145, 149–53), not only to establish a new HR philosophy, but also to recruit and select an 'appropriate' workforce rather than having to work with, and retrain, an existing one (see Preece, this volume; but see also Hendry, this volume, for the potential advantages of brownfield sites where the selection, training and commitment of the workforce are already of a high quality prior to the investment in technical change).

For the first time in the history of Pirelli General, personnel specialists, together with the senior divisional management team, decided to use a variety of personality, attitude and computer aptitude tests, as well as more conventional interviewing techniques, to select *non-management* staff for its new factory. In the event, a substantial number of applicants – including some who had worked in the former Aberdare factory – were turned down, not on grounds of technical competence or experience, but on behavioural and attitudinal grounds. As one shift manager reported: 'If a guy didn't seem to have the right attitude for what we wanted here, the concept of teamworking . . ., then in spite of what qualifications and experience he might have we didn't want him'. Specialist personnel managers played, as one would expect, an important role in the choice of methods of recruitment of new staff, but interestingly they were also part of the management team which developed the selection criteria for the new posts (compare the experience in K-Electric on this issue, see Chapter 7, this volume).

In the selection process itself, personnel and line managers worked closely together at all stages. The first stage in each recruitment round was a joint presentation by both the administration and operations managers. This was followed by a series of written tests and a first interview by the recruitment and training manager and the immediate line manager for the post in question. If applicants were successful in the first interview and in the personality and computer-aptitude tests, they were given a final interview around a week later by the Administration Manager and the senior line manager (for example, the operations manager for production and maintenance staff, the commercial manager for sales). In this way, both personnel and line management brought their experience to bear on, and 'owned', all stages of the selection process.

Recruitment of non-management staff began in the spring of 1987 and was phased in as the machinery was installed, commissioned and became operational. The induction programme (run in conjunction with Aberdare College) lasted between two days and a week, depending on the numbers recruited, and involved college- and seminar-based sessions on the business and technical principles of the factory, teamworking and training other staff, as well as an introduction to cable-making and cable sales and markets. All new staff, including administrators, were given a detailed tour of the new factory and encouraged to familiarize themselves with the layout.

The personnel working group was also responsible for devising a skills training policy to enable new employees to achieve greater work flexibility once they were appointed. The main means of achieving this was to be through the acquisition of 'skill modules' (the models for Pirelli identified by ACAS were Cummins Engineering and Pilkington Glass, see Pottinger, 1989; IDS, 1992). In the production area, for example, a number of modules were identified covering different machine processes, and each employee was expected to train for, and acquire, at least one skill module per year. Eventually, the aim was for staff in each of the three main functions – production, maintenance, administration – to acquire one or more modules from at least one of the other main functions (for examples, see Yeandle and Clark, 1989a). The successful completion of each skill module attracted a non-consolidated payment, initially £250, around 3.5 per cent of basic salary (for a report on various examples of skill-based pay, including that at Pirelli Aberdare, see IDS, 1992). Skill modules at Pirelli Aberdare were thus not only a central component of the system of flexible working and the basic unit of skills training, but also, as it transpired, the only performance-related incentive element in the company's wage pay-ment system. Initially no upper limit was placed on the number of skill modules that could be acquired by any one person, an omission which caused friction at a later stage, as we will see.

Flexibility in Practice

Increases in Functional Flexibility

By the autumn of 1990 (when the first phase of fieldwork took place) the CIM system was up and running and a broadly stable pattern of working had been established for each of the three main occupational groups – producers, maintainers and administrators. Although there are many different aspects of flexibility (see Pollert, 1991b), I will concentrate here on task and job range and job demarcations, often known as 'functional flexibility'.

Looking first at task and job range, by 1990 most producers had acquired around four skill modules and worked on machine processes in at least two of the four main areas of the factory (for example, two different types of machine process in metallurgy and two in extrusion, or two in assembly and two in packing). It should be remembered that many of these machines were tandemized, so that the range of tasks for which a producer would be responsible was significantly greater than in the old Southampton and Aberdare plants. In contrast, maintainers were involved on a day-to-day basis in carrying out maintenance tasks *in all four areas of production*. In addition, mechanically trained fitters regularly carried out electrical (and occasionally electronic) maintenance, while electricians did some mechan-ical maintenance too. Administrators had seen the smallest change in task and job flexibility, tending to carry out traditional tasks (albeit computer-assisted) in traditionally titled jobs such as sales ledger, wages, purchasing and home sales.

Turning to job demarcations, the lowest scope for flexibility was again to be found among administrators. Jobs were highly circumscribed and there was very little flexibility on a day-to-day basis apart from answering the telephone if a colleague was busy. Only two had managed to change jobs by applying for vacancies as they arose. As for maintainers, not one had been required to take on producer tasks, although there had been a substantial relaxation of demarcations within maintenance between fitters and electricians. However, although the initial intention had been to produce all-round flexible maintainers on a unified maintainer grade, electrically and electronically trained maintainers had proved difficult to recruit and retain, mainly because of competition from 'local' companies such as Bosch and Ford. By 1990, in direct response to these pressures, two new maintenance grades were introduced, automation technician for those with some formal technical qualifications (which effectively excluded the fitters) and auto engineer (for highly skilled all-round computer and electronics technician engineers). Both were put on higher rates of pay than the basic grade maintainers. By mid-1990, then, demarcations within maintenance were reasserting themselves and causing substantial friction within the maintenance department. Among producers, as we have seen, most staff who had been employed since 1987 were capable of operating at least four machine processes, and as a result of sickness absences, holidays, training and tight staffing levels, had generally worked in most of their skill module areas during any 6-month period. They also regularly undertook minor maintenance tasks and often worked jointly with maintainers in solving more serious problems.

From Full to Limited Flexibility

By the summer of 1990, the experience of the first three years of factory operation had persuaded manufacturing and shift managers to propose a modification to the original philosophy of full flexibility, and in August of that year they introduced what came to be known as skill module 'capping' (by analogy with government spending restrictions on certain local authorities in the UK). Under this system, narrowly agreed by the workforce after a ballot in July 1990, every member of non-management staff was restricted to a maximum of seven skill modules. Within these seven they would be allocated, after consultation with their immediate line manager, 'primary' and 'secondary' areas of responsibility. For example, some producers would have primary skills in metallurgy (three modules) and secondary in laying up (two modules), while others would have primary skills in packing (two) and secondary skills in extrusion (three). Employees would be expected to work mainly in their primary area (involving, for producers, between three and five machine processes), but could at any time be allocated to their secondary area as required. At a minimum, every employee would be required to work for at least two weeks every nine months in their secondary area of skills.

Limiting Full Flexibility in Practice

There are two immediate points of interest associated with this change. First, the contractually enshrined opportunity to deploy all non-management staff totally flexibly (within the constraints of their level of training) was not only *not* taken advantage of in practice, it was effectively limited by the policy of skill module capping. Indeed, by mid-1990 there had been no flexibility of staff between the three main functions, only flexibility within them, with maintenance having the most flexible patterns of work, followed by producers, with administrators as the least flexible. Secondly, capping at seven was not simply a unilateral management decision, it was accepted as broadly satisfactory and appropriate by around 90% of the non-management workforce interviewed at the time. The fact that there was only a small majority for acceptance of the company proposal was because many staff felt that they had been promised a greater number of skill modules on recruitment, and the company was not prepared to raise the payment for individual modules to counteract the loss in potential earnings arising from capping. Staff were also critical of what they felt was some unevenness between shifts in the rigour and time taken before skill modules were awarded. No manager had responsibility for monitoring the operation of the skill module system as a whole, a fact not unassociated with the lack of continuity in the personnel function on site (a matter to which we will return below).

There are six main reasons for the abandonment of full flexibility. First there was what was known as the '**horses for courses**' principle. Quite simply, many employees were generally more suited to – and interested in – certain areas of work rather than others. Some work, for example in extrusion, involved short bursts of activity and the ability to cope with pressure and analyse problems quickly and clearly, interspersed with periods of 30 minutes or more where long lengths of cable were sheathed in which no operator intervention was required. Other work, such as the cutting and boxing of 100-metre lengths of cable in the packing area, was much more routine, with regular 10-minute cycles in which, say, 100 boxes were produced. Given such a divergence of types of work requirement, both producers and shift managers agreed that it was best for staff to work in those areas which best suited their temperament, skills and abilities.

The second reason for limiting full flexibility was the need for **specialist knowledge**. Rather than allocating employees to areas of work about which they had little or no up-to-date and specialist knowledge, regular working in one particular area allowed the company to use the knowledge and experience of staff to produce high quality work. Staff in overseas sales, for example, who got to know individual customers and their particular problems and payment arrangements, were a valuable asset in customer relations, and themselves enjoyed high levels of job satisfaction from building up their expertise and their personal relations with customers. This is totally consistent with the findings of the Institute for Manpower Studies Panel Study of large manufacturing companies, which emphasized management's awareness of the continuing 'advantages of individuals' being specialised and "knowing what their job is"', adding that excessive job rotation was felt to be disruptive, 'not just of efficiency, but of staff motivation' too (quoted from Elger, 1991: 51).

Thirdly, there was the strong interest of both management and staff in employee '**ownership**' of particular work areas. If employees were allocated duties which gave them overall responsibility for a particular area, there was a greater possibility of a commitment to, and achievement of, high quality work. For example, in the initial phase of CIM implementation when technical problems were numerous, maintenance staff were allocated to duties on a fire-fighting basis as and when problems arose. On reviewing the position in mid-1990, production and maintenance managers found that a number of problems on machines were recurring, but that no maintainer had had day-to-day 'ownership' of a particular area. As a result, faults were often patched up temporarily rather than dealt with systematically and 'engineered out'. In mid-1991, therefore, maintenance staff were allocated primary responsibility for one of the four main work areas, while retaining a general brief to deal with urgent problems wherever they arose.

The fourth reason for abandoning full flexibility was in connection with **training**. From late 1987 until mid-1990, there was a substantial requirement for on-the-job training for new and existing staff, particularly in the production area, and it was vital that the trainers were not only good teachers, but fully up-to-date and knowledgeable about their particular machine process. In a number of cases, management requested certain staff to remain in one area, rather than move around the factory to acquire new skills, so that they could provide training to new recruits. While this need has now reduced somewhat (since most staff have achieved their primary and secondary skill modules), some new training is still likely to take place and all staff will need to undergo regular refresher training to keep up their 'secondary' skills. In addition, as with all advanced technical systems, continual incremental improvements and modifications to software, hardware and production procedures will require a regular updating of staff if they are to continue to be able to work competently in their secondary areas.

The fifth reason for limiting the commitment to full flexibility was to deal with the problem of **skill retention**. In a previous study, we noted that skills could not be utilized adequately if there was too great a gap between skill acquisition and their application in practice (Clark et al, 1988: 113, 121–8). Similarly at Pirelli Aberdare, it became clear that staff were not able to retain a wide range of skills if they were not given the regular opportunity to practise them. The chances, for example, of producers having a regular opportunity to practise skills on, say, ten machine processes across all four areas of production were extremely remote. Virtually all producers interviewed in 1990 accepted that seven skill modules was the maximum they could hope to learn and retain.

Sixth and finally, flexibility was limited by the comparatively **tight staffing levels** in the new high tech factory. In fact tight staffing levels had two contradictory effects on possibilities for flexibility. If we consider task and job demarcations between maintenance fitters and electricians, for example, it is clear that the need for functional flexibility was great given the small number of maintainers employed (on average four to five per shift). This is fully consistent with the finding in the 1984 WIRS survey that the task range of electricians was the greater, the smaller the number of manual workers employed in an establishment (see Daniel, 1987: 169). Conversely, tight staffing levels amongst administrators led to very low levels of functional flexibility because staff in one area (wages, export sales, accounts, purchasing) could not be spared for training in a very different unrelated one. Thus, the pressure to reduce labour costs, from the time of the decision to invest in 1984 through to 1992, was both a limitation on, and reason for, the degree of flexibility in different areas of the plant.

Limited Flexibility as Full Flexibility

In summary, under conditions that were highly favourable to full flexibility – contractual requirement, high level of automation, greenfield site – it has been neither required nor used. However, this does not mean that there has been no significant change in patterns of work. As Hyman has noted, total flexibility in an organization is 'empirically (and probably logically) impossible', since all planned and rational behaviour requires some form of 'stable structural regularities' (Hyman, 1991: 277). The question therefore revolves around the balance between flexibility and regularity, that is, the form and extent of 'flexible rigidities' (the title of a 1986 book by Ronald Dore). If compared with arrangements in the old Southampton and Aberdare plants which it replaced, for example, there has been a significant task and job enlargement, with most employees covering up to five or six machine processes where they previously only covered one or, at most, two. The result is that work patterns at the new plant show only those rigidities which are necessary to achieve high quality human input into the production process.

In addition, it is important not to underestimate the symbolic effect of the company's commitment to full flexibility. The very fact that it placed such a great emphasis, in its single-union agreement and in recruitment presentations, on a commitment to full flexibility has helped create what amounts to a new approach to work. By 1990, the vast majority of production staff interviewed expressed a complete willingness, within the limitations of their training and capabilities, to be as flexible as operations required. In addition, a similar overwhelming majority preferred their new-found functional flexibility to older forms of task and job demarcation. These responses suggest a strong degree of 'normative commitment' to functional flexibility in a geographical area in which traditional job demarcations have been, and to some extent still are, the norm. While this finding appears to contrast with evidence presented by Hyman (1991: 278), it is consistent with the WIRS findings on employees' greater propensity to accept increased flexibility when advanced technical change is introduced (see Daniel 1987: 65–71, 177–80; also Daniel and Millward, this volume). By mid-1990, then, the willingness of the workforce to be totally flexible had been achieved, although it had not proved necessary to go beyond what was, by any standard, a substantial degree of flexibility in both job tasks and job demarcations, mainly within, and to a lesser extent between, production and maintenance. In short: *Pirelli has achieved what it set out to achieve in the single-union agreement, namely full flexibility to do what it wants. In practice, however, to do what it wants it does not need full flexibility.*

Self-Supervision – a Cornerstone of Increased Flexibility

There is an additional element to the flexible organization of work at Aberdare which means that the factory does not simply exhibit 'increased flexibility at the margins', as Elger has reported from Ford and Lucas (1991: 61). That element is self-supervision. Some of the recent UK sociological literature on flexibility has suggested that the redesign of flexible work teams tends to involve 'increased supervision' (Pollert, 1991b: 21). In contrast, the more managerial literature on CIM and flexible work patterns has highlighted examples where day-to-day task allocation duties are delegated to 'self-managing work teams' (Owens, 1991: 53), leading to the creation of a 'new breed of supervisors' or team managers with supporting rather than directly controlling roles (Daly, 1991). As one commentator put it: 'supervision is out, self-management is in' (Dent, 1990: 35). This section looks at self-supervision as one of the cornerstones of the new flexible work arrangements at Aberdare.

There was no mention of self-supervision either in early management drafts of human resource policies for the new factory or in the single-union agreement. However, the delivery of the first machines in late 1986 and early 1987 triggered detailed discussions between personnel, operations and shift managers at the plant on how work would be organized in practice. It had always been assumed that the allocation of individuals to particular work areas on a weekly or fortnightly basis would be determined by the first-line managers for each shift. However, it was soon realized that, with many of the traditional operational management functions (sequence of products to be produced, material flow, quality checks etc.) incorporated into the CIM system and a flat and lean management structure with a ratio of one shift manager to twenty-six producers, the production workforce, as individuals and as teams, would need to 'supervise' manufacturing operations themselves on a minute-by-minute and hour-by-hour basis. Thus was born the idea of self-supervision. To meet this new requirement, an additional question was incorporated into the recruitment interviews: 'What would be your attitude to self-supervision?' The answers were sometimes unexpected. One applicant who replied 'Yes, please, I'll have a slice of that', was not successful!

To identify what self-supervision meant in practice as of mid-1990, it is instructive to cite the views of staff who had previously worked in the old Aberdare factory prior to its closure. In the first two excerpts producers contrast the two systems of organization and management:

> In the old plant it was a case of the foreman was there, the chargehand was there, the boys on the machine, any problems, go and see the chargehand or foreman and he made the decisions. Although the boys could do it themselves then, you weren't expected to do it, you were expected to go to the foreman or chargehand and ask them their opinion or ask them their advice, and they'd go and sort it out for you . . That is a real change. The whole unit is based on a self-supervision attitude.

> In the old Aberdare factory you used to have the foremen, there must have been

half a dozen of them on each shift, there were swarms of them . . . they'd have the whips out to make you work . . . You tend to work harder now they're not on your back . . . I used to spend more time dodging the white coats in the old place.

In the next excerpt, another producer uses an additional comparator – the nearby Hitachi factory at Hirwaun – to highlight the level of trust implied by self-supervision at Aberdare:

It's surprising, I didn't think it would really work, but it does in most cases . . . Now, if you've got a problem, you try and sort it out yourself, or if it's a major problem, of course, you see your shift manager . . . I've heard some of the boys talking about Hitachi . . . Well, I don't think the one or two who worked there were happy. Standing over you all the time. Here, you don't get that. You are self-supervising, they trust you to do your job. That's a good thing.

Teamworking is also central to self-supervision, and the following passage identifies some of the attitudinal changes it requires:

I enjoy coming to work, I think that means a lot . . . because you know you work on shifts and you get used to the boys you are working with. And we do work as a team, and it's enjoyable. You come to work on the machines next to one another, and there's no pressure on you . . . I think it's much better working like that. If you've got pressure on you, you tend to rebel against that, you think 'well why should I?' . . . [The other day] a boy on the other shift came in and he'd left a lot of bobbins out the back of the packing section, just piled up there, and we couldn't move. And I said, 'Well, you move that', and he said 'It's not my job', and I said 'What do you mean, it's not my job, we're supposed to be flexible, there's no such thing'. I said 'You belong to Victorian values . . . you're flexible, you can't say it's not my job to move that'.

Finally, it is interesting to note the views of one of the shift managers. This man had worked for Pirelli for more than 30 years, beginning as an operative, and working his way through the ranks right up to assistant manager at the old Southampton factory. The excerpt begins with him talking about the old factory:

People expected you to give them a programme of what they had to do. There *were* people there who did use their initiative and went beyond, . . . but in the set-up we had there, there wasn't the ability to use it all . . . I find this is an area where they tend to come from more traditional industries, they do find it harder to start making their own decisions . . . When it comes to actually going to tell another guy, 'I don't want you to do that because you're affecting me – if you were to do that you'd help me make my job easier'. They think *I* ought to be doing that . . . I'm pleased to see on my shift a good teamwork, particularly in the metallurgy section, there's four or five lads, they just move up and down and help each other. When there's a breakdown on the rod machine, for example, you'll find two guys will be on it, with no instruction from me. They're the team and I try to preach that and get them to see this. There is a team element on extrusion, too, on a changeover [from one bobbin to the next], they go and help each other, but you're dealing with more individual products on extrusion, whereas on metallurgy it's a group and bank of machines which are all running a similar product all the time.

In all these quotations we can identify a number of facets of self-supervision in the production area at Aberdare: the end of demarcations based on the idea of a fixed 'job'; the expectation that individual operators would take decisions previously left to supervisors; the need for self-supervision at team as well as individual level (although with different degrees of teamwork in different parts of the production process owing to differing technical and operational requirements); the absence of the 'overseeing' foreman role; the high level of trust; the problems with traditional attitudes; the indication that many staff may be working harder (intensification of work); and, throughout, the contrast with more direct systems of labour management and control, whether it be the old factories at Pirelli Aberdare and Southampton, or the Hitachi plant three miles away.

For producers at Aberdare, self-supervision has represented a major change, not only in attitudes to work, but involvement in work. If a problem arises, their first instinct is to seek to resolve it themselves – or in collaboration with other producers or maintainers – rather than calling the foreman or even another member of staff because the work required is not in their job description. Alternatively, if their area of work is running smoothly and can safely be left unattended for a while, then they may well decide to walk round the factory floor to see if they can help out a colleague (this may, of course, also involve having a chat or two along the way!). The vast majority of producers interviewed said that they thought management now had all the flexibility it required, and they also believed that the greater flexibility increased satisfaction in the job and the trust and responsibility vested in them, even though it often involved intensified work effort over the course of a shift. As Elger has observed, intensification of work can go hand in hand with 'real sources of satisfaction' coming even from 'modest forms of job enlargement and flexibility on the shopfloor' (1991: 56). In this case, though, job enlargement and increased flexibility were more than modest. In addition, functional flexibility linked to self-supervision did appear to provide *joint benefits* for management – where it was clearly functional in terms of smooth production flows – and for the workforce – where it has led to increased job satisfaction and interest.

Criticisms of the Practice of Self-Supervision

Nevertheless, producers did express some criticisms of self-supervision in practice. The most common criticism was that a very small minority of staff abused the system, either by poor time management and attendance (taking long breaks, not arriving for work punctually, not helping out when their machine/section was running smoothly, even unwarranted 'sickness' absence which placed greater burdens on the team) or by poor work performance (reduced work effort resulting in smaller production output, failure to repair or clean machines at the end of a shift, making wrong decisions when problems arose). This not only led to low morale, it undermined the basis of the system because staff felt that if one or two individuals could 'get away' with it, then why should they bother? In one respect, too, some producers expressed a preference for the old system over the new, in that when they had a technical problem on a machine, the old foreman had almost certainly worked on it in the past and could give expert guidance. In contrast, only one of the shift managers had previously worked on the shopfloor as a cable-maker and none had experience of shopfloor work with a CIM system.

Line Management and Self-Supervision

Both these criticisms touch on the role of line managers under a system of self-supervision. While this cannot be discussed in detail here, it is worth identifying some of the actual or potential features of the new shift manager role at Aberdare. First, there were a number of **operational/ technical tasks**: setting and monitoring the implementation of broad performance objectives and weekly work plans, such as quality standards and weekly output targets; dealing with major contingencies, such as machine breakdowns, product defects, competing work priorities; identifying and acting on recurrent problems (from 1991 many of these were aided by quality improvement teams under the company's new total quality management programme).

Secondly, there were a whole range of **human resource management tasks**. Some were of a formal kind: work allocation on a weekly or fortnightly basis, team briefing, redeploying staff because of holidays and sickness, working out training plans, organizing training, establishing and enforcing standards of discipline and self-discipline. However, others were more informal – such as walking round the factory at the beginning of each shift, both to find out how production was going, and also to listen to individual problems and suggestions. This latter point was stressed by many producers as a crucial function of first-line management under a system of self-supervision, and they were critical of some of their managers for not being sufficiently receptive to suggestions and complaints and for becoming too distant from operational realities. Some were also criticized for not praising staff where they had performed well and not encouraging them where they were having difficulties. These 'informal' human resource management functions were not seen as a substitute for a formal annual appraisal – which had not been implemented for non-management staff by 1992 despite being envisaged under the 1987 single-union agreement – but as a vital communication mechanism and motivator for self-supervised staff.

Interestingly, while the shift and other line managers have taken on (more or less successfully) this wide range of human resource responsibilities for particular groups of staff, two of the five site personnel specialists at Aberdare have played an important complementary role as what might be called the general 'eyes and ears' of the plant. Not surprisingly, the degree of success in filling this often underestimated function has been very much dependent on the character of the individuals concerned. The first job-holder was an outgoing and charismatic personality, who enjoyed high esteem amongst the staff and made a major contribution to the good atmosphere in the early years of the plant. After a gap of a few months in early 1989 when he left for a major promotion to another company (during which time a temporary replacement was brought in), a third personnel manager was appointed who was the opposite of the first – an assiduous professional who rarely spoke with production staff and spent much of his time in his office on broader aspects of personnel administration. He resigned after less than a year for a higher level job at another greenfield site in South Wales, and, following a further gap of a few months, a fourth personnel officer was appointed. He was much more accessible to staff, going out every day on to the shopfloor and receiving regular visits during the day from staff who would often call in for a chat. He resigned in late 1991, however, again for a major promotion to another greenfield site in South Wales, and a new personnel officer took up his post in March 1992.

There is no doubt that lack of continuity in the personnel function, and lack of a strong personnel presence in the plant between early 1989 and mid-1991, was one of the contributory reasons why the practice of self-supervision was open to the kind of legitimate criticism discussed above. The failure to introduce an appraisal system, and the unevenness in the award of skill modules between shifts and between producers, maintainers and administrators, can also be attributed in part to the lack of specialist personnel management continuity on site. What was clearly absent, according to a senior manufacturing manager on site, was someone to act as a kind of 'auditor' of the performance of line managers in managing human resource issues (this idea is developed further in the concluding chapter in this volume).

This reference to the importance of the personnel function, however, should not detract from the fact that, for most staff, their line manager was 'the management' and thus the main influence on their overall perception of employment relations in the plant. On a site with a delayered and lean management, it is clear that the quality of line management – and a clear definition of its tasks – is crucial. Self-supervision at Pirelli Aberdare does not mean absence of management, but a heightened, more focused and more exposed role for a smaller number of line managers.

Conclusion

The level of functional flexibility at Pirelli Aberdare has fallen significantly short of the original intention of full flexibility between production, maintenance and administration. Six reasons have been given for this outcome: the 'horses for courses' principle, specialist knowledge, ownership of particular work areas, training, skill retention, and – more ambiguously – tight staffing levels.

However, our overall evaluation of the level of flexibility will be quite different if we base our assessment not on comparisons with the original intention, but with previous patterns of working at the factories which were the immediate forerunners of the new plant. On this comparison, production staff at Aberdare experienced a significant task and job enlargement and an increased involvement in maintenance, although the latter was somewhat restricted due to limitations of training and capability. Much of this increase in functional flexibility was directly related to the technical capabilities of the CIM plant, with tandemization of previously separate machine processes, a reduced need for human intervention in computer-aided production processes, and the functionally designed architecture of the new plant. As for maintainers, there was a substantial loosening of traditional demarcations between mechanical, electrical and electronic maintenance, made possible by the greenfield-site agreement under which both fitters and electricians were in the same trade union and required to be fully flexible. There were still degrees of specialization, however, not only because of differences in craft training, but also because of the complexity of the new technology and the inability of any one individual to become expert in all aspects of the machine processes. No maintainer has ever been required to engage in production work.

Administrators experienced the least change in functional flexibility. Many of the reasons for this are the same as those given for the lack of total flexibility in production and maintenance. In particular, extremely tight staffing levels and heavy workloads made it very difficult for staff to spend regular time away from their work learning new jobs. However, the range of different tasks and jobs carried out by administrators was significantly greater than in production, and the integration of administrative tasks with the overall production system at Aberdare (the goal of a 'computer-integrated business') was relatively underdeveloped. This was because a greater priority had been given to integration *within* production and because many administrative processes (sales, billing, materials purchasing) were still coordinated centrally within the company at a lower level of computerization.

Despite these uneven conclusions, there is no doubt that increases in functional flexibility for producers and maintainers have been substantial. If we also take into account the impact of self-supervision on work behaviour and attitudes to work, however, it is clear that the change has been even more fundamental. Under the system of self-supervision at Pirelli Aberdare, employees exercise a much greater level of judgement and decision-making than under traditional forms of working. In practice, this means that first-line managers rarely engage in day-to-day problem-solving and are only called upon if there is a major problem which requires coordination across a number of areas of production. While it would be foolish to suggest that this system operates totally smoothly, or that it is accepted by all staff, the overwhelming support for self-supervision, and the strong expression of preference for it over the old supervisor-driven system, does also suggest that it enjoys the 'normative commitment' of the vast majority of staff.

We have noted how the CIM system chosen, its architecture, technology and lay-out, were conducive to, indeed required, flexible patterns of working and self-supervision. We have also seen that the choice of a greenfield site presented management with an opportunity structure to be innovative and strategic, both in the choice and lay-out of new technology and in the choice of human resource policies and the recruitment of staff. We now turn to the importance of human resource issues in planning, implementing and operating the new plant, and the role of different actors – senior general, line and specialist personnel managers – in shaping the process and outcomes of human resource change.

Human resource issues played no direct role in the initial decision to invest, and there was no specialist personnel involvement on the company board. However, corporate personnel specialists had a well-established position within the company which enabled them to exert a considerable influence on the elaboration of a personnel/HRM strategy at an early stage of the implementation process. As members of the personnel 'sub-group' they were able to use their 'connections', particularly with ACAS and its Work Research Unit, to gain access to information about current best practice and thereby to establish their legitimacy as the 'experts' in the field. The fact that they developed the HRM strategy in close collaboration with the divisional manager-designate, who did not have the expert knowledge, the connections or the time to pursue the issues in detail, meant that human resource issues were 'owned' by senior general management and not simply seen as a preserve of the personnel department. In fact, it was the divisional manager-designate who provided the greatest continuity in the human resource field and came to personify the commitment to a high trust and progressive HR policy when the plant came on stream and corporate personnel involvement was more at a distance.

Moving on to a later stage of the implementation process and a lower level of specialist personnel involvement, the key actors here were line managers and the site personnel manager (divisional administration manager). Close collaboration between them was an important element in establishing the selection criteria for new staff, personnel specialists had full responsibility for putting in place the instruments of selection, and interviews were conducted jointly. However, the absence of personnel continuity in subsequent years meant that the onus for detailed implementation and the development of policies on skill-based pay, monitoring employee performance, training and discipline rested on the shoulders of line managers, who were already overburdened with getting the new plant up and running. As a result, policy and practice in these areas not only fell short of the initial plans, but (by general consensus) left something to be desired. So while senior general managers were instrumental in setting the general framework for the new HR policies, and middle and junior line management were crucial for implementing them on a day-to-day basis, corporate and divisional personnel specialists played important roles in shaping and carrying out the new policies and, by lack of continuity and absence of divisional personnel involvement for a certain period, contributed to a partial failure fully to carry them through.

To what extent can the Aberdare experiment thus far be deemed a success? After many technical teething problems, employees achieved their planned annual production target (17,000 tonnes) for the first time in 1990, a higher annual output than that ever achieved at the old Southampton plant, with around half the number of production staff. On a number of other measures, too, such as sales per employee, the plant has achieved better results than were ever achieved in Southampton. However, from early 1990 to the time of writing (autumn 1992), the UK market for building wires, along with the construction industry on which it is so dependent, has been hit very hard by the recession. In 1991–92 most UK companies in the general wiring field introduced short-time working and redundancies, and in May 1992 Pirelli itself announced thirty redundancies at its Aberdare plant. Under such conditions it is difficult to gauge whether the Aberdare experiment has been a 'success'. If demand rises so that the factory can operate consistently at or near full capacity, the signs are that it will be able to establish itself as the lowest cost producer of building wires in the UK. If it achieves this objective, then human resource management, and personnel specialists at different levels within the organization, will have played an important part in that success.

Acknowledgements

I would like to thank the Leverhulme Foundation and the ESRC-funded Industrial Relations Research Unit at the University of Warwick for financial support of the research discussed in this chapter, and my colleagues at IRRU for comments on an earlier draft. My greatest debt of gratitude is to the employees of Pirelli Cables Aberdare, who gave so generously of their time and so honestly of their views, and to the company (in particular David Yeandle, John Siney, David Gaskell and Bob Nicholas) for allowing me to carry out the research.

Notes

1. The research reported in this chapter is part of a wider study of the implementation of new personnel policies at Pirelli Cables' CIM plant. Two articles describing the new policies and outlining the rationale behind them were published in mid-1989 (Yeandle and Clark, 1989a, 1989b). The first period of fieldwork took place between July and September 1990, during which time interviews were carried out with 94% (137) of the total workforce on site (148). A number of periods of observation were also spent with production staff on the shopfloor. Most of the data discussed here were collected during this period. Since then interviews have been conducted with senior corporate managers from the company, full-time trade union officers etc., and a second period of fieldwork has been completed (in August and September 1992). The author is currently engaged in writing a book telling the story of the factory from its conception in the early 1980s through to the present day.

2. Pirelli General plc was re-named Pirelli Cables plc in 1991.

7

Human Resource Management in 'Surveillance' Companies

Graham Sewell and Barry Wilkinson

In recent research we have been concerned to relate parallel developments in the organization of manufacturing activities and systems of managerial control. Specifically, we have argued that two particular developments – just-in-time manufacturing and total quality control – which are commonly associated with worker empowerment and the devolution of responsibility to the shopfloor through team-based organization are, in some cases, predicated on a simultaneous centralization of strategic managerial control (Sewell and Wilkinson, 1992a, 1992b). Not only is this centralization of control enabled through systems of surveillance and discipline based on new technologies of electronic work monitoring, it is actually enhanced through the very forms of work organization which, rhetorically at least, seek to maximize worker empowerment.

Thus far we have been primarily concerned with examining the impact of these forms of work organization on shopfloor workers – the principal subjects of surveillance and work monitoring – in terms of their changing position within the industrial labour process. In this chapter we turn our attention to the changing role of managers under this form of productive regime. We have previously argued (Sewell and Wilkinson, 1992b) that, within the flattened organizational hierarchies of the companies we researched, some traditional managerial functions – especially those associated with control – had not disappeared but had been internalized by the individual shopfloor workers in the form of self-management. In this chapter we wish to examine the way in which the personnel function has been transformed in these 'surveillance' companies.

Focusing on the personnel function is particularly appropriate given the characteristics of the companies we researched. They were all companies that have adopted or even pioneered some of the best practices associated with human resource management. The rhetoric of HRM acknowledges that responsibility for some of the functions that were previously in the domain of the personnel manager may well be devolved to the shopfloor. Armstrong (1988) has argued that this poses a threat to personnel managers as it undermines their so-called professional status. However, much of the HRM literature puts forward the contrary argument that in allowing certain functions to be devolved the personnel manager is given the freedom to get involved in the strategic management activities that were frequently denied them in pre-HRM regimes (for example, see the reviews contained in Storey, 1992a; and Chapter 1, this volume). No wonder then that HRM should be so enthusiastically embraced by the personnel profession if it appears to elevate them to a place at the heart of strategic managerial decision-making and adds to the validation of their professional bona fides.

In the light of these comments this chapter will explore some of the realities of the transformation of the personnel function. First, we briefly discuss the current debate on changes to the personnel function as it relates to our own work. Secondly, we outline the nature and form of electronic work surveillance and demonstrate how it supports a form of self-management within shopfloor workers which incorporates many of the traditional functions of the personnel manager. We will then go on to examine the actual role of personnel managers within these manufacturing regimes and contrast this with the rhetoric of HRM. Finally, we relate these developments to the continuing debate concerning the current status of personnel management by reference to the wider literature on profes-sionalization. In adopting this framework we will be addressing many of the common themes to be found in this volume, especially those expressed in Chapters 2 and 6, this volume.

From Personnel Management to Human Resource Management

It is necessary to comment briefly on the emergence of new forms of personnel practices because the organization which constitutes the centre-piece of our analysis – K-Electric – has been at the forefront of changes in the personnel function in the UK. Further, we would argue that the technology of surveillance which we describe actually underpins the sorts of changes to organization and management associated with human resource management.

A central plank of HRM is the deployment of a number of techniques and practices which, according to its supporters, enables it to effect the heroic achievement of spanning the gulf between the corporate interests of a company and those of its employees. These include the careful selection and induction of employees which contribute to the establishment of a homogeneity of values, a pay and appraisal system which integrates individual and strategic company interests, a carefully designed internal labour market which gives employees an interest in the long-term success of the organization, etc.: in other words, exactly the sorts of 'good' personnel practices documented in, and advocated by, countless personnel management textbooks. There are two extra dimensions, however, which are supposed to distinguish HRM from personnel decisively. One relates to organizational culture, the other to the location of the personnel function.

On the first dimension, HRM is claimed to be concerned with *the generation of trust, responsibility and commitment* which arises when employees' values fall in line with the employer's organizational values. Of the practices that make for a break from the preoccupation with 'contracts management', the existence of charismatic or transformational leadership is crucial, along with the fostering of an organizational culture which is characterized by widely shared and strongly held implicit and explicit values (Legge, 1989a). Organizations held up as models of this strong version of HRM (that is, HRM which extends beyond concepts of sound personnel management) are typically the 'excellent' North American companies and the large Japanese corporations (Pascale and Athos, 1981; Peters and Waterman, 1982). In these companies the role of the organization goes so far as to provide a source of meanings and superordinate goals for its employees previously found in religion and community. Within organizations, HRM is presented as a method of 'releasing untapped reserves of labour resourcefulness by facilitating employee responsibility, commitment and involvement' (Keenoy, 1990c: 4). It is part of a new organizational form which transcends bureaucracy and the role of employee as 'cog in the machine': organizations should be flat, accountability centres set up, responsibility pushed to line management or team leaders at the point of production or service delivery, and everyone should have a customer, whether internal or external, to ensure quality by exerting a form of consumer sovereignty on the relationship. These help give organizational members a sense of ownership leading to commitment and, therefore, the possibility that management may trust the workforce.

The second of the distinguishing dimensions of HRM – *the location of the personnel function* – has already been implied. Personnel loses its role as a specialist activity as line managers are empowered to make their own decisions – or at least be involved in decisions – on the procurement, appraisal, development and even separation of their own members. Production supervisors become 'supporter', 'guide', 'coach' and 'communicator' to their employees rather than mere 'production chasers' dependent on specialists for 'servicing the contract' between employer and employee (Wickens, 1987). As one observer of the Nissan plant in North East England put it:

> In customary British practice, the nitty gritty of production is the business of the engineers, while the workers are in the domain of personnel. The supervisor overlooks both, but controls neither . . . In terms of traditional British manufacturing, this scene [at Nissan] is revolutionary – because of the power of the supervisor to control production. (Popham, 1992: 28)

Incidentally, the new-found 'power of the supervisor' is dependent also on breaking what in some companies is the traditional role of the shop steward in communicating between management and workforce. As Wickens (1987) puts it, 'he who communicates is King', and there is no room in an organization that admits no differences of interest between employer and employee for communications relays that might distort the message.

While our own research at K-Electric has uncovered both an HRM rhetoric and a real shift in responsibilities which has made the team leader key in the employer–employee relationship, it has not uncovered grounds for accepting the notion that 'commitment' and 'trust' are essential features. On the contrary, our study of the technology of surveillance at this company would suggest, if anything, the operation of a *low trust* system of production. After describing the company, we will return to the question of the nature and changing role of personnel management. We would argue that this cannot be understood in the absence of a consideration of the mechanisms of surveillance which necessarily underpin the new organizational form and ensure a predictability of behaviour in the absence of traditional bureaucratic control mechanisms.

A Case Study of Work Surveillance

Company Background

K-Electric was established in the UK approximately 10 years ago as part of the Japanese parent's strategy of establishing transplant factories within its major world markets. The plant, which produces electronic consumer goods, was previously British-owned and was reopened by K-Electric, with much of the same 're-recruited' workforce on new contracts, after being closed for several months. K-Electric supplies the European market, and it has sister plants in Japan, Singapore, Mexico and the United States. In line with market demand, production at K-Electric has increased rapidly and consistently through the 1980s and into the early 1990s. The factory, which now employs over 700, is basically an assembly plant; the direct–indirect ratio is around $3.5:1$, with 70 per cent of the directs and 50 per cent of the indirects being women. Between fifty and seventy people work on temporary contracts, the number varying to meet seasonal changes in demand. Only five Japanese nationals are permanently engaged in the plant. One of these is the assistant managing director, but the managing director and all other directors are British. Close contact is, however, maintained with the head office in Japan, and most managers have spent time in Japan as part of their training and development.

The Framework for Personnel Management

K-Electric is not untypical in its human resource management practices compared with other Japanese companies in the UK (for general accounts and examples see Yu and Wilkinson, 1989; Gleave and Oliver, 1990; Wilkinson and Oliver, 1990). Selection is rigorous, and includes tests for dexterity (which is crucial to many of the assembly jobs) together with interviews which look for commitment, enthusiasm, willingness to work overtime and an ability to work in a team. Previous attendance records (from school if the candidate is a school-leaver) are closely scrutinized.

Recruits have a one-week induction – which includes on-the-job instruction in a training facility – before being put on the line. All the time the team leaders, who are in part responsible for their own selection and induction, are 'getting a feel' for how and where the recruits would best fit into the team. Before the end of the induction week recruits are invited to give their impressions and to confirm that they will be happy with a job in which attendance, attention to detail and quality are strongly emphasized. Many recruits select themselves out at the end of the first week; those who remain are likely to stay with K-Electric for at least several years. In the panels section, which employs around 350 – and is the focus of our analysis – K-Electric has a turnover of around four people per month.

Pay levels for comparable jobs are well above average compared with the consumer electronics industry in the UK and the local economy. The company is among the top five in the pay leagues on both counts. According to one manager this was the quid pro quo for being employed by 'pretty tough task masters . . . In [K-City] K-Electric is known for being strong on quality and on attendance and absenteeism'. Operators are paid by a straight time rate. There is no piecework and there are no bonuses except for a small attendance bonus paid twice a year. However, there is an appraisal system which applies to every worker. The appraisal is carried out annually by the team leader or immediate supervisor, and it includes subjective assessments of cooperativeness, teamwork ability etc., as well as objective measures of performance and behaviour. The results of the appraisal directly affect the worker's pay level, and can feed into considerations of promotion, transfer and even redundancy.

The company has a single-union agreement which is characterized by a strike-free clause, a flexibility provision which stipulates complete managerial prerogatives over the deployment of labour, and a Company Advisory Board which makes recommendations on issues such as pay and working conditions (and redundancies) which would normally be the preserve of collective bargaining in the UK (Wilkinson and Oliver, 1990). The Company Advisory Board is also used to impart company information to the workforce, and is part of a comprehensive system of communications in the company which also includes company newsletters and team briefings at the start of every working day. Of course, this massively reduces the shop steward role in communicating between employer and employee. K-Electric operates a single status policy. Everyone is issued with the company jacket, and toilet, canteen, car parking etc. facilities are shared in common. Such policies, from the beginning, meant K-Electric had all the characteristics of companies setting up on greenfield sites (cf Chapter 5, this volume) making questions of 'will we get this past the union or workforce?' superfluous.

It is important to point out that this company is not untypical, at least among recent Japanese investors. Such a framework for personnel management has in fact been established consistently by Japanese companies setting up in the UK during the 1980s. In a recent comprehensive study of

Japanese manufacturing transplants in Wales, for instance, most of the features described above were commonplace (Morris et al, 1992).

Production and Materials Control

The three main production sections are: 'machining', where printed circuit boards (PCBs) are prepared and some components inserted on automatic machines; 'panels', where more components are manually inserted on to the PCB on production lines; and 'assembly', which includes sub-assembly of some components and final assembly. There is a final test facility within the assembly section. Certain high-value components are bought in, but K-Electric is in the process of establishing its own production facilities for some of these.

Since taking the plant over K-Electric has gradually moved towards just-in-time production and supply. Work-in-progress has been reduced from a 6-week to a 3-day average, and many components are now delivered to the factory one or two days before they are used. K-Electric tries to develop its suppliers' abilities and has rationalized the number of suppliers – many parts are now single sourced – but the company faces difficulties in improving JIT supply because of continuing local supplier incompetence and because of the complex logistics involved in obtaining parts sourced from overseas, including Japan.

Materials procurement is closely integrated with production and sales. A production, sales and inventory (PSI) plan is produced and revised on a monthly basis, and goes forward 12 months. The accuracy of the PSI depends on the accuracy of sales information, and K-Electric go to great lengths to ensure distributors' orders are both accurate and firm. A production schedule is derived from the PSI (using a PC) and this indicates a line-by-line loading on a daily basis for the following month, together with procurement requirements. After detailed production meetings, the company is then committed 3 months forward on labour and materials.

Productivity and Quality

Productivity and quality improvements are sought constantly through a Total Productivity Improvement Programme (TPIP). This is based on weekly meetings of team leaders, each of whom is expected to produce one 'measured' suggestion every week. These should originate from, or at least be tried out in discussion with, team members. These are then progressed by the facilities engineering department. Within a few days of the weekly meeting team leaders are told what action will be taken, and if the idea is not pursued then facilities engineering is obliged to give an explanation. This information is relayed by the team leader back to team members. Those improvements that are accepted and successfully acted upon are often publicly displayed on notice boards in prominent positions around the factory.

While K-Electric simply inherited the technological hardware of its predecessor, a great many incremental improvements have been made, and added together they are significant. Over a two and a half year period between 1987 and 1990, the following improvements were attributed to TPIP:

- Reduction of work-in-progress by 35 per cent
- Internal cutting of lead times
- Reduction of standard times by 15 per cent
- The saving of 11 per cent of floor space
- The saving of fifty-seven staff members.

More importantly, productivity and quality are maintained and improved by careful and constant monitoring of performance and by taking action immediately any problem comes to light. It is in this area of surveillance that the Japanese have had a decisive influence. Production levels and quality are the responsibility of the production department, and team leaders (and ultimately team members) are held accountable for any problems occurring within their control.

The Panels Section

Having broadly outlined the company background, the framework for personnel management, and production control, we now turn attention to the focus of our study, the panels section, which employs around 350. Most employees are women, working on nine production lines, each line making up a team of around forty. Each team has a team leader and around three or four 'senior members' who also work on the line and who are paid slightly more than ordinary members. Above the team leader is the production manager who is assisted by one superintendent. The vast majority of employees in this section are women, including all the team leaders and the superintendent and production manager.

The team leader has extensive responsibilities. Member selection, on-the-job training and appraisal have already been mentioned. The leader is also involved in the details of production scheduling, and is responsible for labour deployment, meeting production targets and maintaining a high level of quality. Each leader is responsible to a 'customer' in the final assembly section, and the leader's job is frequently defined in terms of 'meeting my customer's requirements'. Similarly, the panel section production manager has her customer in the form of the final assembly section production manager. The production manager, and most of the team leaders, were internally promoted from operator level and have an enormously detailed knowledge of shopfloor operations.

Complete workforce flexibility is possible in theory – managerial prerogatives over labour deployment are indeed specified in the single-union agreement. In practice operators work mostly within their section, and again most tend to remain within their team. Many operators are trained in more than one skill, recognized by a higher pay grade, and these are used mostly within but sometimes between teams in the case of absence, lateness, demand fluctuations etc. The team leader is responsible for maintaining both discipline and morale on the line.

Management Information Systems for Production Control

The day at K-Electric's panel section begins with the production manager and team leaders looking at their schedules and 'customer' (final assembly) requirements for the day. The labour they have available is determined by a Labour Hours Analysis which, based on production schedules (derived from the PSI – see above) and standard times, gives the number of labour hours required in each area on a month-by-month basis. A shopfloor PC will tell team leaders and the production manager their precise labour needs for a given level of efficiency in the light of the day's schedule. It is worth describing how these are derived.

The Labour Hours Analysis, carried out on a PC with internally developed software, takes account of operator efficiency, attendance ratios, 'non-productive work' ratios, learning curves on new models etc., based on retrospective information. Production managers and team leaders are then expected, on a monthly basis, to agree to targets with a specified amount of labour. Standard times are produced in Japan with a simple work factor method and are indicated in precise detail. Times are provided to K-Electric for a whole unit of finished goods, for the sections of the factory, for activities within each section, and right down to the level of components to be assembled or inserted in fractions of a second. Allowances are carefully built into the calculation for things like differences in machinery and equipment.

Assembly manuals, which include detailed standard times broken down to the level of individual component insertion, are regularly up-dated in Japan in the light of improvements in methods. Whenever an overseas factory makes an improvement, this fact, and the new method, is relayed back to Japan and the improvement is passed on to all group factories the next time the manual is up-dated. Some improvements come from TPIP and some from management.

When workers arrive at the start of the shift they are briefed by the team leader on targets for the day and any special problems which might arise. Immediately the team leaders then check for absences and consider how best to 'balance' the line. There is no slack labour, so if necessary decisions have to be made on how to redistribute tasks on the assembly line to cover for those operators missing from their work stations. For some operators this often means increasing the number of components per panel they have to insert as the panels move past on the line. Occasionally team leaders cope by coming to an agreement among themselves and with the production manager on a redistribution of available labour between work teams, and in exceptional circumstances overtime becomes necessary to meet targets because of absence.

Because of the problems absence causes in the context of tight staffing, the matter is taken very seriously. An absent member, on return to work, is automatically interviewed by the team leader, and the reasons for the absence and any action taken against the absentee are recorded on the employee's personal file. Employees are invited to sign the statement indicating that they agree that that was what was said to them. Frequent absence, even if due for instance to chronic illness, will lead to dismissal. The names of absentees together with the dates and reasons for absence are publicly displayed adjacent to each production line, a practice documented in other Japanese companies in the UK (Wickens, 1987; Oliver and Wilkinson, 1988; Morris et al, 1992).

The pace of work on the lines is intense, and within working hours the lines rarely stop. Each operator inserts an average of eleven to thirteen components in each PCB (panel) which passes by, and with present line speeds this means an average of around ten components every 30 seconds. Each operator has in front of her a panel blueprint with her own components marked in bright yellow. One commented: 'You get used to it; it's when the line stops – you think it's going backwards'. There is a 10-minute break in each of the morning and afternoon working periods, and operators must not leave the line before a buzzer sounds to indicate the start of the break. After 9 minutes the buzzer goes again and the operator must be back at her work station at the sound of the next buzzer exactly 1 minute later. (Until a year ago the operators could remain in the canteen for the full 10 minutes. One minute was forfeited as part of a 9 per cent pay deal.) Within these 10 minutes there is a frantic scurrying to and from the canteen. (It takes another 30 minutes for the pall of cigarette smoke to clear from the area. Smoking, eating and drinking are strictly prohibited on the line.)

Efficiency ratings are displayed at the end of each assembly line and these are regularly up-dated by the team leader using information from the shopfloor PC. If any team is performing below expectation, then the production manager is expected to take appropriate corrective action. Team leaders are encouraged to compare their performances with other teams, which leads to a degree of competition between them. This does not, however, necessarily lead to inter-team conflict over labour deployment, because the efficiency ratings take account of exactly who is working where at any particular time. The system depends, of course, on accurate information on labour deployment being fed into the labour calculation, the importance of which is constantly impressed on all team leaders and section managers. Each team leader is expected to keep an 'ins and outs' book (presently being computerized) to record all details of labour movements, any downtime and the reasons for it etc. Management selectively uses information from these books to feed into the efficiency calculations, and to examine possible solutions to problems identified.

If a team is performing *above* expectation, management will look very closely at the reasons why. According to one manager, 'We try to keep them going at 110 per cent and get them to pass on the savings'. Sometimes this will involve a time study which is conducted without warning. In this manner, continuous improvement is built into the system of production. A final aspect of production information systems worthy of mention is the monitoring and visual display (on a TV screen) of planned, accumulative and actual output of finished goods on an hour-to-hour basis. This is updated regularly during the working day and gives management a detailed picture of the state of production at any one time. TV screens displaying this information are located at various places in the factory, including the panels section, which gives teams an idea of how their own production is matched (or otherwise) with their customers in final assembly.

The impact of such detailed monitoring and control of production on the line is summed up by one operator who said: 'They pay you well but you have to work for it'. Other typical comments were: 'You reach your targets and they just push you harder and harder'; 'It's terrible, it's always like this'; and

> They make you work every second in the day here . . . the times come down from up there, they're all on paper; they should come down on the line and see how they like it . . . If they spot you doing something faster they put the targets up . . . they find out. Now and then they come with a watch, and if they catch you doing it faster you have to do it all the time – it's not fair.

Team leaders also face heavy demands. One, commenting on a particularly hectic period, commented: 'I used to think, Jesus Christ, I don't know whether I'm on my head or my feet . . . With [the previous British owners] we had two or three thousand people with far less output than we have today'. Unaware of the theoretical framework we were eventually to use in our interpretation, she continued: 'Don't get me wrong, the people here are not prisoners'.

Management Information Systems for Quality Control

At the same time as 'waste' is ruthlessly eliminated and labour productivity pushed to its limits, quality has to be carefully maintained. One operator felt there was a contradiction here when she commented: '. . . when you're interviewed they ask you what's the most important – quality or quantity. They want you to say quality, but when you get on the line you see they want both. You can't have both'.

In-process control is the responsibility of manufacturing, and sections are held accountable for any quality problems. Within the panels section the great majority of quality problems are related to faulty insertion of components on the panel. Each team conducts its own visual and electronic inspections on the panels and an attempt is made to take corrective action before they go to the customer in final assembly. As the panels section production manager said, 'We want to keep our problems in here on our own doorstep; we don't want them [final assembly] to see it'. Any mistakes identified by line inspectors are attributed to the individual operator responsible, and charts at the end of each line display how many assembly defects were caused by each operator.

Some defects do, none the less, get through to final assembly, to be discovered on the final electronic test. Here a probe is inserted into the completed good, and a screen flashes 'pass' or 'fail'. Where it states 'fail' it automatically gives information on the nature of the fault, and this allows the tracing of the fault immediately to the individual culprit. Senior members from the panels section visit their 'customer' every hour to collect defect information, which is used to up-date charts indicating team and individual errors.

For individuals, quality performance is recorded on charts above their heads at the work station. A green A4-sized card which reads 'good' indicates zero defects the previous day. An amber card reading 'caution' indicates between one and four defects. And a red card which reads 'danger' indicates five or more defects. Also alongside each operator is a daisy chart which indicates quality performance for each day of the whole month. The in-section inspectors also have cards which indicate the number of faulty components which they should have identified but allowed to pass by. Under such a regime it would be difficult to imagine, and we certainly did not document, individual selective control over information, poor time management, or other forms of resistance (as are documented in Chapters 6 and 8 of this volume).

The production manager commented that the card system 'makes people nervous a little bit. Nobody like the red, I'll tell you that for a fact. I've only had one person feel as if she were back at school. I had to explain that we were only doing it to help her'. A team leader explained enthusiastically how the system was introduced with the help of engineers from Japan. She commented, 'The girls don't mind the cards, they think it's a good thing. When they see caution they go "ooh, maybe I could do a bit better"'. Where someone is identified as having a quality problem (not a difficult job) the first step is counselling. The team leader takes the offender off the line to the canteen (the line is re-balanced meantime) and tries to get to the root of the problem. As one team leader said, 'I ask them "Have you got a problem? Have you got a personal problem?" They could have something on their minds and it's best to find out why'. While discussing counselling sessions, another team leader said 'Sometimes I don't feel like a manager; I feel like a social worker, a solicitor, a policeman'.

More than twenty defects in a month results in a verbal warning under disciplinary procedure, and repetitions ultimately lead to dismissal. Where an operator is found to have made three or more mistakes on the same batch of panels (batches are typically between 500 and 1,000) she is taken to the final assembly area (her customer) and requested to do a manual check on the whole of the batch. This can cause disruption for an hour or two for her fellow team members, who have to take on her tasks. This practice of demonstrating the impact of an employee's mistakes on their customers has been noted in other Japanese companies in the UK (Takamiya, 1981; Reitsperger, 1986).

Within teams, operators attempt to 'look out for each other'. The observer standing by a production line will hear every 2 minutes or so a shorthand message such as 'knock-out on P39' or 'C330 reverse' which is repeated operator by operator up the line until the operator making the mistake can see her fault and make amends. In the meantime, downstream operators will try to correct the faultily inserted components before the panels reach the solder bath and the visual inspectors so that the mistake is not recorded. With such relentless repetitive work – work cycle times are typically around half a minute – and considering each operator is likely to insert over 8,000 components in any one day, it is not surprising that mistakes occasionally occur. One operator commented, 'Sometimes you just slide them in the wrong way round or whatever without knowing, and suddenly somebody shouts it up the line. You don't know how you did it'. Another said, 'Twenty rejects mean you get taken to the coffee lounge for a warning; we do eleven per panel, 800 panels a day, sometimes 980, twenty rejects isn't many'.

The latter comment tells us something of the experience of work in a surveillance firm. It also tells us something of the power of the first-line production manager (the team leader) which derives from an efficient system of surveillance and her role in disciplining the workforce. Indeed, throughout our description of K-Electric we have noted the line manager's extensive role in personnel matters – from selection, induction, and training through communications, counselling and discipline. Working within a framework established by senior management, supported by an information system which provides the most accurate information on behaviour and performance, and impelled by a set of targets and perform-ance measures, the strong task orientation of the team leader is an orientation which embraces all aspects of employee relations.

The Changing Nature of the Personnel Function: Professionalization vs Proletarianization

The Growth of Professionalization in Personnel Management

Since its formal constitution in 1947 the Institute of Personnel Manage-ment (IPM) has been centrally involved in a process of legitimating the personnel function as a profession. Despite the problematic nature of defining the personnel function and the lack of any real consensus on the fundamental day-to-day role of the personnel manager (Tyson and Fell, 1986), the IPM has been successful in its objective in the sense that few would now seem openly to question the professional legitimacy they have sought to construct. In order to fulfil its desire to become a self-regulating sovereign body which controls access to the profession and progress within it through a hierarchy of membership, the IPM has followed the classic strategy identified by Wilensky (1964). This involves accrediting programmes of education and training in recognized institutions where different levels of attainment correspond to different positions in the membership hierarchy. However, at the very time that personnel management appears to have become consolidated as a profession, the new 'paradigm' of human resource management has meant the issue is once again under scrutiny. After examining the nature of 'professions', we will go on to examine how the role of the personnel manager is being transformed within surveillance firms.

The Process of Professionalization

If asked 'what is a profession?' few people could give a definitive answer, yet there is a strong sense that they might recognize one if they saw one. Indeed, some of the most powerful allusions to professional status are of the visually symbolic kind – one only has to think of the doctor's white coat and stethoscope, the lawyer's wig and gown and even the male accountant's pin-striped suit and red braces. However, most systematic accounts of the professions focus on what Saks (1983) calls the 'taxonomic approach'. At the crudest level this simply involves drawing up a list of occupational groups which are presumed to be professional, usually on the basis of prestige or socio-economic status (Raelin, 1985). A more sophisticated approach involves drawing up lists of common or comparable functions and characteristics which can be used to identify professionals and professional groups. Kerr et al (1977) summarize much of the literature adopting this method of definition by identifying six general characteristics. Thus, professionals are seen to display:

1 **Expertise** based on the command of a body of abstract knowledge gained by engaging in a prolonged period of study and/or training
2 **Autonomy** through possession of the freedom to identify problems and prescribe solutions (that is, to have direct influence over ends *and* means)
3 **Commitment** through the display of a primary interest in one's chosen specialty
4 **Identification** with fellow professionals, both within one's own chosen specialty and between other professional groups, through formal structures of association or through external referents
5 **Ethics** based on an accepted code of conduct which allows emotional detachment from the client and precludes a conflict of interests
6 **Standards** through committing oneself to helping maintain the standards of other professionals' conduct through peer review.

Central to the establishment and maintenance of these characteristics is the existence of the professional association – run by its members – which acts as the custodian of 'professionalism'.

The principal criticism of the taxonomic approach is that, although it may be meaningful at the group level, at the level of the individual there is the problem of consistency in roles (Ritzer, 1972). The nature of this problem is particularly apparent in the occupation we are discussing here, given the ambiguity that still exists over the role of the personnel manager. Thus, although the IPM may well consider itself to act as the custodian of professionalism, for individual personnel managers in different firms, their understanding of what it is to be a professional will be diverse. This represents what Hall (1968) has identified as the structural/attitudinal dichotomy. In this situation, although there may well be a structural validation of professionalism (for example, through formal educational standards, examinations, entrance requirements etc.), if individuals do not possess any coherent and shared identity relating to their own roles then they do not *feel* professional. Thus, although developing a taxonomy of professional occupations may serve some analytical purpose in a categorical sense, it makes little contribution to developing an understanding of the actual dynamic of the process of becoming a professional and creating professional knowledge.

An alternative approach to the issue of professionalism centres on the way in which professional groups go about obtaining and perpetuating the power to create status and autonomy and maximize their social and economic position in the labour market (Larson, 1977; Klegon, 1978). Child and Fulk (1982) suggest that the origin of professional power stems from the ability to retain autonomy and occupational control within organizations. This is achieved by demonstrating that there is a domain over which they exercise influence where their technical contributions, formulated on the basis of privileged access to a body of knowledge, are sufficiently indeterminate that no one else could make them. This interpretation of professionalism strongly echoes the earlier work of Johnson (1972), who argued that the extent to which the professional can maintain this indeterminacy depends on the power of occupations to impose 'their own definition of the producer/consumer [professional/client] relationship' (Johnson, 1972: 45). Thus, Johnson argues that we should not constitute professions in terms of static traits, rather we should take a 'processual' view of professionalism as 'a peculiar type of occupational control rather than an expression of the inherent nature of particular occupations. A profession is not, then, an occupation but a means of controlling an occupation' (Johnson, 1972: 45).

In the light of this comment, the principal role of a body such as the IPM is not simply to carry out tasks like controlling access to the profession and validating examinations but something much more complex – the creation and defence of an aura of indetermination in relation to the activities of personnel specialists which protects them from external scrutiny, evaluation or control (Boreham, 1983). Another way of expressing this is that in order to maintain the asymmetry of power between themselves and the client, the professionals must be able to define the ends *and* the means. Clearly, this is the case between doctor and patient: although an individual may present feeling unwell, he or she is not officially considered unwell until diagnosed by a medically qualified practitioner who then has control over treatment. In the case of the personnel manager this is particularly difficult, for commonly they are in control of neither means nor ends and, as Guest (1991) has pointed out, are themselves frequently subject to close control by a non-professional group, namely general managers.

The relationship between the personnel manager and general manager is itself indicative of a wider dilemma faced by professionals working in an organizational context of bureaucratic control. This relates to the challenge posed to the autonomy of professions by developments in what are defined – in managerial terms, at least – as impersonalized systems of rational control (Miller, 1967).

Under the development of bureaucracy, professionals see the domain of their personal discretion and power continually encroached upon by the advancement of the means of rational evaluation and measurement. Therefore, professionals must fight a continual battle to preserve the indeterminacy of their activities. Clearly, this throws into stark contrast the differing objectives of personnel managers as an aspirant professional group and general managers as bureaucratic administrators.

The contradiction between the objectives of professionals and bureaucrats is taken up in the debate which can be characterized as 'professionalization vs proletarianization'. As Wilensky (1964) points out, as the number of occupations claiming professional status increases, so the universal status of professions becomes devalued. However, proletarianization does not necessarily involve the degradation of status. Rather it centres on the desire to make professionals accountable to bodies other than their professional association (Haug, 1973) and to reduce professional actions to a set of rational tasks (Oppenheimer, 1973). The combined effects of these tendencies is to undermine indeterminacy and autonomy and deskill professional occupations. The key to both is the ability to specify those tasks and subject them to rational measure, thus exposing an external bureaucratic control on the professionals, for if their performance can be closely scrutinized and evaluated then their power to be judge and jury of their actions is seriously eroded. For many professions it has long been the case that there may be some external control over the ends aspect of professional conduct – one only has to think of the budget constraints faced by medical professionals in the NHS. In response some professions may learn to tolerate external control over ends in return for continued internal control over means, which is then to be jealously guarded (Raelin, 1985). Once that guard is breached and control of means is lost then, for some of the less well established professions at least, the professional game may well be up.

The Role of the 'Professional' Personnel Manager in 'Surveillance' Companies

How far has the role of personnel managers been transformed under the influence of the surveillance technologies we found in our research? As we have already demonstrated, the operation of workplace electronic surveillance supplants the need for the traditional bureaucratic hierarchy comprising relays of control. Furthermore, the operation of the disciplinary mechanism on the subjectivity of individual workers instils a sense of self-management. Thus, many of the traditional functions of the personnel manager are devolved to the shopfloor with the team leaders assuming a pivotal role.

With the disappearance of the traditional domain over which personnel managers exercise direct influence, the question emerges – do they assume the strategic role as predicted or are they increasingly marginalized? In order to answer this we must examine the actual functions of the personnel manager observed in our case study. One of the principal roles centres on the process of selection and recruitment. As we have previously noted (Sewell and Wilkinson, 1992b), the search for 'docile bodies' – that is, the a priori identification of workers who will conform to company goals through the use of instruments of selection – is of central importance in establishing a workforce that will be amenable to the forms of work organization deployed in surveillance firms. Clearly, if personnel managers are involved in the development of selection criteria and hence in the formulation of corporate goals, then it would be fair to say that they have assumed a strategic human resource function. However, it was our experience that personnel managers were simply responsible for the administration of so-called rational instruments of selection. By this we mean the range of psychometric, aptitude and dexterity tests which claim or at least allude to scientific validity. In this sense, the primary role of the personnel manager has been deskilled to a formal set of tasks imposed from above. This tendency is clearly in accord with the proletarianization thesis which stresses the way in which indeterminacy and hence autonomy are undermined. Personnel managers simply become gate-keepers employing other people's selection criteria.

Being administrators of selection does not necessarily provide conclusive proof that personnel managers have been marginalized, especially if they have some role in workforce planning. However, this does not appear to be the case in K-Electric, where a further challenge to the autonomy of personnel managers stems from the control of the performance information generated by electronic surveillance. The generation of the labour hours report was a key instrument in centralizing strategic contrrol. However, the configuration of the surveillance apparatus means that responsibility for collecting and disseminating workforce performance measures does not reside with the personnel manager. Indeed, personnel managers are directly bypassed. This supports Armstrong's arguments (1988, 1989) concerning the role of performance information in circumventing the autonomy of personnel managers. However, it is at this point we diverge from Armstrong for, instead of elevating the role of management accountants, in our experience the responsibility for this aspect of the management of the human resource resides with production managers. This is particularly interesting given the traditional status of production engineers in UK manufacturing (see Child et al, 1983). For the personnel manager, however, it may well be immaterial who takes responsibility, for the direct effect is that the already partial nature of their influence in directly controlling the human resource is further eroded.

Another area where the rhetoric of HRM seems to offer expanded opportunities for the personnel manager is under the guise of what Storey (1992a) calls the 'change-maker'. Strongly influenced by the work of Kanter (1984), here the personnel manager is seen as performing a crucial role in the area of strategic organizational development. However, even in this area, the forms of continuous improvement employed in K-Electric mean that the tactical dynamic of development is in the hands of the team, while the strategic initiative again resides with production managers. This concurs with the finding of Daniel and Millward (Chapter 2, this volume) that professional personnel managers are marginalized from the innovation process, and at K-Electric even the residual 'fire-fighting' role suggested in that chapter is not in evidence.

Conclusion

The foregoing discussion supports the argument that the professional role of personnel managers, in 'surveillance' companies at least, is being undermined. Principally, this can be traced to the extent to which many traditional functions of personnel management have been devolved to the line, while the remaining responsibilities (particularly recruitment and selection) have become deskilled and subject to external control. This concurs with the proletarianization thesis which predicts that continuing professional status is placed under increasing strain as discretion and control over means and ends are eroded. However, we have not commented on the other element of the proletarianization thesis which relates to the possible rational measurement of personnel functions themselves. Although it is the shopfloor workers and teams who are subjected to the closest surveillance (Sewell and Wilkinson, 1992a), we have in this chapter identified the possibility of managers also being placed under scrutiny. Thus, the performance of personnel managers (in their role as gate-keepers) can be indirectly monitored in that the workers' performance as individuals and as teams can be used as a benchmark for the success or otherwise of the personnel manager's implementation of the rational instruments of recruitment and selection.

Acknowledgements

The authors gratefully acknowledge the support of the Joint Committee of the Science and Engineering Research Council and the Economic and Social Research Council of Great Britain in funding this research. A special thank you must also be extended to Ian Kirkpatrick for his invaluable help on the literature concerning professionalization.

8

Introducing On-Line Processing: Conflicting Human Resource Policies in Insurance

David Collinson

This chapter explores the contribution of corporate personnel managers to the implementation of on-line processing (OLP) by examining two inter-related case studies from the insurance industry. It confirms Daniel's findings (1987, and Chapter 3, this volume) that employees and trade unionists strongly support the anticipated introduction of new technology. However, the analysis contrasts with Daniel's conclusions (1987) regarding the role of personnel managers in technical change in two important ways. First, the chapter reveals that personnel specialists in the study company *were* centrally involved in managing the process of technical change. They did not merely react to problems that emerged after technology had been implemented, as Daniel discovered. Secondly, their policies were found to be mutually inconsistent and to produce counter-productive consequences. This contrasts with Daniel's survey findings that the early involvement of personnel managers in the change process is generally positive.[1]

The chapter analyses two different human resource policies, one concerned with grading, the other with staffing levels, designed to anticipate and implement the transition to OLP. The first case illustrates the positive potential of personnel specialists' contribution to the manage-ment of technical and organizational change. It describes how the deskill-ing and degrading effects of new technology were anticipated and overcome through the implementation of a **regrading/flexibility scheme**. By recognizing the importance of retaining skilled and experienced insurance clerks at a time of significant organizational change, corporate personnel managers were proactive in smoothing the way for technical innovation.

In contrast with Guest's model of HRM (1987; see Chapter 1, this volume), however, human resource policies prove not always to be coherent, consistent and/or integrated when implemented in practice. A second case study illustrates how the positive effects of managing the regrading scheme at this company were largely offset by corporate personnel's policy on **staffing levels** before and during this period of technical change. The corporate refusal to approve recruitment placed enormous strain, pressure and stress upon those employees who were trying to utilize the new technology. The HRM objective of the regrading scheme, to retain skilled employees, was therefore inconsistent and in conflict with the staffing policy which was concerned to avoid recruitment. Hence, the empirical analysis suggests that the early involvement of personnel specialists in technical change is not always positive, since it may both reflect and reinforce the ad hoc and discrete character of particular HR policies. The broader implications of these findings are considered in the conclusion. Before examining the two case studies, the chapter begins with a brief outline of recent technical and organizational change in the insurance industry and in the particular organization studied.

Change in the Insurance Industry

The 1980s was a period of considerable market, legal, technological and organizational change in the insurance industry. Legislation deregulated product markets, which in turn intensified market competition and product diversification. Consumer demand increased particularly in the areas of private health insurance, pension products and unit-linked investments. Equally, deregulation encouraged several significant takeovers and mergers. During this period, something of a technological transformation also occurred with the old systems of batch processing being replaced by the new technology of on-line processing (Barras and Swann, 1983; Rajan, 1984; Rolfe, 1986). The transition to OLP was accompanied by widespread organizational restructuring in which some personnel specialists played an increasingly important role. There have been dramatic reductions in the size of branch networks and work has been reorganized according to the separate markets of commercial and personal customers.

Partly as a result of these changes in the 1980s, the insurance industry experienced a rapid increase in incoming business and associated enquiries (Barras and Swann, 1983; Rajan, 1984). In a bid to generate greater market share, companies became more willing to accept risks. Some companies even offered discounted rates on premiums that did not adequately cover the risk involved in particular policies. This growth in business volumes therefore reflected and reinforced greater price competition, intensive marketing and differentiated products within insurance markets that, in turn, significantly eroded profits. In 1984, for example, underwriting losses in the UK exceeded investment income, resulting in an overall trading loss of £83m in general insurance (Sturdy, 1990). Yet this rapid erosion of profitability meant that insurance managements became less concerned with improving market share and more preoccupied with the control of operating costs. Of these costs, around 70 per cent are attributable to staff salaries (Storey, 1987). In consequence, recruitment was curbed across the industry. Between 1980 and 1985, for example, insurance employment grew by only 3 per cent, whereas output increased by 35 per cent. Much of this growth in employment merely reflected the recruitment of data processing and life assurance sales staff (Sturdy, 1990), while it also concealed a simultaneous decline in clerical employment (Rajan, 1984).

This period of increased cost controls and intensification of clerical labour also marked the onset of a wave of new technology initiatives, in particular the replacement of 'batch' processing with on-line processing systems. Most insurance companies have followed a similar path using parallel technologies (Rolfe, 1986; Storey, 1987; Sturdy, 1990). Indeed the considerable costs of investment in new technologies reinforced the managerial sensitivity to labour costs. Batch processing had enabled the computerization of data storage. Using this system, clerks could enter information about policies on to a computer input form. These forms were then sent in batches to head office where the information was punched into the mainframe computer. This system was protracted and fragmented. It was therefore very time-consuming, as well as being prone to errors because of the duplication of data input. However, it did afford a degree of discretion to clerks who could use their actuarial skills and rating guide book to calculate insurance premiums.

By contrast, full on-line processing eliminates much of the discretion of the clerk and the possibility of errors in the policy data. By locating the computer connected directly to the mainframe on the desk of the clerk, data can be punched in just once, thereby reducing processing time. The possibility of errors is all but eliminated by the computer's enhanced processing capacity which facilitates the cross-checking of all input data. Once the information has been stored in the form it prescribes via the menu-driven input system, the computer automatically calculates the appropriate insurance premium. With the exception of the most complex of policies, discretion as well as errors are weeded out of the processing system and information is transmited directly to the main head office computer.

The actual process of data input is no faster than the old batch processing. However, the new system dramatically reduces delays that occur from data loss/errors or confusion, which in turn result in extensive time-consuming enquiries within the company. In addition, it eliminates both the duplication of data and the search for missing paper-based information. By compressing the long chain of batch processing, the single automated procedure of OLP provides instantly available, accurate and current information. Thus most managements have come to recognize the significant advantages accruing from on-line processing. Yet this new computer technology was being implemented into the insurance industry against a background of work intensification and increased managerial sensitivity to cost controls. It was precisely these conditions that characterized the study company in its transition to OLP, on which this chapter concentrates.

This major insurance company is a public limited organization wholly owned by a multinational corporation. It is known as a 'composite' insurance company because it offers both life assurance (as well as pensions and private health insurance) and general insurance (fire and accident, motor and marine, aviation and transport). The company is one of seven major composites in the UK that together comprise almost 50 per cent of all insurance premium income. The evolutionary and incremental transition to OLP at this company occurred between 1984 and 1988. Some departments were fully on-line more quickly that others.

In 1984, the group's net written premiums amounted to £664.6m. Although this was a record year, 1985 proved to be even more successful. By the end of April 1985, for example, new home insurance business alone had risen to £33.6m, an increase of over 52 per cent on the same period for the previous year. Commenting on these developments, a senior management report stated:

> New business production has been at record levels and we are having to handle an unprecedented number of new enquiries. We are not alone in this situation and the fire and accident departments of the major composite insurers in particular are all faced with administrative problems.

Despite this growth in business, these companies were also faced with trading losses, particularly because of the large number of claims in most areas of business. This reinforced the intensification of work for the current labour force because of a steadfast reluctance by management to recruit additional staff. At the case study company, recruitment had all but ceased after 1981. In the following three years one-third of the high street branch network was closed and 800 employees were lost through normal wastage. Branches were redefined as 'profit centres' reflecting the greater focus on cost control.

In a survey of all employees, conducted in 1984–5, 65 per cent of both men *and* women believed that new technology would have a positive effect on their work (Collinson, 1987b). This is completely consistent with survey findings on the same issue (see Daniel and Millward, this volume). Expectations were high because employees hoped that on-line processing would reduce the pressure of work in general and the level of backlogs in particular. However, as the following analysis reveals, these expectations were not fully realized.

At the time when the transition to OLP commenced, the company had approximately 6,500 employees working in 100 branches throughout the company. The branches constitute regional processing and marketing centres which administer policy proposals, accounts and claims, handle enquiries, amend policy details and generate new business. Within each branch are individual departments (fire and accident, motor etc.), which in turn are split into several sections comprising between eight and ten clerks organized by a section leader or supervisor. The latter reports to the superintendent of the department.

The professional personnel function, which is well resourced with over thirty staff, is located at the corporate headquarters in the south of

England. Day-to-day HRM and personnel matters in the branch locations are the responsibility of the administration manager. He or she deals with recruiting, training, discipline and salaries, while the branch manager concentrates on marketing and the acquisition of new business. It is their joint responsibility to ensure that staffing levels and budget limits are not exceeded. Typically, administration managers have progressed through the actuarial technical grades. They rarely have any professional training or qualification in personnel or human resource management. The extent of their in-house training is likely to be courses run at head office on particular topics (for example, appraisal, equal opportunities, selection skills etc.). Hence, as is the norm in insurance generally, personnel management practices in operating units are in the main conducted by ex-line managers, while professional personnel managers are largely restricted to the construction and monitoring of policy from corporate level. Full-time HRM professionals are therefore extremely remote and detached from the everyday practices of insurance work.

This geographical distance can create serious organizational problems, not only in the context of selection and equal opportunities (Collinson, 1987a, 1991), but also for the implementation of new technology. Corporate personnel's geographical distance often precludes them from detailed and reliable knowledge and understanding of local conditions and practices. Consequently, it was frequently difficult for personnel professionals in this company to anticipate the likely localized consequences of new technologies and HRM policies devised at corporate level. Yet it was the responsibility of corporate personnel to manage and implement the organizational and HRM changes that inevitably accompany the introduction of new technologies.

To evaluate local conditions and the possible effects of new initiatives, corporate personnel managers relied heavily upon information from local line managers. As the second case study below will illustrate, the reliance on line managers for information about branch-level matters is likely to produce at best a highly selective set of data and at worst a wholly distorted and overly positive picture of local conditions. Communication between corporate personnel and local line management might therefore be problematic. Typically, the latter are used to exercising extensive control over their own branch. They may be antagonistic to monitoring and policy-level prescriptions disseminated down from personnel professionals at head office. In addition to their dependence on line managers for local-level information, personnel professionals in insurance have to rely on them for the actual implementation of new technology at branch level.

Typically, therefore, corporate personnel managers in insurance retain an ambiguous relationship with line managers – one of potential tensions, defensiveness and distance, yet also mutual interdependence. Partly because of these communication difficulties, corporate personnel managers at this insurance company recognized that trade union representatives might also provide useful information and experience regarding the local conditions and likely consequences of new technology introduction. This is illustrated below in the first case study, where corporate personnel's policy of communication and widespread consultation *prior* to the implementation of technological and organizational change was crucially important in facilitating the change process. Technical decisions regarding the nature and extent of technological innovation are largely the preserve of senior managers in the data-processing department. However, the overall management of the change process is primarily the responsibility of the corporate personnel department. The introduction of on-line processing raised two key human resource issues that professional personnel managers took steps to resolve, namely grading and staffing. Each will be discussed in turn.

Regrading, Flexibility and Employee Communication

As the foregoing discussion suggested, OLP eliminated the need for a great deal of clerical discretion, knowledge and experience in the processing of insurance policies. Much of the basic underwriting knowledge was now incorporated into the technology. With the new machines able to calculate premiums in an instant once the data had been accurately punched in, it was recognized that OLP would result in a deskilling and degradation of insurance clerical work. In particular, the new technology would have a detrimental impact on the clerical grades 1–6 which were primarily occupied by women. OLP would be detrimental because the in-house company job evaluation scheme was weighted in favour of actuarial/ technical insurance skills. The scheme gave little value to keyboard competency, precisely the type of skill that the company now expected from its clerical grades. Under the conventional job evaluation scheme, the regrading panel (consisting of representatives from management and trade union) would have had to reduce clerical grades 4, 5 and 6 to approximately grade 3 level. Hence, because of the job evaluation scheme, OLP would lead to significant salary reductions in clerical grades 1–6.

Corporate personnel recognized the paradoxes and dangers of introducing a highly expensive OLP system that deskilled and de-motivated the very employees on whom the company relied for its effective and speedy incorporation into everyday production practices. With strong encouragement from the trade union, corporate personnel managers sought to anticipate and overcome these potentially detrimental effects. After extensive negotiations, consultations and communications throughout the company, a regrading scheme was devised and agreed for workers in the 1–6 grades. The scheme was implemented on 1 July 1985.

The regrading scheme provided employees in the 1–6 clerical grades with a new generalized job description. They would now be located within three new graded bands roughly equivalent to the old 1–6 structure, as follows:

New grade	Approximate equivalent old grade
A	1 and 2
B	3 and 4
C	5 and 6

These arrangements would facilitate employee flexibility, the primary theme of the regrading scheme. Clerical employees were now required to be able to *transfer* across tasks and departments, for example from fire and accident to the motor or claims department. They now had to be flexible within all areas of work previously performed by clerical grades 1–6. In return for this greater employee flexibility, corporate personnel agreed to protect current levels of pay, be committed to employment security and provide all necessary training to facilitate employee movement between tasks.

A management circular outlining the new scheme stated: 'The overall purpose of the restructuring is both to improve efficiency and provide security of employment . . . in a period of change'. Corporate personnel managers argued that the regrading scheme could reinforce the security of *employment*, but not of specific jobs, since these were likely to be changed dramatically by OLP. While unable to commit the company to total job security for employees, corporate personnel stated in their explanatory booklet: 'Greater versatility and adaptability should increase security of employment for staff'. In addition, they did guarantee employees' current salary by adhering to the principle that the company was paying for their flexibility, experience and knowledge regardless of whether these were currently being fully utilized.

It was also stipulated that the annual appraisal of grades 1–6 would be replaced by an automatic incremental pay increase at the end of each year. Evaluation would simply be in relation to performance on the continuum: very good, satisfactory, unsatisfactory. Anticipating possible problems related to the contractual flexibility requirement, corporate personnel ensured that this evaluation should also take account of the individual's experience and the length of time spent on current work responsibilities. So, for example, performance might now be evaluated higher where the employee had only recently been transferred to this task. Equally, it was stipulated that where staff were performing to the standard of 'outstanding', but were then required to change job function, this would not have a detrimental impact on their salary progression. Managers were provided with a facility to make an appropriate recommendation to the personnel department. Corporate personnel were also very keen to reassure existing clerical staff that their opportunities to progress beyond the old grade 6 into the senior technical grades would *not* be reduced by the regrading scheme. They stated repeatedly that staff who demonstrated sufficient skills capability and commitment would continue to be considered for promotion.

Corporate personnel managers were therefore able to anticipate and overcome many concerns of employees that are often associated with significant organizational change. The effective implementation of the regrading scheme alongside OLP was the outcome of extensive communication and consultation throughout the company. Prior to the implementation of the scheme in July 1985, corporate personnel conducted an extensive consultation exercise. In collaboration with line managers and members of the union executive committee and divisional council, they developed and then revised the detailed regrading policies and procedures. Having incorporated various comments regarding possible problems with the initial proposal, corporate personnel specialists then prepared the launch of the restructured grading scheme. They were acutely aware of the importance of the scheme for the introduction of OLP and of the need for the change process to incorporate extensive communication with, and involvement of, all concerned in order to produce a final policy that benefited both management and employees alike. That way, resistance to the changes could be minimized. Prior to the launch, all line managers were informed that 'presentation and communication will be a major consideration if the benefits and objectives of the new arrangements are to be achieved'.

The new structure was launched with extensive explanatory literature, procedural instructions and booklets distributed to all employees affected by the changes. A video was produced and distributed throughout the branch network. This was disseminated through a two-stage exercise to communicate the policy. Stage one consisted of a programme of seminars at each main branch or head office location at which representatives of the personnel department were present. Stage two comprised announcement circulars, briefing meetings by local management, a special booklet and video presentation. In advance of the launch, all line managers received seminars on the new structure so that they, in turn, would be able to conduct appropriate briefing meetings within their locations.

At the stage one seminars, corporate personnel specialists were able to alleviate anxieties and clarify uncertainties. For example, they emphasized that the flexibility requirement did not mean constant transfers, but that it simply removed the traditional barriers to movement between departments and different jobs. 'Team spirit' and 'working together' were equally vital and would not be prejudiced by the restructuring exercise. Furthermore, clerical employees were informed that where their salary did not coincide with a sub-level point within the new grading scheme, individuals would receive a salary increase that would relate them to the next higher sub-level point.

To summarize, from the perspective of corporate personnel the regrading changes were successful both in conception and implementation. Employee anxieties had been anticipated and overcome. Line managers had been thoroughly briefed, thus enabling them to communicate the policy to their own staff. The changes paved the way for the transition to OLP without damaging employee morale or losing experienced and skilled staff. Consultation and communication had been extensive before, during and after implementation and vested interests had not been threatened. Much of the potential 'downside' of technical change (for example, blocked promotion opportunities, particularly for women, the deskilling and downgrading of their work and the segregation of 'punchers' from 'thinkers') had been anticipated and measures were introduced to overcome practical difficulties and union/employee concerns and anxieties. Corporate personnel specialists were able to overcome their geographical distance from the branch network via a strategy of cooperation and consultation combined with their own willingness to be flexible and amend the initial policy proposals. This in turn facilitated the introduction of OLP and associated changes in working practices. However, the contradictions and ambiguities of corporate personnel's position, geographically detached from operational practices, often without sufficient status and authority within the managerial structure, did not always facilitate the successful management of new technology implementation, as the second case study now illustrates.

Staffing Levels, Work Intensification and Employee Resistance

In the mid-1980s, corporate personnel managers were aware of the unprecedented backlogs of unprocessed policies in the branch network. These resulted from the severe intensification of work in the clerical grades, combined with management's refusal to recruit and the pressure of the difficult transition period when staff had to be trained and familiarized in the new OLP technology. In a 1983 report to management, the fire and accident superintendent at the Manchester branch referred to 'enormous backlogs' of 1,000 policies. Yet, by 1986, during the transition to OLP these had risen to 3,500 (Sturdy, 1990). In order to reduce the amount of unprocessed business, corporate personnel introduced a monthly 'state of work report' to be completed by sections, departments and branches. At the end of each month, a 'work count' was conducted of policies received, processed and outstanding. This information was forwarded up the branch hierarchy until it reached corporate personnel. On the strength of these figures, the company compiled and issued a league table of all branches according to production and backlog performance. A 'branch of the month' with the lowest backlog level was then identified. This increased surveillance from head office, and visibility for the branches (particularly those at the bottom of the league) was intended to motivate and discipline employees to work more quickly. It was widely believed in management that most employees would work harder to avoid being identified as at the bottom of the pile.

Informed by these monthly calculations, the staffing section of the corporate personnel department conducted an annual country-wide exercise to evaluate current and future staffing needs and to define the expected staffing levels for each branch, within which they were expected to keep. In the context of the heavy investment in OLP, the increasing managerial sensitivity to reducing costs, but also the anticipated future labour-saving effects of new technology, the staffing section was seeking to exercise tight control and discipline over branch-level recruitment. By contrast, clerical employees and trade union officials regularly stated that there were too few staff trying to process a massive and increasing number of new policy applications and enquiries.[2] While staff were doing extensive (paid and unpaid) overtime, this was not compensating for the general under-employment levels in the branches to meet product demand at a time of significant organizational and technical change.

In practice, the league tables and staffing level policies generated three different responses from employees. First, the work counts increased the competition between branches, superintendents, section leaders and even section staff. Many employees dealt with the growing production pressures by working harder and by trying to process policies even more quickly. This became known as '*shifting*' work (Sturdy, 1990). In order to overcome the unremitting sense of pressure, many employees tried to intensify their work output so that once and for all they could 'get on top of the backlog' and generate a sense of control and job satisfaction for themselves. Many staff worked evenings and Saturdays and some even did unpaid overtime.

Yet the increasing flow of processing work combined with the pressures of utilizing unfamiliar new technology meant that the option of shifting work could not fully succeed. The more that was shifted, the more that arrived on work desks requiring attention. For some, the objective of clearing their desk by the close of the work-day remained a strong incentive regardless of the fact that policies would again be stacked high on their desk the following morning. For others, however, shifting work against almost impossible odds only generated disillusion, cynicism and even burnout. This response was particularly likely in those departments with the highest workloads and the lowest staff levels. Rather than generating motivation, the league tables were rejected by many on the grounds that their comparisons were invalid and unfair (particularly between different types of business and policies), the criteria for perfor-mance evaluation were inconsistent between branches, and the whole exercise for many was simply 'a farce' (see also Sturdy, 1990). Paradoxi-cally, the branches achieving greatest growth in new business were likely to be subject to the most intense backlog pressures. The departments with high backlog levels were also likely to receive the most customer telephone complaints. A vicious circle could quickly set in. The constant stream of complaints distracted staff from their current task as they tried to respond to the customer's concerns. Almost inevitably, work slowed, standards slipped and complaints increased further (see also Storey, 1987).

In these frustrating and demotivating conditions, informal *resistance* through work avoidance could take many forms.[3] During the course of the day, staff might disappear from their section in order to 'go to the filing room' or 'to see the inspectors or surveyors' to discuss the details of a specific case. These visits could be extended and in many instances staff would then find their way to the toilets, always a safe haven for those seeking to avoid work (Goffman, 1968; Linstead, 1985; Collinson, 1992). Equally, some clerical workers resisted customers as well as the processing of policies. They could leave their desk as the telephone started to ring or drop the receiver immediately after picking it up, thereby redirecting the call to another telephone or back to the main switchboard.

In more extreme cases, when the anxiety of the work count was most intense immediately before the end of the month, certain employees either placed particular types of *unprocessed* work straight in the rubbish bin or took them home where they were disposed of later. These would be short pieces of work such as endorsements (i.e. policy amendments/changes) that were of less importance than new business policies. When brokers or customers would later complain, the 'chaos of the backlogs' constituted a useful excuse for the failure to make the appropriate changes. Work was distributed in such a way that it was impossible for section leaders to identify precisely who was responsible for processing which work. Here again, the backlog pressure precluded the possibility of monitoring work distribution.[4] Ironically, the backlogs themselves became not merely a condition, but also a legitimation, justification and facilitator of branch-level resistance. Work intensification generated extensive negative consequences for the company in terms of low employee morale, which led to subtle and covert forms of resistance that avoided and even destroyed outstanding work. In turn, this intensified the number of complaints from customers and brokers alike.

Many of these practices of resistance or 'escape attempts' (Cohen and Taylor, 1992) provide only temporary relief from the incessant, negative work pressures. In the longer term, they tend to reinforce greater surveillance, for complaints are then directed further up the hierarchy and staff have to account for their actions to a higher level. Yet the backlogs provide employees with an ideal alibi for their oppositional practices. Suffice it to say that senior management's attempts to increase competition and thereby productivity through the 'work count' and league tables were not always successful. Moreover, corporate personnel's distance from local conditions meant that they were unaware of these self-defeating effects of their motivation strategies. Work intensification generated a paradoxical and simultaneous response of 'shifting' and/or resistance.

The same is true for the third employee response to the intensified work conditions. This involved a combination of shifting and resistance that had the unintended and unacknowledged effect of creating further and deeper staffing problems. As a result of the work count, employees would seek to reduce their backlogs towards the end of the month. One widespread strategy was to select work that could be shifted quickly. Although management stipulated that policies should be processed in the chronological order in which they were received, staff frequently selected smaller, less complex policy applications that could be processed at speed. They would defer more complicated and time-consuming tasks until the next month. This widespread end-of-month practice was often effective in eroding backlog figures.

Of much greater significance in the context of this chapter was the tendency of employees at various levels of the hierarchy to under-calculate the extent of the backlogs on their desk in their formal report to those in authority within the section department and/or branch. In the absence of any alternative system of accountability or method of verification, the backlog levels that were communicated up the hierarchy were increasingly reduced the higher they went. Yet these figures were treated by corporate personnel as an *objective* statement of actual production and backlog levels. Hence they were the fundamental basis on which staffing levels, and recruitment and training policies, were decided. In turn, selection and training were crucially important for the management of new technology implementation.

Yet if the practice of understating and reducing backlog figures was as pervasive across the entire country as some employees and trade union officials contended (in confidence), then the backlog data reaching the corporate personnel department were dramatically under-reported. This practice had important interrelated implications for both the calculation of future staffing levels and for managing the transition to OLP. Most employees seemed unaware of precisely how corporate personnel calculated staffing levels. While the main priority of staff was to protect themselves from the critical attention of authority by under-reporting the extent of backlogs, corporate personnel managers in turn underestimated future staffing requirements which, paradoxically, then had the effect of further intensifying work for branch clerical workers. Very soon a vicious circle was established, as Figure 8.1 describes.

Employees working in various regions of the branch network and several trade union representatives confirmed that it was normal practice for individual actuaries and clerks to report that they had, for example, thirty-five pieces of outstanding work when in fact the actual figure was nearer to fifty. Concerned about the league tables and their own personal annual appraisal, section leaders too had good reason to understate the level of backlogs reported to the superintendent. Equally, superintendents and even branch managers were under similar pressures of increased competition and personal evaluation in the annual appraisal system. The 'no problems here' discourse in which managers frequently invest (e.g. Jenkins, 1986) was facilitated by corporate personnel's geographical distance from operating units, making closer monitoring and scrutiny difficult if not impossible.

Nevertheless, despite this, corporate personnel showed little interest in improving the accounting procedures for the 'state of work report'. When trade union representatives informed corporate personnel managers of the likely inaccuracy of these statistics, the latter's response was: 'Are you telling us that our line managers are lying to us?' Perhaps their unwilling-

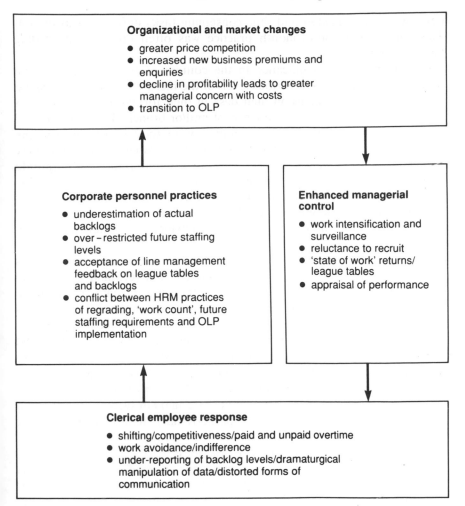

Figure 8.1 *The vicious circle of staffing and backlogs*

ness formally to accept this information was because, even on the reported data, the backlog levels looked serious. Higher backlog figures would certainly have reinforced the case for further recruitment, thereby flying directly in the face of formal human resource policy. In addition, the staffing policy of corporate personnel was informed by the assumption that most shortfalls on the recruitment and workforce profile were a short-term problem that would be resolved by the labour-saving effects of the new technology. In practice, these assumptions were only partly validated.

Once OLP was fully operational and employees were familiar with its capacities, the technology did indeed facilitate some reduction of backlogs (see also Rolfe, 1986). However, this effect, like the introduction of OLP itself, was impaired by the HR policy on staffing levels. Recruitment remained highly restricted. In consequence, the initial positive employee response to the capacity of the new technology for shifting work was increasingly replaced in many cases by disillusion and/or disenchantment. For example, the early enthusiasm for OLP of a section leader in one branch was tempered 12 months later following a massive increase in business volumes that was not mirrored by commensurate recruitment: 'You see yourself going backwards, the pile gets higher and higher . . . It's just getting too much. Everyone is disgruntled because it's so intense' (quoted in Sturdy, 1990: 347). Hence the continued intensification of work and rigid staffing policy tended to erode in some cases the initial positive employee response to OLP well after the completion of the transition period.

Between 1987 and 1992, the company made considerable redundancies, primarily in the supervisory and lower managerial grades (predominantly men). Management also increased its surveillance, for example by monitoring employees' use of the telephone (to eliminate personal calls) and by closely scrutinizing employee absenteeism patterns. State of work returns were calculated on a weekly basis and disciplinary procedures were immediately instigated where mistakes were found in work performance. Yet, in November 1992, the processing of policies was still characterized by extensive backlogs. The company encouraged staff to undertake overtime, while employees complained that the considerable costs of overtime could have been invested in the recruitment of additional staff. When backlogs became excessive, individual clerks were placed in an office and instructed to 'shift' policies without being 'distracted' by colleagues or telephone calls. The anticipated improvements in the quality of working life through the introduction of new technology had not been realized. As one employee observed:

> The problem of backlogs is still with us even now. There is a lot of overtime being worked. The other month they had to stop all overtime because of budget problems. Then they rely on taking people out of the department and making them work in an office on their own without any distractions. The real problem of not having enough staff is never tackled.

This case study suggests that the competitive and evaluative pressures on employees at various hierarchical levels resulted in the under-reporting of backlog levels. The intensification of work, discipline and surveillance generated a 'dramaturgical' response from many employees who sought to manage a particular impression for those in authority (Goffman, 1959, 1968). The transition to full OLP and its potential effects in reducing backlogs were both impaired by corporate personnel's rigid and restrictive staffing policy. The widespread employee expectation that OLP would reduce both work pressures and backlogs was not confirmed in practice. As a result, the positive effects of corporate personnel's efforts to involve all employees in the regrading exercise were significantly diminished by the detrimental consequences of the staffing policy. Within and between the HR policies devised by the corporate personnel department to manage the transition to OLP, there appeared to be deep-seated inconsistencies, conflicts and contradictions. Paradoxically, the persistence of backlogs intensified employee anxiety and demotivation, rendered the monitoring of work flows all but impossible, generated resistance and increased customer complaints.

Conclusion

What are the implications of these two case studies for HRM? The experience of this major insurance company suggests that technical change may often be much more complex than is suggested by Daniel's broad-sweeping and generalized conclusions (1987, and this volume). Rarely, for example, is it possible *in practice* to make a clear analytical separation between technical and organizational change.[5] In practice, the two are frequently inextricably linked. Accordingly, it is perhaps less surprising to find personnel managers involved in planning and managing these change processes. The empirical analysis revealed the initial effectiveness of corporate personnel in anticipating the transition to OLP by introducing a regrading/flexibility scheme after extensive consultation and communication. In so doing it shows how proactive intervention by a personnel/ HR department and extensive consultation with the workforce can prevent advanced technical change leading inevitably to deskilling (Braverman, 1974).

The foregoing case studies also raise broader questions for HRM scholars and practitioners about the effective introduction of technical and organizational change. Does the concern with employee flexibility lead to upskilling or work intensification? What are the training implications of new technology implementation? How likely is it that mutually inconsistent and even contradictory HR policies and practices may characterize other organizations and industries both in the UK and elsewhere?

Within the HRM literature, recent debates on functional flexibility have been influential. Some writers have argued that employers' concern with flexibility can lead to a general upskilling of employees (Atkinson and Meager, 1986). This process has been termed 'polyvalence' by Child (1985: 125–9). In his view this is a form of work organization where 'workers perform, or at least are available to perform, a range of tasks that cut across or extend traditional skill and job boundaries' (1985: 125). Although he notes that polyvalence may sometimes have to be 'forced through by confrontation with the trade unions' (1985: 127), the converse was discovered in the company studied here, where the unions were so involved in the design and management of the scheme that they could best be described as its joint authors. Wilkinson's study (1983) of polyvalence through job rotation also has certain similarities to the analysis presented here. He found that the management of a manufacturing company recognized the potentially negative effects of deskilling craft work and consequently introduced flexible working through job rotation. These arguments are supported by the regrading scheme at the insurance company, which facilitated the introduction of OLP by involving employees through the consultation process and producing agreed measures on flexibility that did not threaten vested interests.

Nevertheless, other writers have rejected the upskilling thesis. They contend that employee flexibility is nothing more than an employer strategy of work intensification (e.g. Pollert, 1991a). The foregoing examination of staffing policies and their branch-level effects provides some support for this view. Corporate personnel's role in managing the change process was only partly successful. Other HRM practices had the effect of intensifying work. These generated significant problems at branch level and some were also in conflict with one another.

Corporate personnel managers had considerable control over the job evaluation scheme and the grading of jobs. These could all be evaluated at head office. However, their lack of knowledge of local conditions and practices resulted in an under-calculation of the extent of backlogs across the branch network. They failed to recognize how employee evaluation systems such as the 'work count'/league tables and personal appraisals generate insecurities that individuals manage by selectively controlling their communication of information (see also Collinson, 1993). Motivation and intensification through the fear of a negative visibility (for example being 'bottom of the league' or having an 'unsatisfactory' appraisal) is a double-edged sword for managers. The insecurities and defensiveness that it produces might indeed facilitate the 'shifting' of work, but only at the cost of *simultaneously* reinforcing resistance practices (such as dramaturgical communication, work avoidance, counter-cultures of indifference, resentment and criticism of management).

Managerial assumptions about the labour-saving effects of advanced technical change have not been realized in the sense that severe backlogs persist in company branches at the end of 1992. The failure to eliminate backlogs reinforces the argument that management's practices were part of a deliberate policy of work intensification through technical and organizational change. Corporate personnel's under-calculation of backlogs combined with their inflexible staffing policy reinforced enormous pressure on employees. Paradoxically, the very staff who had been involved and protected by the regrading scheme were the same employees who bore the considerable brunt of the work intensification and blocked recruitment. Hence management's objective of generating employee cooperation and loyalty through the regrading scheme was entirely inconsistent with the concern to intensify production and minimize costs which informed the corporate staffing policy.

O'Reilly (1992) argues that a clear distinction needs to be made between a deliberate strategy of upskilling and a more ad hoc process through which tasks are expanded and work intensified. Yet, in the foregoing case study, *both* upskilling (to avoid downgrading) and work intensification (to avoid recruitment) *simultaneously* characterized the personnel department's practices. These practices were not so much *alternative* objectives, but were rather simultaneously embedded in the different HR strategies and policies of corporate personnel. Of crucial importance here were the ambiguities and paradoxical effects of personnel's practices. These have been neglected in debates on flexibility.

Equally within the personnel/HRM literature, there seems to be little recognition of how different HRM policies can simultaneously have inconsistent and opposing objectives and effects (see Legge, 1989a). In managing the transition to OLP at the case study company, corporate personnel managers produced separate but overlapping HR policies and practices which in some cases were in conflict with one another. These conflicts and contradictions were experienced most acutely at branch level. The objectives and effects of the regrading scheme contradicted those of the staffing policy. The 'state of work report' and evaluation systems (i.e. league tables of branches and personal appraisal) distorted personnel's calculation of future staffing levels, while also partially legitimizing the flawed current recruitment policy. Work intensification reduced employee morale and generated forms of resistance that impacted negatively in the product market by intensifying customers' complaints and dissatisfaction. This, of course, could result in a loss of important business.

These contradictions between different HR policies also impacted on training practices within the organization. The extensive backlog levels created such intense workplace pressures that the commitment to train, which had been guaranteed by the regrading scheme, was often abandoned at local level. In the context of the league tables and other evaluation systems, branch-level managers and supervisors were forced to prioritize production over and above staff training and development. Here again, other HR practices suffered the consequences of an inflexible staffing policy. Similar findings regarding the vulnerability of training initiatives have been identified by recent studies (e.g. Keep, 1989; Rainbird, 1990).

In the final analysis, HR practices were driven primarily by accounting preoccupations with minimizing costs. The contradictions which were a condition and consequence of corporate personnel policies were a direct outcome of this prioritization of these narrow economic considerations. Where a broader set of objectives informed HR policy construction, as in the regrading scheme, implementation was more successfully achieved.

The notion that HR policies *are* therefore internally consistent and integrated (see Guest, 1987) may well be fundamentally mistaken. The idea that they *should* be integrated may simply reflect a naive liberal hope or the legitimating occupational ideology of personnel management that 'good' HR practices are *automatically* beneficial for companies and their employees alike. As this chapter illustrates, these practices can be produced in isolation from one another and without *full* regard for their overlapping and cumulative effects. This evidence therefore suggests that ideal models of HRM might be precisely that, simply models. In practice, HR policies may continue to be ad hoc and isolated, with unintended and unacknowledged effects that are inconsistent and even contradictory.

So how generalizable are these findings? It could be argued that the contradictions in these HR policies, in turn, reflect both the persistent structural and identity problems of personnel professionals in contemporary organizations (e.g. Watson, 1977; Hyman, 1987; Armstrong, 1989; Legge, 1989a; Hollway, 1990; Collinson, 1992; Sisson, 1989c) and, more broadly, the contradictory objectives of managerial control strategies in capitalist enterprises (e.g. Cressey and MacInnes, 1980; Hyman, 1987). Personnel specialists frequently do not have the power, status or technical knowledge to ensure that their formalized models are implemented in practice (Sisson, 1989c). Equally, personnel managers are often simultaneously concerned to generate employee commitment, cooperation and loyalty on the one hand, while also exercising control, maximizing productivity and minimizing costs on the other. Despite liberal claims to the contrary, in many cases these objectives are incompatible. The contradictory nature of such managerial HRM objectives and practices is by no means unique to the UK insurance industry.[6] It seems to be true of other UK organizations (see Child, 1985; Hyman, 1987) as well as companies in North America (see Juravich, 1985) and Japan (Kondo, 1990). Research therefore suggests that the internally inconsistent HR practices critically examined in this chapter[7] may have implications that are applicable or generalizable to a wider constituency of organizations. Shaped primarily by the financial position of the company and the wider economic conditions in product and labour markets, corporate personnel policies and practices are thus likely to reflect and reinforce the primary contradictions of contemporary organizations and of their own position within them. There seems to be little indication that this is likely to change in the foreseeable future.

Acknowledgement

I would like to thank P.K. Edwards for helpful comments on an earlier draft of this chapter.

Notes

1. The case study material is drawn from a longitudinal research project in one large insurance company. It is based on both quantitative and qualitative methodologies. Unlike Daniel's study, it does not only rely on the responses of managerial and trade union representatives, but also draws on interviews with those in more subordinate hierarchical positions. With the support of the Banking, Insurance and Finance Union and of corporate personnel, 5,000 staff were surveyed in 1985. This first stage in the project examined the subjective experience of staff with regard to a range of employment issues (see Collinson, 1987b). Subsequent qualitative research focused upon selection practices in the company and throughout the insurance industry (Collinson et al, 1990). I also acted as a consultant to the trade union between 1985 and 1988. In addition, I was involved in a parallel research project in this particular company which examined gender and new technology (Sturdy, 1990). In

1992 I returned to the company to conduct further interviews in order to update the empirical findings.

2. In their study of technical change in insurance, Batstone et al (1987: 70) also found that trade unions criticized management heavily for reducing the number of staff prior to the transition to OLP.

3. These practices of workplace resistance raise important methodological issues in relation to the WIRS surveys. It could be argued that the empirical analysis presented in this chapter is consistent with the WIRS findings of resistance in large-scale organizations. However, it is difficult to see how the sort of data on workplace resistance described in this chapter could have been uncovered by the WIRS methodology. The latter relies on a large-scale questionnaire survey of senior organizational members (managers and trade union officials). It therefore neglects the perspectives *and* practices of those in more subordinate positions within organizations. Yet it is at this level where resistance often takes place. If I had relied on a questionnaire survey (of senior employees) alone in conducting this study, the resistance practices described here would not have been uncovered. As the analysis emphasizes, corporate managers were unaware that such practices were common in the branch network. In addition to interviewing employees in more subordinate positions, I also observed various oppositional practices during periods of non-participant observation in the company. In sum, I would argue that the WIRS methodology inevitably underestimates the extent of workplace resistance. Even though surveys may find no evidence of resistance, it cannot be concluded that there is an absence of resistance in a particular workplace.

4. Section leaders and supervisors could have spent a considerable part of their day manually calculating and monitoring the amount of mail and telephone enquiries received, their allocation to section staff and the latter's completion rates. This, however, would have reinforced the level of backlogs, because supervisors would have been distracted from the processing of policies. There was no way that minor changes to the software could have resolved this problem. More detailed management information about the flow of production required a considerable increase in manual labour. In 1992, management still do not closely monitor the flow of policies. It is a relatively straightforward matter to monitor 'terminal workload' (the quantity of work keyed into the computers), but this constitutes only one element of the processing of policies.

5. It could be argued that the workplace resistance identified in the WIRS survey was an employee response against organizational rather than technical change. However, as the foregoing case studies indicate, technical and organizational change are frequently inextricably linked in quite complex ways. Rather than seek to identify their differences, it may be more analytically fruitful to examine their complex interrelations. Equally, the unravelling of particular employee motives of resistance is itself highly problematic (see Collinson, 1993).

6. A very pertinent illustration of similar contradictions between technical change and understaffing occurred in late 1992 in the London Ambulance Service. A new computer system for managing emergency calls went fully on-line in October 1992 at a cost of £1.5m. This was against a background of considerable cuts in ambulance personnel and control room staff in anticipation of the labour-saving effects of the technology. Unfortunately, major difficulties emerged in the computer system. With too few staff to manage, ambulance crew members reported that a number of deaths may have occurred in the first 36-hour period of the computer's operation due to ambulance delays in reaching emergency calls. Within days, the chief executive of the London Ambulance Service had resigned.

7. Another illustration of unrecognized contradictions within quite different HRM practices is, on the one hand, the current interest in 'succession planning' and on the other hand, the emphasis on equal opportunity practices. The nurturing of particular individuals who are identified as having 'senior management potential' reproduces an elitism and tiering in the internal labour market that directly contradicts the principle of equal opportunities and equal competition for available places. This tension between equal opportunity practices and managerial control concerns appears to characterize UK (Collinson et al, 1990) and US (Martin, 1990) organizations alike. Tensions within the *same* HRM practice are documented

in Geary's study (1992) of pay and appraisal, which reveals how different elements of a payment system can be pulling in opposing directions. The co-existence of a plurality of payment systems, one emphasizing individual reward, the other focusing on collective remuneration, led to employee confusion regarding the dominant purpose of management's payment strategy.

9

Technical Change and Human Resource Management in the Non-Union Firm

Ian McLoughlin

Amongst the many findings from the British Workplace Industrial Relations Survey in 1984 was the surprising observation that establishments that recognized trade unions were more likely to have introduced advanced microelectronics-based technology than their non-union counterparts (Daniel, 1987: 34–6, 47), a finding repeated in the 1990 survey (Daniel and Millward, this volume). Against these findings can be set the well-documented trend of the fall in aggregate trade union membership since 1979. This decline has fuelled the increasing interest in new 'human resource management' techniques derived from the United States, which appear to offer management a sophisticated means of managing without trade unions. Significantly, one of the theoretical 'pay-offs' from adopting HRM techniques is said to be greater employee commitment and flexibility, which in turn facilitate technical change (Guest, 1987).

Thus we are faced with something of a paradox. On the one hand non-union firms appear to be less conducive than their unionized equivalents to technical change. On the other, they have been increasingly highlighted as the locus of a set of techniques for managing employee relations designed to secure the kind of organizational conditions which would promote the adoption and effective use of advanced technology. The aim of this chapter is to try to unravel some elements of these apparently contradictory views.

This task is aided by new empirical data from the first in-depth study of industrial relations in non-union firms in Britain. The chapter begins by examining some conceptual ideas which may assist in understanding the significance of non-union status and HRM for technical change. The links between non-unionism, the management of employee relations and the adoption of new technology are then explored with reference to empirical evidence from the 'high technology' sector.

Technical Change and 'Employee Voice'

The survey evidence cited above clearly challenges the simplistic notion that the absence of trade unions automatically gives the non-union employer an advantage when introducing new technology. Indeed, one might go as far as to suggest that it indicates that the absence of unions is a source of disadvantage. This raises some interesting questions about the significance of 'employee voice' in the process of technical change in the non-union workplace.

A broad picture of the way the introduction of advanced technical change has been managed in non-unionized workplaces is provided by Daniel (1987: 119–21, 137–8; also Daniel and Millward, this volume). This evidence suggests that managements in non-union establishments are less likely to consult their workforce, especially through formal channels. In the cases where some form of consultation takes place, this tends to be on an informal basis, through discussions with individual workers or group meetings rather than formal channels such as joint consultative committees or specially constituted committees. A similar pattern is reported for office workers. However, office workers in non-union workplaces are much more likely to be consulted through informal channels, such as individual discussions or ad hoc meetings, than their counterparts in unionized settings.

Why are managements in unionized establishments more likely to consult employees over technical change than their non-union counterparts? In their well-known work, Freeman and Medoff (1984) challenge the neo-classical assumption that union organization leads to lower productivity because wages are raised above competitive levels and restrictive work rules are maintained. They argue that, although union organization can have these 'monopoly effects', their presence can also have productivity-enhancing outcomes. These derive from the 'collective voice' effect associated with union presence. This provides a formal institutional mechanism for articulating grievances, passing information and resolving conflict and leads to lower labour turnover (employees feel it is worthwhile seeking redress rather than quitting). It also induces management to adopt more efficient policies and practices, raises employee morale and improves managerial response.

In so far as improved productivity can be regarded as a potential outcome from adopting new technology, these arguments can readily be adapted to cover the process of adopting and implementing technical change. For instance, a 'monopoly effect' would suggest that trade unions will resist management plans to adopt technology, or put management off the idea altogether. If this fails, unions would then seek to extort the maximum 'price for change' from management through devices such as pay increases or guarantees on job security. Once implemented, unions would seek to defend, as far as possible, existing work practices viewed by the employer as inefficient. On the other hand, a collective voice effect might also occur. Union presence would provide both formal and informal channels of communication, consultation and possibly negotiation, smoothing the path of implementation, fostering employee commitment to the new technology and promoting acceptance of changes in work organization. As the inevitable teething problems occur during implementation and initial operation, information provided by employees would be critical to management in finding optimum ways of operating the new system and organizing work around it.

Whereas non-union settings may be free of the potentially damaging 'monopoly effect' and conducive to introducing advanced technology without having to make concessions on pay, job security and so on, the absence of unions would also mean the absence of the 'collective voice' effect and its associated benefits. Thus, under no pressure to consult and with no formal means of communication, the tendency in non-union settings may well be for managers either to fail to talk to their employees or to do so only through informal channels. This line of argument, also, suggests one explanation of why non-union settings may be less conducive to technical change, at least in terms of their capacity to implement and use new technology effectively.

However, the Freeman and Medoff thesis assumes that union organization will always have similar 'monopoly' and 'collective voice' effects, while in reality union behaviour is highly variable and contingent upon other factors such as union policies, the nature of the production process and management strategy (Edwards, 1987).. The mirror image of this criticism can be applied to non-union settings. Here management behaviour will also be variable and subject to influence from contingent factors. In particular, management approaches in some non-union settings may in fact be more conducive to the adoption and effective use of advanced technology than in others, especially where a deliberate attempt is made to 'substitute' for the absence of trade unions by providing relatively sophisticated informal and/or formal means by which consultation with employees can take place. It is therefore necessary to develop a more differentiated conceptualization of the approaches that can be taken to the management of employee relations in non-union settings, which in turn involves a consideration of what is distinctive about HRM techniques and how these might support technical change.

Managing Employee Relations in Non-Union Firms

There have been a number of attempts to develop and refine conceptual models that seek to identify different styles or approaches to the management of employee relations. However, prior to the current interest in HRM, these have usually been directed at unionized settings and have only dealt with non-union firms as a byproduct. Approaches to the management of employee relations at a conceptual level have tended to concentrate on the notion of 'management style'. For Purcell this is a corporate steering device that provides 'a distinctive set of guiding parameters, written or otherwise, which set parameters and signposts for management action in the way employees are treated and particular events handled' (Purcell, 1987: 535). In a development of earlier work, he has advanced a typology

in which two separate dimensions of management style are identified
These are **individualism** – 'the extent to which the firm gives credence to
the feelings and sentiments of each employee and seeks to develop and
encourage each employee's capacity and role at work' (1987: 536) – and
collectivism – 'the extent to which the organization recognizes the right of
employees to have a say in those aspects of management decision-making
which concern them' (1987: 537).

A management style which emphasizes the value of employees as
individuals will view them as a resource to be developed and nurtured, and
individual relationships between managers and employees will involve a
strong human relations component. A firm which does not stress the value
of the individual contribution of its employees, with little priority given to
security of employment and an overt emphasis on direct managerial
control and the cost of labour, will tend to view them as a 'commodity'.
Between these two poles is a more paternalistic management style where
the emphasis is on 'caring for' rather than developing human resources.

Firms which recognize their own employees' right to collective representation will regard the existence of democratic structures representing
employees as legitimate. The collective relationship will be seen as:
cooperative, for example where the emphasis is based upon developing
constructive relationships through integrative bargaining with trade
unions; **conflictual**, where the emphasis is placed on adversarial bargaining; or **unitary**, where the legitimacy of collective arrangements is called
into question by managers.

A number of difficulties with Purcell's approach have been identified by
Marchington and Parker (1990). In a study of unionized firms, they found
the empirical identification of 'individualism' as a 'discrete aspect of style',
and as a policy goal distinct from 'collectivism', problematic (1990: 234–5).
In a later article, Marchington and Harrison have suggested that it is
inappropriate to distinguish between individualism and collectivism as
discrete aspects of management style in so far as 'the amount of individualism . . . can vary across different aspects of the employment relationship,
and any convincing theory must recognize the existence of these' (1991:
288). This is an important point, since 'individualism' and 'collectivism',
although analytically distinct, are unlikely in practice to be mutually
exclusive features of management style. Both are likely to be present in
any employment relationship, in varying degrees. As Marchington and
Parker (1990: 80) themselves point out, Purcell's formulation suggests
firms may alter their styles along both dimensions at the same time. Thus
one would expect a 'mix' that might prove difficult to disentangle
empirically. However, this does not necessarily undermine the analytical
usefulness of attempting to locate management styles in these terms.

The 'collectivism' dimension also poses problems for Marchington and
Parker because, in their research, the presence of unions was not wholly
explained by management commitment to collectivism. Union presence

also reflected management's lack of capacity to resist union organization. In addition, the actual depth of commitment of managers to trade union representation was variable, with significant differences between the intentions of senior management and the attitudes and behaviour of workplace managers (1990: 235–6). Following from this, Marchington and Parker have argued for a more expansive definition of management style, suggesting that it should not be conceptualized exclusively at a corporate level, but can have 'meaning in all workplaces, irrespective of policy pronouncements', as an influence on the management of employee relations in the workplace (1990: 232–3). This is a useful point since, rather than just focusing on senior management intentions, it takes into account the actual attitudes and behaviour of managers at workplace level which, as already noted, may well be at variance with that intended by senior managers.

Put another way, as already noted in Chapter 1 above, an important dimension of the way employee relations are managed is constituted by the degree of 'strategic integration' (Guest, 1987, 1989). Guest identifies this as an important and distinctive feature of HRM techniques where personnel policies exhibit 'strategic integration' in terms of their internal coherence, integration with overall business strategy and influence on line management decision-making. In other words, full HRM involves an explicit and tight coupling between strategic intent and managerial attitudes and behaviour at the workplace. This can be contrasted with management styles where such couplings may be far looser, that is, where strategic intent may be implicit rather than explicit, vague and ill-formed rather than clearly formulated, and where there may be scope for line and other middle and junior managers to develop (or not develop) their own approaches to managing employees.

With these observations in mind, a conceptual distinction has been made in our own study of non-union firms between the degree of 'strategic integration' in management approach and the extent to which emphasis is placed on individual or collective approaches to regulating different aspects of the employment relationship (see McLoughlin and Gourlay, 1992). The suggestion is that approaches to the management of employee relations in non-union settings can first be analysed in terms of whether 'strategic integration' is high or low. In the former case there is a 'tight coupling' between relatively proactive, formalized and integrated strategic intentions and workplace practices. In the latter, there is little formalization or integration, indicating the possibility of a wide variety of mainly reactive practices. Secondly, approaches can be analysed in terms of whether individual or collective methods of regulation are employed with reference to particular substantive and procedural aspects of the employment relationship. 'High' levels of individualism do not necessarily imply the exclusion of collective approaches to job regulation, merely that one is more predominant in the 'mix' than the other (see Figure 9.1).

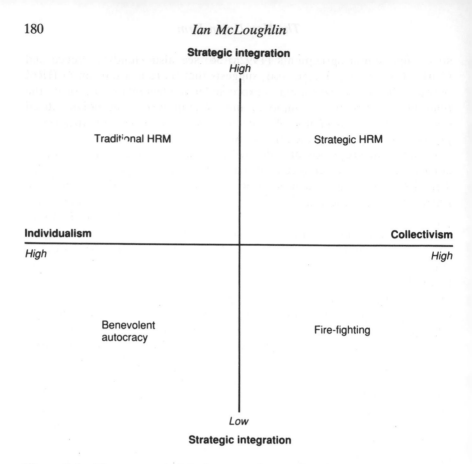

Figure 9.1 *Management style in non-union settings*

HRM and the Non-Union Firm

Human resource management is an approach which has frequently been linked to non-union firms or firms seeking to change fundamentally their relationship with existing trade unions (Foulkes, 1980; Kochan et al, 1986; Storey, 1992a). However, whether an HRM approach is incompatible with trade unions has been a matter of some dispute. According to Guest, for example, HRM may 'leave little scope for collective arrangements and assume little need for collective bargaining' and 'therefore poses considerable challenge to traditional industrial relations and more particularly to trade unionism' (Guest, 1989: 43). On the other hand, HRM is not, in Guest's view, anti-union in so far as key elements, such as strategic integration and an emphasis on management recognition of the value of employees as human beings, appear to be consistent with collective approaches. Storey goes much further and suggests that it may even be debatable to characterize HRM as 'unitarist', since it appears possible that trade unions could be accommodated within the model if a more cooperative relationship is posited, for example in the forms exemplified by new-style single-union agreements (1992a: 36; see also Hendry, Preece and Clark, this volume). Legge, too, suggests that there is a tension in HRM between the *normative* emphasis expressed in management rhetoric on the relationship between the employer and the employee as an individualized one, and the *practical* use of collective forms of work organization or problem-solving, such as teamworking, quality circles (1989a: 35–6).

Rather than a rejection of collectivism *per se*, therefore, it may be that it is particular forms of collectivism that are called into question by HRM. Thus HRM is perfectly consistent with a mix of individual and collective regulation where the latter is of a non-union character or a cooperative type of unionized arrangement. HRM approaches are not therefore confined to non-union settings and may well emerge and co-exist alongside collective bargaining and trade unions. However, where this does occur, it is possible that, over time, traditional adversarial union organization will be modified significantly.

Given these observations, the identification of HRM as a single management style is obviously misleading. Storey (1992a) provides the best attempt to date to provide a means of differentiating types of HRM. He locates the various meanings given to the term HRM on two dimensions 'weak/strong' and 'soft/hard'. In analytical terms, the least useful of the versions of HRM are those which lie at the 'weak' end of the 'weak/strong' dimension. Here HRM constitutes little more than a cosmetic relabelling of what hitherto has been termed personnel management. Storey suggests 'soft' variants of HRM stress the need to manage 'human relations' effectively as part of their business objectives. In contrast, the 'hard' variants focus on achieving the 'best fit' between the management of human beings as 'resources' and the requirements of the business.

Using an apparently similar approach to Storey, Keenoy (1990a) identifies three versions of HRM – traditional, strategic and neo-pluralist – each with different implications for unions. **Traditional HRM**, in Storey's terms a 'strong/soft' version of HRM, has as its basic assumption that 'investment in people is good business, if not the basis of good business' (Keenoy, 1990a: 5). Investment in human resources is held to lead to a situation where union representation is not perceived as necessary by employees. If such a need arises this reflects, in management eyes, failings on their part. **Strategic HRM**, approximating to Storey's 'strong/hard' version, starts from the question, 'what HRM strategy will maximize competitive advantage, optimize control, and minimize unit and labour replacement costs?' (1990a: 5). The relevance of union presence is assessed in these terms. **Neo-pluralist HRM**, in Storey's terms a 'weak' version of HRM, seeks to regulate the employment relationship by eliciting commitment and generating consensus through increased employee involvement and participation. For Keenoy this approach is applicable in both non-union and unionized settings as a form of 'non-adversarial collaborative relations' (1990a: 6).

It was noted earlier that, in principle, non-union firms are faced with a problem of how to deal with the absence of the potentially beneficial effects of union presence when technical change occurs. In other words, how can non-union firms come to terms with the absence of institutional mechanisms that support the collective voice effect? One obvious response is, of course, to do nothing, and there is clear evidence that this is what occurs in at least some cases. For example, nearly a fifth of manual workers in non-union establishments are not consulted over the introduction of advanced technology (Daniel and Millward, this volume). Alternatively, if HRM is a feature of the management of employee relations in at least some non-union settings, then some form of 'union substitution' might be anticipated.

This raises the question of specialist personnel involvement in the management of technical change. On the one hand, the high profile given by HRM to 'human resource' issues within overall business strategy would appear to place personnel issues at centre-stage in the management of change – technical change included. On the other, the focus on the management of human resources may also shift responsibilities from the specialist personnel function to line managers, who as the direct interface with employees are regarded as better placed to manage the human element of any change process (see Legge, this volume).

It must also be noted, however, that personnel specialists are present in only the minority of establishments. Moreover, they are probably even more likely to be absent in non-union establishments in so far as the presence of personnel specialists is positively associated with union presence (Daniel and Millward, this volume). In other words, in most non-union settings, not only are employees less likely to be consulted, but personnel management is likely to have less influence, if only because specialists are absent. A further point is that if, as UK evidence suggests, early personnel involvement is linked to the smooth introduction and acceptance by workers of technical change, then implementation problems and worker resistance might feature even more in non-union workplaces.

In the case of 'traditional HRM', management attempts to avoid the need for union representation are usually underpinned by policies designed to produce terms and conditions of employment superior to those that a unionized workforce might expect, i.e. 'market leading' pay and conditions and high levels of job security. In addition, sophisticated methods of information disclosure, communication, consultation and grievance handling are likely to be features of management approach. In effect, these provide individual or informal non-union voice mechanisms.

At the same time collective or formal non-union voice mechanisms might also be developed. As suggested above, in certain circumstances, 'strategic HRM' would not be inconsistent with the collective regulation of the employee relations issues highlighted by technical change. For instance, procedural arrangements such as JCCs or elected works councils might well become forums for dealing with some of these issues. Thus, a 'strategic HRM' approach to managing technical change involving union substitution could take one of two forms, either individually based or collective, depending upon what management saw as the 'best fit' with internal and external contingent circumstances. In principle, either approach would have beneficial effects when advanced technology is introduced, since both provide a 'substitute' voice mechanism.

These different HRM approaches also suggest different kinds of specialist personnel involvement, both in the management of employee relations as a whole and more specifically in the management of technical change. Storey provides a useful schema for differentiating types of personnel involvement. He identifies four distinct roles (Storey, 1992a: 168–9):

- **Change-maker**: where personnel involvement is both strategic and interventionary
- **Adviser**: where personnel acts as a non-interventionary adviser to line management
- **Regulator**: where personnel intervenes on a tactical basis to maintain jointly agreed rules and company procedures
- **Handmaiden**: where personnel acts as a non-interventionary servant to line management.

Clearly the more strategic roles of change-maker and adviser suggest themselves as most consistent with HRM-type approaches. For example, in his study of large non-union firms in the United States, Foulkes found that the personnel function took a proactive and influential role in the development, implementation, maintenance and monitoring of HRM-type policies. Significantly, personnel specialists were involved in strategic policy-making and also acted as 'expert advisers' to line managers in dealing with human relations issues. In contrast, in his study of large unionized firms in the UK, Storey found that the personnel specialist usually acted in the role of regulator, intervening to manage discontent in the organization and maintaining joint rules and procedures through temporary and tactical truces with organized labour. Significantly, in developing an HRM-type approach, senior and middle line managers in many of Storey's companies had assumed a broader remit and taken the lead in determining how human resources were managed, thus effectively downgrading the contribution of the personnel specialist.

Turning directly to our own study of non-union firms, a number of questions now arise. First, what kind of approaches to the management of employee relations are taken in non-union settings? Are these of an HRM type as often claimed, or do other approaches exist or even prevail? What are the implications for technical change of these approaches to the management of employee relations? Do they provide effective non-union employee voice mechanisms which compensate for the absence of unions, or is the absence of unions actually a source of difficulty in non-union settings in the context of advanced technical change? Finally, what role do personnel specialists play in the management of employee relations and technical change? Are they strategic change-makers or advisers, or do they play a less significant and more subservient role in supporting line management through tactical interventions?

Technical Change and the Management of Employee Relations in a 'High Tech' Setting

The 'high technology' sector provides a good prima facie case for exploring many of these questions.[1] First, it has been suggested that the sector is disproportionately non-union (Beaumont, 1986; Beaumont and Harris, 1988).[2] Secondly, many US-owned firms in the UK, such as IBM and Digital, which are seen as at the leading edge of imported HRM practices, are located in this sector (Beaumont, 1987). Finally, almost by definition, firms in the high technology sector are at the core of technical change, and it is widely assumed that they are able to implement technical change smoothly with high levels of employee acceptance.[3] In addition, we chose to focus our research in the South East of England. In part this was because this geographical area has been shown to have lower levels of union density and organization (Millward and Stevens, 1988) and is noted for significant concentrations of 'high technology' industry along major motorway routes such as the M3/M4 corridor.

The issues raised earlier in the chapter will now be explored with reference to a new data-set. This comprises a postal questionnaire survey of 115 establishments in the 'high technology' sector of the South East of England; a follow-up questionnaire and interview survey at thirty of the establishments; detailed case studies of management policies and practices at three firms (two of which were drawn from the original sample) based on semi-structured interviews from managing director down to supervisory level; and questionnaire surveys of a sample of the workforce at each of the three firms. Fieldwork was conducted between 1988 and 1991. Findings are reported in part in McLoughlin and Gourlay (1990, 1991, 1992) and in full in McLoughlin and Gourlay (1994). This chapter draws mainly on the postal survey and follow-up interviews.[4]

The survey asked questions similar to those used by Daniel (1987) about the extent and nature of advanced technical change and technology-related organizational change. Respondents were asked whether there had been any major changes involving the use of microelectronics or information technology in the production of products or provision of services since 1980 and what proportion of employees of various grades worked with the new systems. In order to assess future developments, respondents were also asked similar questions about innovations planned for the next three years. An attempt was also made to gauge how far technology-related organizational changes had accompanied technical change. This is important, since it is widely recognized that, in order to gain the full benefits of advanced technology, innovation in management organization and work design as well as production/service processes is required (see Buchanan, 1989; Bessant, 1991; McLoughlin and Clark, 1993). Respondents were therefore asked if there had been any associated organizational changes – in particular involving working practices, supervisory functions or management structure – as a result of technical change.

Our results confirm that the 'high technology' sector is a high innovation one. Eighty-four per cent of the surveyed establishments had introduced major changes involving the use of microelectronics or information technology in the production of products or provision of services. Fifty-two per cent of establishments stated that major changes involving the use of advanced technology were planned in the next three years.[5] On the key question of the presence/absence of recognized unions our findings replicated the general picture presented by previous research (Daniel, 1987; Daniel and Millward, this volume). Our high technology establishments which recognized trade unions were more likely to have adopted microelectronics than the non-union establishments. Differences in establishment size and ownership did not effect this relationship. Presence or absence of union recognition, however, made little difference to the proportion of employees using new technology, although for cases with less than 200 employees there was a tendency for a greater proportion of workplaces with union recognition to have less than half the workforce using new equipment. Plans for future change were, though, far more likely to have been made in non-union establishments than in their unionized counterparts.

When technology-related organizational change is considered, a more complex picture of the implications of the presence/absence of recognized unions emerges. Overall, 40 per cent of establishments that had introduced microelectronics had also made changes in working practices, supervisory functions or management structures as a result. In general, however, this technology-related organizational change appeared to have taken place less often in unionized establishments. When size of establishment was taken into account, a different pattern was evident. Where unions were recognized in smaller establishments, it appeared that technology-related organizational change had not taken place, but that in larger establishments union recognition made no difference as to whether such change occurred.

Two main conclusions can be drawn from this evidence. First, it confirmed existing findings that unionized establishments are more likely to have undertaken advanced technical change than non-union establishments. Secondly, it demonstrated that when technology-related organizational change is considered, union presence appears to be more of an inhibitor, especially in smaller establishments. Significantly, non-union status appears to confer no advantage either in terms of the adoption of advanced technology or, apart from the case of small establishments, in the ability to introduce technology-related organizational change.

In order to explore how the management of employee relations was related to technical change, a follow-up interview survey was undertaken at thirty of the establishments, usually with personnel managers or persons responsible for personnel matters, and also sometimes with a line manager as well. In addition a further questionnaire on human resource policies and practices was administered. Using this data the approaches to managing employee relations at the thirty establishments (seven of which recognized unions) were classified according to the 'strategic integration' and 'individualism/collectivism' dimensions outlined above. This procedure is described in more detail in McLoughlin and Gourlay (1992), but it can be noted that, amongst the items used to locate individual cases on the 'strategic integration' scale, were (i) the presence/absence of specialist personnel managers at establishment and board level in the firm, and (ii) the extent and timing of any specialist personnel involvement in technical change. The findings can be summarized as follows:

1 A third ($n = 10$) of establishments exhibited management approaches of the **high strategic integration/high individualism** type. None of these establishments recognized trade unions and all were part of non-union firms. Personnel policies and practices were typically tightly coupled to overall business requirements. In most instances relatively sophisticated individual non-union voice mechanisms were in evidence. Interviews with specialist personnel managers usually revealed strong statements of individualistic and unitary values, coupled with a view of unions as irrelevant to the needs of both employer and employee. Significantly, only four of these establishments were foreign-owned. In addition, all had under 500 employees, and eight had under 20 per cent of manual employees. Half had been founded since 1979 and only three conducted manufacturing or assembly operations at the location. The management approaches in this category appeared to approximate to the 'traditional HRM' model.

2 In a fifth of cases ($n = 6$) the management of employee relations could be classified as a **high strategic integration/high collectivism** type. Three of these establishments were non-union and part of non-union firms. The other three all recognized unions to varying degrees and were part of firms that did likewise. Employment policies were a mix of individualized and collective rules, frequently varying in emphasis according to the segment of the workforce concerned or reflecting an increased individualization of hitherto collective employment relations. In one notable example (a firm with recognized unions for both manual and non-manual workers), a takeover by a US firm and rethinking of business strategy had prompted a new emphasis on the individualization of employment relations. However, despite the introduction of a mission statement and a new emphasis placed on individual appraisals and the like, the establishment management still saw an important role for unions as a voice mechanism. Taken as a whole, the six establishments tended to be larger and older than the others in the follow-up survey; three were UK-owned and three US-owned; all bar one had a significant manual workforce; and all conducted manufacturing and/ or assembly operations at the site. Management approaches in this

category appeared to show some features of the 'strategic HRM' approach, taking a contingent view of the relative merits of collective, as opposed to individual, regulation of the employment relationship for different groups of employees.

3 In five further cases the approach could be classified as **low strategic integration/high individualization**. Four of these did not recognize trade unions and were part of non-union firms, the other establishment had recognition for one category of the workforce (manual employees, who constituted a minority), but was also part of a firm that did not recognize unions elsewhere. Personnel policies and practices were fragmented and lacked formalization. The employment relationship was viewed in most instances as a strictly individual one. There was a reliance on informal methods of communication, for example through the management chain or even the office 'grapevine'. Typically, the establishments in this category had under 500 employees, carried out manufacturing and/or assembly at the location, but under 20 per cent of the workforce was manual, the majority being white-collar or professional technical staff. None of the versions of HRM seems to apply here, and this management approach is perhaps best described as a variant of 'benevolent autocracy' where unilateral management control over the employment relationship is mediated by the need to retain high skilled and valued human resources (Goss, 1991).

In one case, a US-owned computer supplier – subsequently studied in more depth as one of our detailed case studies – this approach was combined with some scepticism towards the human resource function and the explicit HRM approach of the US parent. Management interviewees recounted how strenuous attempts had been made in 1978, when the company was established in the UK, to keep unions out. They emphasized that the preferred approach was to treat employees as 'valued individuals'. However, UK line management was also particularly suspicious of personnel as a specialist management function and only at the time of fieldwork in 1990 was a personnel manager appointed. The deep suspicion of the US parent's human resources function appeared to have quite a lot to do with this and to have inhibited the development during the 1980s of the most basic of personnel administrative procedures at the UK location. This suspicion appeared to be shared by senior management in the US company. The UK managing director recounted to us his experience on asking the vice-president of the US parent what he thought of the role of the human resources function. The VP replied with some candour: 'Well if you ask me they're all a bunch of fucking social workers!'

4 In just under one-third ($n = 9$) of establishments the management approach was of a **low strategic integration/high collectivism** type, in which employment policies were fragmented and lacked formalization. Five of these establishments recognized no unions and were part of non-union firms. Two recognized unions for some categories of employee and did likewise elsewhere in the firm. Of the two remaining, one was a non-union

establishment that was part of a unionized firm, and the other a fully unionized establishment that was part of a fully unionized firm. In many of these cases human resource issues were given little priority. Regulation of the employment relationship tended to be a mix of collective and individualized approaches, with the emphasis on the former in the non-union cases (for example through job evaluation, payment by results and annual collective pay reviews). In two cases, unions had been de-recognized in the early 1980s, but management still retained a predominantly collective approach. Establishments in this category were the most likely to have a large manual workforce (although six establishments still had under 500 employees) and to carry out manufacturing and/or assembly operations. Again, this type of employee relations management did not approximate to any of the various versions of HRM discussed earlier and is best typified as a variant of conventional reactive and opportunistic 'fire-fighting'.

Thus, various versions of the HRM model were evident in the interview sample establishments, in particular 'strategic HRM' and 'traditional HRM' approaches. However, these were by no means predominant, and what have been termed 'benevolent autocracy' and 'fire-fighting' approaches were also in evidence.

Turning once again to the question of technical change, two propositions suggest themselves in the light of the earlier discussion. First, the establishments with an HRM-type approach ('traditional' or 'strategic') would be expected to be more likely to have undertaken technical change and to be using it more effectively through making technology-related changes in organization. This is because these establishments would be more likely to involve specialist personnel managers, either as 'change-makers' or 'advisers', at an early stage in technical change. At the same time, where unions were absent, non-union voice mechanisms of a collective or individual nature would be likely to be present, thus compensating for the absence of the positive benefits that could be associated with union presence.

Secondly, those exhibiting the 'benevolent autocracy' and 'fire-fighting' approaches would be less likely to have undertaken technical change and, if adopting, more likely to be using new technology at sub-optimum levels because they had not introduced technology-related organizational change. This, it could be suggested, is because the lack of early specialist personnel involvement in change would encourage the predominance of technical issues in the management of change. At the same time, in the non-union cases at least, the absence of adequate voice mechanisms would mean that problems associated with this approach would be exacerbated. How far do our data support these propositions?

In fact there were no discernible differences between those establishments adopting an HRM-type approach and those adopting a different approach to the management of employee relations in terms of whether advanced technical change had occurred. Overall, twenty-nine out of the thirty establishments in the follow-up survey had introduced advanced technology since 1980. The only establishment not to do so was part of a Japanese-owned firm with a 'traditional HRM' approach. In this case, though, there were extensive plans to introduce advanced technology over the next three years.

Differences were apparent, however, in respect of organizational change. While eleven of the total of thirty establishments had not made technology-related organizational changes, eleven out of the fifteen establishments which had an HRM-type approach to employee relations management had. In these establishments specialist personnel involvement in change was the norm, usually at an early stage, although this was normally as a provider of advice to line management rather than as a 'change-maker'. It is also worth noting that, in many of the cases where personnel had not been involved at early stages in the past, there were plans to change this in the future.

In the case of the establishments with a non-HRM approach to employee relations management ('benevolent autocracy' and 'fire-fighters'), nine of the fourteen had also introduced technology-related organizational change. The 'fire-fighters' were the least likely to have made organizational changes as a result of adopting advanced technology, although five out of nine establishments had. However, closer inspection of these five cases revealed that in two establishments technical change and organizational change were very limited, affecting only a very small number of employees. In a third case, a specialist personnel manager had not been involved in the introduction of advanced technology at all (even, according to the personnel manager, when it concerned the computerization of the personnel department!). The other two cases, however, appeared to be genuine examples of early and full personnel involvement, although again in the 'adviser' rather than 'change-maker' capacity.

In the cases where no organizational change had been attempted the personnel function was generally either excluded or involved in later stages of change. In the case of the 'benevolent autocrats', where the introduction of advanced technology with organizational change was the norm, specialist personnel involvement appeared to be a function of a variant of paternalism, reflected in a desire to 'take valued staff along with management' by engaging in some kind of communication and consultation with the workforce. In the main, however, the management of change appeared to be exclusively in the hands of line management, with little or no personnel involvement.

Conclusion

In sum, it was possible to identify at least four distinct approaches to employee relations management in the interview survey establishments. Two of these were versions of HRM, the other two were not. The type of approach to employee relations management did not seem to influence whether advanced technical change had occurred or not, since practically all establishments were adopters. However, the introduction of technology-related organizational change as a result of adopting advanced technology did seem to be linked, in terms of both its occurrence and its character, to the style of employee relations management. Establishments with an HRM-type approach were more likely to have made such organizational changes, and although this was by no means excluded where employee relations management was of a non-HRM type, the instances of organizational change were often less significant. Despite the high levels of such change, there was little evidence that specialist personnel managers acted as 'change-makers' in their organizations, even in establishments which adopted an HRM-type approach where this might have been thought most likely. In the main specialist personnel management in these circumstances appeared to play a more reactive role, responding to the requirements of line management as 'advisers'.

Finally, let us return to the question posed at the start of this chapter as to whether non-union settings are more or less conducive to technical change than their unionized counterparts. What has been suggested is that the approach taken to the management of employee relations is a critical variable determining how effectively management in non-union settings responds to technical change. On this point, the evidence from our high technology interview sample revealed that most non-union establishments in the interview survey had introduced advanced technical change. However, whether this was accompanied by technology-related organizational change was strongly related to the approach taken to the management of employee relations. In general, where this was of an HRM type, then organizational change was more likely. However, personnel specialists normally acted, not as 'change-makers', but as 'advisers' to line management. Where non-HRM-type approaches were evident, then organizational change was either less likely or more limited, and the role of personnel specialists was at best as servants to line management, or at worst non-existent.

Acknowledgements

The research reported in this chapter was supported by grants from the National Advisory Board and the Economic and Social Research Council (Award No. R002311164). Their support is acknowledged, as are the helpful comments of Neil Millward on earlier versions of this chapter.

Notes

1. Although not without its problems, the official definition of the 'high technology' sector was followed (see Butchart, 1987).
2. Beaumont and Harris make this suggestion on the basis of a secondary analysis of the WIRS data set. However, the 1990 survey shows that this holds true only if all workplaces

(i.e. including public sector workplaces) are considered. If just private sector workplaces are considered then those in the 'high technology' sector are no more likely to be non-union than 'non-high technology' sector workplaces. In fact, they are more likely to have recognized unions present. I am grateful to Neil Millward for supplying this information.

3. This point is confirmed by the 1990 Workplace Industrial Relations Survey which shows that 55 per cent of establishments in the 'high technology' sector had adopted advanced technology between 1987 and 1990, compared to 39 per cent of 'non-high technology' private sector establishments.

4. The postal survey found that 80 per cent of the surveyed establishments did not recognize trade unions; 56 per cent of employees in the sample were employed in the non-union establishments; and over two-thirds of the establishments not recognizing trade unions (accounting for 39 per cent of employees in the sample) also had no union members. These findings run counter to a survey in the Scottish electronics industry (albeit based on a narrower definition of 'high technology') which found most employment to be in unionized establishments (see Sproull and MacInnes, 1987, 1988). In addition, the suggestion from our data that the 'high technology' sector exhibits an above average level of non-unionism, at least in the South East, is not supported by the 1990 WIRS survey, provided public sector establishments are ignored.

5. These results can be compared with those of Daniel, who found that only 31 per cent of manufacturing workplaces had experienced advanced technical change (1987: 13) and 53 per cent of private sector offices (1987: 40). Obviously, the difference may reflect the later timing of our survey. However, the more recent survey data on microelectronics use in manufacturing suggest our findings for high technology are still above the norm (Northcott and Walling, 1988). See also note 3 above.

10

Towards Factory 2000:
Designing Organizations for
Computer-Integrated Technologies

John Bessant

Background

Recent years have seen an upsurge of interest in the question of appropriate organization design for manufacturing firms. Changes in both technology and market environment have been discontinuous and there is a need to find alternative models better suited to these conditions (Child, 1987; Clark and Staunton, 1989). In particular there is a school of thought which sees such changes as representative of a paradigm shift away from the mass production pattern which has dominated organization design for most of this century (Freeman and Perez, 1989). However, while the arguments about the limitations of the old paradigm are well articulated, there is less agreement on the form which the new one might take.

This question of organization design is of particular interest to manufacturers because of:

- The increasing incidence of failure of investments in advanced manufacturing technology (AMT) where there was no parallel organizational change
- The significant opportunities opened up by alternative organization designs
- The lower cost of organizational change as compared to capital investments in AMT.

Despite growing pressures on firms from an increasingly competitive market, the early 1980s could be characterized as a period of technological optimism. While industry was being challenged to produce more flexibly, with higher quality, more frequent product innovation, better delivery and service to customers etc., there was a growing awareness of the potential of new manufacturing technologies to meet this demand for improved performance. In particular, the possibility was emerging of using such technology in *integrated* rather than discrete form, taking advantage of advances in communications and networking technology to facilitate the emergence of linked manufacturing *systems*. Such systems went beyond what might be termed 'substitution innovation' – replacing what was always done with equipment that performed the task a little better – towards radically new ways of carrying out the task or even making possible totally new tasks (see on this Miles et al, 1988; Bessant, 1991).

The emerging pattern of 'computer-integrated manufacturing' (CIM) promised significant improvements at a strategic level, not just improving the performance of particular tasks or functions, but enhancing the overall performance of the firm in terms of reduced response times, better quality control, faster new product development and lower inventory levels. Not surprisingly there was a surge of growth in interest and investment in what appeared to offer the solution to industry's problems.

This picture of an ideal marriage – between the challenges facing manufacturing industry and the potential of AMT – represented a myth to which many parties happily subscribed. Users wanted to believe in it because it seemed to offer a simple (albeit expensive) way of meeting the needs of an increasingly demanding market. Suppliers wanted to foster it because they would sell more systems. Governments and other agencies concerned with industrial development jumped on the bandwagon and promoted aggressively the adoption of AMT with both the carrot of financial support and the stick of dire warnings as to the consequences of failing to keep up with international competitors.

If the early part of the 1980s was characterized as optimistic, the latter part revealed a growing disillusionment with AMT and the realization that a successful marriage needs both hard work and a willingness to adapt if it is to succeed. A variety of studies have indicated disappointment and dissatisfaction with AMT's ability to live up to its full potential, and while there have been few total failures, many systems throughout the world are operating at less than their full potential (Jaikumar, 1986; Burnes, 1988b; Ettlie, 1988; Bessant, 1991). Analysis of the causes of these failures suggests that, although there have been 'teething troubles' associated with the technology itself, the majority of the problems have been due to a failure to take a strategic approach to such investments and to recognize the need for significant parallel organizational change (Ettlie, 1988; Bessant, 1991). The dimensions of such changes range widely, from requiring new and multiple skills, through changes in work organization towards more teamworking to restructuring of the vertical and lateral relations within the firm and beyond. Experiences of this kind have led to a resurgence of interest in variations on a socio-technical design theme and to particular interest in the developments – which appear to have their roots in a Nordic model of shopfloor organization – of 'anthropocentric production systems' (Brödner, 1985; Wobbe, 1992).

At the same time there has been a growing awareness of the potential performance improvements which can be gained through alternative organizational arrangements – often in the absence of any investments in AMT. Examples include various applications of the principles of just-in-time manufacturing and total quality management together with long-established models for teamworking, group technology and cellular manu-facturing (Schonberger, 1985; Imai, 1987; Kaplinsky and Hoffman, 1992). Recent interest has focused on 'lean production' systems, so called because they use far fewer resources than traditional systems. In their comparisons of car assembly plants worldwide, Womack et al (1990) found that automation levels were not significantly different and that these did not account for the wide differences in performance between lean and traditional assemblers. However there were major differences in human resource practices and production organization models, particularly in areas like teamworking, employee participation in problem-solving, multi-skilling and training.

Making such changes involves disruption, training and physical reorgan-ization, but evidence suggests that the resulting benefits quickly outweigh the costs and that the establishment of new organizational features such as continuous improvement groups can contribute major long-term returns (Imai, 1987; Bessant, Burnell et al, 1992). Faced with this kind of experience, manufacturers now have a growing interest in exploring alternative forms of organization design in manufacturing. However, recognizing the need to change and being able to identify and implement appropriate and relevant changes are not the same thing and a number of questions need to be raised about the dimensions, extent and rate of change in organizational design.

A Change of Paradigm?

Manufacturing can be viewed as moving through a period in which previously accepted 'best practice' conditions for industrial performance may no longer apply. In particular, it appears that mass production models of production and consumption which dominated the first half of this century are giving way to more fragmented patterns of demand and more flexible modes of production. Such models are incompatible with older forms of organization, especially those stressing division of labour and rigid bureaucratic organizational forms, and we are seeing the emergence of alternative, more flexible arrangements based on networking and decen-tralization.

There have been many attempts to explain this change, but all have in common models which suggest a change of 'paradigm' (Bessant, 1991; Piore and Sabel, 1982). This involves a discontinuous shift in the 'rules of the game' triggered by a combination of major technological and environ-mental change. Earlier examples of such turning points in industrial history include the transitions associated with the emergence of steam power, of railways and communications, and the development of mass production in the first quarter of this century (Freeman and Perez, 1989).

Under these conditions it may be difficult to specify what form new organization designs should take; there is unlikely to be a single, clear blueprint, but rather an evolving pattern and a period during which both old and new patterns co-exist. Liu et al (1990) suggest that there are 'life cycles' to technology systems, with three phases. In the first there is a transitional process in which many innovations take place and overturn old techniques and processes of production. In the second phase the technology system establishes itself, develops and matures, while in the third, stagnation phase it declines and begins to give way to a newly emerging system. They suggest that stagnation arises from at least two sources, 'in part, because the actors involved do not know how to manage the process of change. It also comes about because the designers of existing technology share a frame of reference about how organizations should be designed, i.e. they share a paradigm for organizing that is based on a stagnating technology' (1990: 8).

Organization Design for Factory 2000

If companies are to move to more suitable organizational forms appropriate to a new paradigm, then some indication of the dimensions and extent of these changes is needed. Elaborating this appears at first sight to be a daunting task, but it is possible to draw upon three sets of clues to help in the process. First, we have a fairly clear idea of the likely technological shape of the factory of the future. From a combination of R and D studies, prototype projects, extrapolation of current trends and examples of early pioneer users we can build up a picture of the likely technological skeleton. Irrespective of the products being made such a factory is likely to make extensive use of integrated automation and to employ networking technology within and between firms to a much greater extent than currently (Bessant, 1991).

Secondly, we can draw upon an extensive body of research in organization design dating back over the past seventy-five years or so. However, conventional organization design theories have significant limitations, not least their preoccupation with maintaining an equilibrium rather than sustaining continuous change. Most organization theory dates from the 1960s and organization design as a subset of this has followed models which emphasize the pursuit of efficiency as an implicit or explicit rationale for organizations. Clark and Staunton (1989) suggest that this is flawed in that it sees innovation as a deviant case, an occasional exception to which the organization adapts before returning to its equilibrium position. Emphasis in recent research and theory is now shifting to seeing innovation as continuous and as important as efficiency in the context of increasing uncertainty and change in environments and technology etc. For example, Lawrence and Dyer (1982), in their review of a number of sectors of US industry, suggest relative success or failure in performance is directly related to the adaptability of organizations within these sectors to cope with the simultaneous demands of efficiency and innovation.

Consequently emphasis may shift from looking at formal structural relationships as might appear on an organization chart, towards the processes and underlying cultures of adaptive organizations, for this may be where more useful models for designing the factories of the next century will be found. For example, increasing demands for flexibility and adaptability are more likely to be met by fluid coordination and organizing processes embedded in an organic culture than in a formally structured bureaucratic pyramid. At the same time, there is growing recognition that major transitions between different organization designs do not occur smoothly (Miller and Friesen, 1984) and there is often considerable friction in shifting between forms.

The third set of clues which might be of value are early experiments aimed at finding alternative forms of organization design. If we are seeing a shift in paradigm then we would expect there to be extensive experimentation taking place (not all of it necessarily successful) with different arrangements. Although it is inevitable that each firm will develop its own particular solution to the design problem, it is likely that some basic design trajectories (Nelson and Winter, 1982) will emerge which define the pathways along which other firms will move at a later stage.

The MOCIT (Manufacturing Organization for Computer-Integrated Technologies) Project

This last point provided the motivation for a two-year research project carried out between 1988 and 1990 by researchers from Brighton and Sheffield Business Schools (for further details, see Bessant, Levy et al, 1992). The intention was to try to follow some early experiments towards new organizational forms and to try to derive from these broad design trajectories emerging in the new paradigm. In particular we looked at the case of integrated and networked systems of the type which we expect to become widely used during the next 10–15 years. The underlying hypothesis was that stand-alone technologies would generally be accommodated without major organizational change, whereas the shift to integrated systems challenged the firm to change along several dimensions. This is consistent with other research findings which suggest this first step toward integration is the most difficult and is usually inhibited by organizational rather than technical problems (see on this Bessant, 1985).

From the outset the research was designed as a mapping exercise, trying to pick up some indication of experimentation taking place towards a new paradigm, rather than a detailed diffusion study or one aimed at accurately measuring the dimensions of change. Through case studies of integrated technology applications we looked for evidence of various types of organization design artefacts which the literature suggested would provide indicators of a shift.

In selecting companies for study we concentrated on those that had successfully implemented computer-integrated technology (although we recognize the difficulties in defining 'success' (see Voss, 1986)). Operationally we chose companies which the trade press or the Department of Trade and Industry (DTI) had recommended to others as exemplars of 'how to do it'. Inevitably this is a crude measure, but it does have the virtue of incorporating some sense of peer acclaim which is of direct relevance to the process of paradigm transition. The companies were selected from a broad spectrum across the UK ranging in size, age, ownership, turnover, industrial sector, product range and complexity, and types of technical application; we were able to study twenty-eight of the fifty companies approached, resulting in a total of forty-six applications.[1]

Main Findings

The detailed findings of this research have been reported elsewhere (Bessant, Levy et al, 1992), but an overview of the design trends will be given here. We included metrics on twenty dimensions related to specific focal points; as an indicator of a paradigm shift we would expect to see changes across these on a wide scale. The findings are broken down into three different operational spheres – work organization, management organization and inter-organization relations. We also measured shifts in coordination by re-interpreting our data in terms of Mintzberg's dimensions (1989). Table 10.1 indicates the findings in summary form. Due to limitations of space, only the dimensions concerned with work organization and management organization will be considered here.

Work Organization

Our expectations were that changes within the area of work organization would centre upon individual operator skills and responsibilities, training received, work relations with other operators, the organization and nature of supervision, and the nature of the reward systems operating. Responses varied, but most were moving in the same general direction. If there was a single common theme, it was a changed perception of the role and value of the shopfloor workforce, with managers talking of how they had considerably undervalued and consequently under-utilized the resources of their workforce. As one planning controller observed, the perception was changing to one which recognized that 'with every pair of hands you get a brain free!'

One area of particular interest was the way in which operator skills were changing with the introduction of CIT, and the data indicate that across the board, machine operators were moving from single-skill machine minding to multi-skilled practices. Multi-skilled practices were not confined to existing job tasks, but applied to a wider set of functions. They varied according to situations and particular companies, yet they had a number of facets in common. These included changes in job title, teamworking, greater responsibility for quality and machine maintenance, an involvement in continuous improvements and responsibility for sequencing work processes. In some situations developments included a range of team-

Table 10.1 *Dimensions of organizational change*

Dimensions of change	Extent of change (% of firms reporting)
1 Work organization	
(i) From single skill to multi-skill developments	96
(ii) From high division of labour to integrated tasks	93
(iii) From long skill life cycle to short skill life cycle	86
(iv) From skill life = employee life to skill life < employee life	82
(v) From individual work/accountability to teamwork/accountability	82
(vi) From payment by results to alternative payment systems	86
(vii) From supervisor controlled to supervisor supported	82
(viii) From low work discretion to increased flexibility/autonomy	89
2 Management organization	
(ix) From sharp line–staff boundary to blurred boundaries	86
(x) From steep pyramid to flat structure	60
(xi) From vertical communication to network communication	89
(xii) From formal control to 'holographic adjustment'	86
(xiii) From functional structures to product/project/customer-based	78
(xiv) From status differentiated to single status	68
(xv) From rigid and non-participative to flexible-participative	78
3 Inter-organization relationships	
(xvi) From tight boundaries between firms to blurred boundaries	50
(xvii) From 'arm's length dealing' to cooperative relations	54
(xviii) From short-term to long-term relationships	58
(xix) From confrontational to cooperative relationships/partnerships	54
(xx) Lack of customer involvement to 'customer is king'	75

organizing skills, including negotiation skills for staff relations in other areas of the organization. Other companies described the development of multi-skills for the purpose of looking after group technology/cell configurations, for minor machine maintenance, and for quality. This is exemplified by the works manager of one company who described his operators' skill profile in terms of three levels: basic (rules, methods of cutting), intermediate (setting, cutting, sizing, tooling) and top (thinking skills, sequencing). In his view the development of automated processes had led to basic skills still being valid, while intermediate skills had disappeared, and thinking skills had increased.

Another issue was whether a shift was taking place, away from the high division of labour epitomized by 'scientific management' principles and towards work design focused upon integrated tasks and the development of skills and responsibilities for operating integrated task sequences. We found extensive evidence for this; many of the new manufacturing applications such as group technology, cell developments etc., involved operators managing a sequence of processes, including minor maintenance work to reduce downtime. As one respondent put it, 'job descriptions have been redrawn to cover the cell objectives of producing a finished product, rather than relating to a particular skill . . . this required substantial training'. It was also clear that the integrated nature of the automation being introduced provided a strong pressure for the design of more integrated jobs.

If skills were being outmoded and consequently needing to be updated with increasing frequency, we would expect to find a reduction in the life expectancy of a set of skills. From the data it was clear that this was taking place; multi-skilling was changing the pattern of skill life. The demands required to improve competitive edge created an expectancy that production processes would change rapidly and that skills would be updated and changed more and more frequently. We also found a shortening of individual skill life cycles, coupled with a broadening of the potential to gain a wider set of skills within the overall organizational skill profile.

The development of multi-disciplinary/cross-functional project teams appeared to be a major aspect of organization re-design. We found several variations, including 'process improvement groups', 'quality circles', 'task forces', 'focused teams', 'quality improvement teams', 'multi-disciplinary teams' and 'cross-functional teams'. An expected feature of the response to the new technological configurations was the development of teamworking to replace individual work practices. Such developments could focus around 'cells' or be multi-disciplinary problem-solving or improvement teams. For example, one such development within an FMS cell was staffed 'by a flexible team of operators who rotated amongst the various tasks required . . . the supervisor worked in a support role to the team allowing them to self-manage work allocation to suit cell and individual needs'.

This example highlights another development, the devolution of responsibility and power to operator teams. Areas for decision-making varied – for example, how to organize work teams? which jobs are to be done, in what order? – but the common element was management's decision to devolve power, responsibility and accountability to the operator teams: 'In the past we had high absenteeism . . . operators did only one job . . . now we have multi-skilled teamworking . . . the sharing of responsibility is a key element'. Here the manager quoted gives credit to the new work design, particularly the introduction of shared responsibility, for reducing high absenteeism in his company, though that was not the prime reason for the new set-up.

Multi-skilled teamworking was found to be a common feature across the research sample. Several companies were moving beyond the integration and sequencing of technical skills, and were now investing highly in the area of people management. Not only were managers trained in new personnel practices, supervisors, team leaders and operators were also included in such developments. The commitment to investing in organization, team and people skills throughout the organization was demonstrated by several companies.

In two major international companies similar models of shopfloor staff development were being introduced. Individuals could choose to train in any one or all four elements of the skill range (people, engineering, production and business skills) and to one of four levels. Selection for training was based on assessment of the needs of the individual together with the needs of the team. These developments contain two major resourcing implications; a high investment in training, and fundamental changes in appraisal/reward systems.

Changes in reward systems were seen as 'high priority' for achieving new work structures. The findings showed shifts from payment for 'output achieved', primarily based on individual piece rate plus bonus with lower rates for downtimes, to payment for 'skills and quality', a rate often higher than achieved through piecework topped up with bonus systems. The new reward system was described by one manager as 'the bedrock on which the attainment of extra flexibility rests'.

Changes like these can take a considerable amount of time and effort to be developed and implemented. Negotiations were often difficult where industrial relations practices were deeply embedded within the conflictual model of 'us and them'. Major efforts were being made to shift away from this and to work cooperatively with the workforce and their representatives. Such changes in work practices, expectations and industrial relations demonstrated the significant shifts in the cultural beliefs and practices occurring in these organizations. Management had to show they meant well by the workforce, an expectation which many managers felt the workforce had legitimate reasons to doubt.

Variations in the payment systems introduced were common; in general, payment for individual skills and quality played the central role, sometimes with team, group or company-wide bonuses attached. The importance of achieving such changes was confirmed by those who had not gone down this path. For example, one company described in detail the problem they had in implementing a new payment structure in line with the desired job/ work re-design for their division of the company:

> The real problem is that the grading differentials are so great that they create serious resistances to change . . . Management have spent three years on talks to get 'payment for flexibility' . . . obtained union agreement locally but central HQ personnel put the brakes on . . . we want to change the reward system, shift to single status and reduce the range of grades . . . but blocked by HQ.

This indicates how important it is to have the full understanding, ownership and commitment of all those who can affect the organization-wide changes taking place. Of the companies researched, this aspect – 'who owns the company?' – has had more influence on such matters as the restructuring of the reward system than we originally thought it might.

One of the most critical points for change was the supervisory role. Our predictions suggested a likely shift from monitoring/control functions to collaborative, support functions. Such changes indicated a fundamental rethink in management's view of its workforce, to one that valued and encouraged the potential and actual skills of the workforce. The direction

f change included creating space for operators to work more flexibly, to
nandle aspects previously the province of the supervisor, or to use their
initiative more. As one respondent commented,

> Managers are now seen as a resource and as providers rather than as monitor
> controllers . . . they are more involved in corporate thinking, as system
> developers, as skill developers . . . The introduction of CIM has seen an increase
> in supportive relationships and less of the old style of the controlling manager.

In most cases the change in supervisory role saw a shift in the level of
responsibility down to the operators in order to allow them to do what was
necessary to achieve the job. This included flexibility and the right to go
direct to those who may assist in solving a problem, rather than going
through the supervisor/manager.

> Give people a job and let them get on with it . . . As managers we only get
> involved if something is seriously wrong.

> Don't see myself as a manager but as a leader . . . pass down responsibility . . .
> in the previous culture we decided what they wanted to know, now we ask.

An important associated development was the creation of team leaders
within the team replacing the old-style supervisor placed above individual
operators.

> [We] got rid of supervisors . . . now have team leaders in manufacturing cells
> who run the teams . . . needed to pass down more responsibility . . . shifted
> from telling to consulting . . . supervisors who couldn't cope with the new way of
> supporting teams left . . . more recently new team leaders have come through a
> natural selection process whereby they are selected by the teams themselves.

Moves to utilize the potential and actual skills of the workforce were likely
to involve a shift from low work discretion to increased flexibility and
autonomy. We looked for shifts in such areas, asking who had control over
what could be done, when and how? Did team/group meetings exist, and
did they discuss how to do the work more effectively? Where did the
problem-solving, quality and continuous improvement groups fit into the
process?

Significant instances of increased flexibility and autonomy have been
developing and we saw a number of interdependent changes. Managers
wanted their workforce to solve problems in the shortest time possible and
saw increased flexibility and autonomy as a necessary requirement to do
the job.

> Operators self-managed their activities around the various work stations . . . the
> FMS cell was manned by a flexible team of operators who rotated amongst the
> various tasks required . . . the supervisor/shop manager worked in a support role
> to the team allowing them to self-manage work allocation to suit cell and
> individual needs.

Against this background, managers saw the need to shift the emphasis of
their work from 'fire-fighting' to overall planning and strategy: 'Managers

are widening their responsibilities . . . now more participative . . . they ar
involved in training on a large scale to develop people skills, to shift from
fire-fighting to planning and organizing, to decentralization of skills'.

Management Organization

The next level of analysis concerned changes in management organization
and included seven measures of change centred upon: the boundary
relationships between functional departments; the levels in the management hierarchy and the span of control of managers; the type of
communication systems operating; control structures; and conditions of
service, including status and management/union relationships.

The organization design implications of stand-alone and integrated
systems of AMT are, in our view, quite different. Our evidence suggests
that little change occurs between line/staff boundaries for stand-alone
applications. Conversely, the successful implementation of a fully integrated flexible system across the company leads to a blurring of boundaries
between previously separate functions – for example, overlapping of job
specialisms, an increase in the use of multi-disciplinary teams, or the
overlapping or integration of previously separate functions such as design
with manufacturing. It may be expressed at the individual job level or may
have resulted in the amalgamation of previously separate departments.

Some departments were less enamoured with the changes than others,
for a variety of reasons, but often to do with loss of status differentials and
power and the loss of some skills to other groups. Those more immediately
affected were those butting up to the production process, such as
maintenance, fitters and quality inspectors, rather than those in sales or
accounts. One company in particular instanced a degree of resistance to
change as engineers cooperated only slowly in 'giving up precious skill
areas that give them status'. Behind these developments lay concerns
about integration and the partial loss of control it entailed for individual
departments. In a few companies the blurring constituted significant moves
towards integration across functional boundaries, and for one it had
progressed so far that there were now formally only two departments, one
supplier-orientated, one customer-orientated. Both were outward looking,
each having various multi-disciplinary product teams. One manager
described it in the following way: 'The whole operation has few if any
functional demarcations . . . no private offices for anyone . . . no private
physical boundaries to demarcate professional or job differences'. Similar
strategies were being considered in other companies where the reasons
given were primarily to reduce the lead time between design and production. A common approach was to allow functional departments to continue
to exist but for staff to work regularly in cross-functional/multi-disciplinary
project teams. Sometimes this would be described as a matrix type system,
at other times as a product- or customer-focused organization approach.

This shift from functionally orientated departments to product/customer orientation was one of several driving forces in the moves towards the blurring of boundaries. While computer-integrated technology (CIT) plays a major part, it normally constitutes only one of several forces in the process. Our evidence suggests that companies are moving along a continuum, loosening the boundaries between functional departments progressively to the point where it makes sense formally to merge them. Parallel to this has been the focusing of departmental or work groupings around product and customer groups rather than around professional expertise.

The more responsibility, decision-making, autonomy and flexibility is located at the point where it is needed, the less will be the need for several layers of management to monitor and control processes. A feature of CIT is that it incorporates many of the monitoring and control aspects of bureaucracy within the technology. In theory this will make such practices less significant components of managerial posts. Linked to this trend is the likelihood of wider spans of control, which is tending to reduce the number of middle managers. Our findings suggest a commonly emerging belief in the importance of flatter hierarchies, but variations in the extent to which this view has been translated into practice.

Several of the companies described themselves as having a flat structure. In two cases that meant having three levels only. In another it meant five levels, in another, six. Clearly size of the company has a part to play, those with extremely flat hierarchies (that is, three levels) being firms with up to 150 employees. Two particular areas were affected by the reduction of hierarchical levels: the number of shopfloor grades and jobs (reduced from twenty-four to only four), and the number of levels within management (reduced from eight to five).

Certain types of job were commonly removed. These included the old charge-hand, who used to help inexperienced operators set machinery, the supervisor, now made part of the team of operators, and the removal of one or two from a group constituting foremen, superintendents, shopfloor managers, production managers and works managers.

Central to the issue of flexibility and the reduction of time delays were arrangements for direct communication with those who can help to get the job done. Within the sphere of work organization we saw the way shopfloor operators talked more and more to other operators or staff in other departments to solve problems. This was in preference to the bureaucratic process of going up the management tree and involving several intermediaries between those who need to talk to each other. Similar shifts were demonstrated within the sphere of management organization, where the blurring of boundaries contributed to a move from vertical communications to network communications. Several features are worth recording from these developments.

There was a distinct shift towards consulting with staff whose contributions were previously ignored. Engineers were described as increasingly involved in encouraging open exploration of issues with the shopfloor, while managers were described as 'always walking around, talking'. Vertical communications were also improving and had much more of a two-way flow character. Managers talked of wanting to know what their workforce thought rather than telling them what they ought to think or assuming they knew already.

Another area of change related to the way an organization got its message across to its workforce about its basic values, beliefs, aims, strategies and practices. We expected to see shifts away from formal control systems to a more 'holographic' approach (defined as the principle of 'everything is in everything else') where a set of values permeate the whole organization in terms of a shared purpose (see Morgan, 1986).

Various examples supported the notion that companies were taking seriously the need for full commitment to a shared purpose, investing considerable resources to put the message across and achieve ownership by the total workforce. Philosophies such as TQM (total quality management) or JIT (just-in-time) were recognized by several companies as ways of achieving shared purpose and values. 'There was a feeling that there was now, as a result of these kinds of communication and the ways in which they had been carried out, a much more realistic appreciation of the market environment . . . by everyone . . . management, shopfloor, unions, everyone'.

Company values were also expressed in changes in working conditions and facilities. These included such artefacts as car parking or restaurant facilities, physical working conditions or conditions of service such as holiday, training, sick leave entitlements or payment structures, and were also reflected in the practice of industrial relations. It was clear those who had gone a long way to achieve their aims had taken the question of single status seriously. In many cases provision of restaurant facilities presented a symbolic as well as a real statement regarding management's commitment to single status and improved conditions. Two companies each spent over £1m on refurbishing restaurant facilities to provide excellent quality service for all staff. Similarly, others had created 'one restaurant for all' provisions. By contrast, in another company separate restaurant facilities for different staff were maintained, the Golden Grill for directors, the Silver Grill for senior managers, and another for 'the rest'. The provision was not seen as a minor issue by staff. It was experienced as a real and symbolic statement of how top management viewed its workforce. As the works manager put it, 'The MD wants us to develop a total quality organization, yet keeps status differentials . . . the answer is . . . contradictory messages won't take your workforce with you'.

Another measure was the extent of employee contribution to the improvement processes within the companies and the degree to which management saw the usefulness of suggestions or contributions from any source. Vehicles for such continuous improvement included quality circles and process improvement groups and indications were that at least some companies were reaping the benefits. 'The enthusiasm was palpable . . .

men came back with ideas for modifications, some of which they had the satisfaction of seeing incorporated . . . there was a recognition that the future lay down this path'.

Coordination Mechanisms

Using Mintzberg's six categories (1989) and the twenty measures of change described above we also noted shifts in coordination mechanisms. Our hypothesis of a move away from mechanistic and direct supervisory control and towards more ad hoc arrangements with high levels of informal mutual adjustment was broadly confirmed.

Three measures (flatter hierarchies, the location and role of supervisors and new operator roles) were selected as indicative of the declining use of direct supervision as a coordinating mechanism. The pattern was one of considerable integration between levels and within functions, with extensive devolution of responsibility and an increase in the use of mutual adjustment as opposed to direct supervision. Further indicators of this shift in coordinating mechanism included the use of autonomous or semi-autonomous teamworking, together with shifts in supervisor role from control to facilitation. Managers regularly talked of the increase in 'informal face-to-face problem-solving' and of 'operators going direct to the person that can help them and not necessarily through their supervisor'.

Control through standardization of work processes has traditionally been the province of technical/support/management services, supporting the line management function. Evidence of changes included the decreasing size of services and declining use of procedure manuals. In one company work scheduling devolved to the shopfloor and in others operators were regularly involved in quality/process improvement teams. Coordination through standardization of outputs was enhanced through the operation of the technology installed which fundamentally improved and increased control over quality of output. Additionally there were reductions in the numbers of specialist departments – such as quality control – while at the same time major investments were taking place to increase the skills and responsibility of direct operators in the management of quality of output.

Growing use of coodination by standardization of skills/knowledge was particularly apparent in the increased amount and direction of investment in training. All companies espoused the value that training was important; more importantly the majority had invested substantially in a wide spectrum of training (86 per cent). The range included: multi-skilling of operators, widening and deepening their skill/knowledge base; giving them responsibility for quality, machine maintenance and sequencing of integrated tasks, for team management and for involvement in continuous improvements. Management and supervisory training included corporate strategy and teamworking approaches and training skills. Another important ingredient was the development of a commitment to core values such as the use of a TQM philosophy.

Evidence of ideological coordination could be found in the methods used to obtain 'shared purpose' through the promotion of core values, strategies and programmes throughout the organization (86 per cent), often by the use of training programmes. Examples include the development of TQM as a major component of achieving business aims, while one company talked of JIT principles as the overriding new philosophy for the company. Other evidence included displaying messages such as 'excellence through people', 'quality improvement teams', 'monthly awards to winners'.

A new paradigm?

Most companies included in our sample reported making wide-ranging changes in the design of their organizations. It is noticeable that the levels of change in work organization were higher than in management organization and these in turn were higher than in inter-organizational relationships. This suggests that there may still be significant problems to be overcome in facilitating changes at middle management level and in inter-firm relations – a view confirmed by several other studies (see, for example, Lamming, 1992).

The role of technology in shaping these changes is interesting; while it is clear that they are by no means a direct result of particular changes in technology, they do reflect some common themes which suggest an underlying *trajectory* of change. In particular the theme of integration runs through the pattern at a number of levels, reflecting the dominant technological trend. This raises the question of the extent to which organization design is influenced by technological change as opposed to other factors such as size or environment (for a review of this, see Clark et al, 1988: 9–15).

Research exploring influences other than technology (for example, Starkey and McKinley, 1988) suggests similar directions for organization design change to those reported here. This is consistent with the view of paradigm changes as involving shifts in technology, environmental and institutional frameworks and underlying values and beliefs (Freeman and Perez, 1989). None the less we cannot discount technology as having no shaping role in the emergent pattern. Technology may not directly determine structure, but characteristics of technology – especially in its more systemic forms – create the space within which design choices can take place. In this connection it is important to remind ourselves of the broad nature of 'technology', embracing not only tangible artefacts such as computers and machinery, but also intangible elements like skills, knowledge and work organization. Noble captures this well:

> Although it may aptly be described as a composite of the accumulated scientific knowledge, technical skills, implements, logical habits and material products of people, technology is always more than this, more than information, logic,

things. It is people themselves, undertaking their various activities in particular social and historical contexts, with particular interests and aims. (1984: 43)

This multi-dimensional nature of technology was central to the development of the 'socio-technical' school of organizational theory (Miller and Rice, 1967) which recognized that changes in the hardware or software will inevitably have an effect on other – organization design-related – dimensions of the broader technology system.

Arguably technology also includes a particular philosophy about how it should be used – for example, to exert and maintain increasing managerial control over the worker and the workplace (Braverman, 1974). Our view is that, although we should be aware that there will be particular views and philosophies 'embedded' in particular technologies, the actual process of organization design in relation to those technologies is more fluid. Certainly there will be characteristics which may push design thinking in a particular direction, but these will be balanced by other considerations and the views of other actors in the process.

We believe that there is no single 'best' way but rather a set of choices which are made as a result of negotiations around a 'design space' (Bessant, 1983); there is no guarantee that the model which emerges will be optimal. (For example, Wilkinson and Sewell report in Chapter 7, this volume, on a significantly different pattern of organization design from that discussed above – yet the technological changes involved were broadly similar.) Furthermore, the broad frameworks within which detailed designs are worked out are likely to be strongly influenced by particular environments and technology. So, in simple terms, highly uncertain environments would not be well served by simple rigid organizations, but rather by those which are flexible and able to respond quickly. These are likely to have more organic decentralized structures. By the same token, integrated technologies which span organizational boundaries – like CAD/CAM – will need integrated organization structures which support such boundary-crossing, such as matrix designs (Winch et al, 1991).

McLoughlin and Clark (1988) argue that complex technologies – 'engineering systems' – generate their own strong imperatives for certain aspects of work and organization and establish constraints and opportunities for others. Clark and Staunton (1989) make a similar case, arguing that there is likely to be a degree of 'soft determinism' associated with organization design around advanced and complex technologies which arises from their basic nature. This pattern appears to emerge in the cases studied, where the underlying technological trajectory is matched by an emergent organization design trajectory.

Implications for Human Resource Management

What are the issues raised by this changing pattern in the area of human resource management? The first point which emerges strongly is the changing role for human resources within the factory of the future. Far from being considered as a cost, a necessary evil which can gradually be eliminated through automation, people are beginning to be seen as an asset, to be developed and upgraded on a continuing basis. While not yet widespread, there is a belief that such investments can offer high returns through smoother and more flexible operation and increased problem-solving capability. This arises from two sources in particular; first the experience with complex automated systems which increasingly require human intervention at critical judgemental points and have led to a revaluing of tacit knowledge and experience and a movement towards the design of 'anthropocentric production systems' (Wobbe, 1992). Secondly, it arises from the growing recognition of the value of human resources in participative problem-solving and product/process improvement activities (Melcher et al, 1990; Bessant, Burnell et al, 1992).

This changing emphasis means that the organizational systems designed to procure, develop and maintain such resources are likely to increase in importance. Employee recruitment is becoming a key issue, especially in many 'greenfield' operations where attempts are being made to use psychometric and other selection techniques to ensure a good match between the individual and the demands not only of the task itself but also of working in teams, contributing to problem-solving and continuous improvement etc. (see Chapters 5, 6 and 7, this volume). Training and development is shifting towards a regular pattern of continuous updating of skills, with a number of firms using sophisticated profiling techniques for identifying individual training needs. One of the main levers for effecting changes like the shift to teamworking is the design and implementation of alternative appraisal and reward systems and the development of new grading and career development pathways.

Another area which is likely to become more prominent is the long-term development of employees (beyond basic skills training). Here two trends emerge as significant – the increasing rise in importance of developing 'people management and interpersonal skills' and the changing roles of key groups such as supervisors, where a shift from controlling to facilitating is involved.

A third, longer-term implication is that organizational development may well become a key strategic resource. Discussions of strategy have increasingly recognized the importance of aligning the organization design with the firm's strategic posture, and this is given greater weight when considering the need to design a continuously changing and adapting organization rather than a stable form. Establishing and extending such capability will require considerable efforts in embedding OD skills, tools and techniques throughout the organization and may well make this field one of the key areas of strategic competence in the next century.

Most of the foregoing suggests that personnel *issues* are likely to become central in the future, assuming considerable strategic importance. While technological change at a substitution innovation level may have been relatively easy to introduce with only minor organizational adjustment, new generations of integrated technologies will involve by their nature extensive shifts in organization design. Yet as Daniel and Millward point out (Chapter 3, this volume), organizational change of this kind is far more likely to attract resistance. Thus a critical role needs to be played in effectively managing the transition. Even 'greenfield' projects of the kind described by David Preece (Chapter 5) involve considerable planning and organization design activity, whilst Chris Hendry's description of Hardy Spicer (Chapter 4) suggests that successful change may depend on having a long-term foundation of attention to personnel issues.

A main theme in the emerging trajectory is the blurring of boundaries – between different skills and competencies at the individual level, and between functions and departments at the organizational level. Thus the question must be raised of the responsibility for looking after these issues – will it be that of an expanded and more strategically involved specialist personnel management function, or will it become a part of the professional training and development of all individuals within the organization?

Certainly the skills of the 'traditional' specialist personnel manager – in design and implementation of recruitment, selection, appraisal and reward systems, and in training and employee development – will be increasingly in demand. There will also be increased need for counselling, coaching and facilitation skills which could be met by personnel professionals whose training and experience equips them for this role. In the area of long-term organizational development it is unlikely that external change agents or lone internal OD specialists will be a sufficient resource to manage the required changes and there is thus an opportunity for significant expansion of the role of the specialist personnel manager.

At the same time it appears that coordination mechanisms are also changing and factories of the future will increasingly be held together by a shared professional perspective, backed up by relevant skills and knowledge. Human resource management may thus end up as a central part of the training and practice of everyone in the enterprise. Certainly there is a precedent for this; the trend is already clear in the move towards cellular manufacturing in which each cell becomes a 'factory within a factory' and replicates key functions like purchasing, planning, maintenance, quality management etc. within the cell.

In the cases which we explored, the role of personnel specialists was ambiguous. Sometimes they played a central role, leading and shaping organizational transformation – for example, in developing a company-wide strategy to support the implementation of a flexible manufacturing facility. However, their ability to contribute strategically in this way required, amongst other things, a detailed grasp of the issues related to technology as well as more traditional personnel matters. Equally there were instances where production and engineering managers took responsibility not only for the technological implementation but also for many of the organization design and personnel-related issues.

These shifts need to be related to the changing context of professional training and development. Increasingly technologists are being trained in a broader set of managerial skills, some of which represent what might traditionally be part of the formation of a personnel specialist (Bessant, Levy et al, 1992). The increasing emphasis on qualifications – for example, many cell leaders and shift supervisors are now holders of first or even postgraduate degrees – may well mark the beginning of an absorption of what was once a specialist function into the general duties of a first-line manager. This process has already happened in areas like quality management and industrial engineering where the specialist professional has begun to disappear as the function becomes part of the general responsibilities of production staff. Advanced technology enables such a shift because it relieves them of many of the direct control and 'fire-fighting' problems which previously preoccupied them.

The reverse could, of course, happen, whereby specialist personnel managers become more actively involved across a wider range of technology-related issues. But if they are to play such a strategic role, or to become an essential part of the manufacturing cell team in the next century, then the content and delivery of professional training in personnel management will need careful review.

The research reported here was focused on UK experiences but similar patterns emerge in studies of the United States (Zammuto and O'Connor, 1992) and elsewhere in Europe (Brödner, 1985). They confirm the general picture of a shift away from the old paradigm, associated with Ford and his contemporaries and a very different set of environmental conditions, towards new ways of designing and operating manufacturing organizations. Managing this transition, which depends increasingly on a different view of the role of people, will require considerable skill and experience across the whole range of activities which traditionally involve the personnel specialist. Thus there is considerable potential opportunity for this group to take a strategic role, shaping and enabling the direction of change. Achieving this will depend on such specialists' taking a much broader view and developing an understanding of the technological, financial and business context in which they will be operating. The alternative is that their expert professional territory will increasingly become colonized by other groups, with an accompanying decline in status and influence.

Manufacturing has much to gain from the early and strategic involvement of personnel specialists in the process of major technological change. But personnel specialists have much to lose if they fail to adapt and develop relevant new perspectives and skills so that they can contribute to the process. In many ways the factory organization models of Henry Ford represented the high point of functional specialization amongst professional groups. The question now is whether the moves towards a post-

Fordist model signal the beginning of the decline of such specialization and the possible disappearance or submergence of the personnel profession.

Acknowledgement

The research described in this chapter was supported by a grant from the ESRC/ SERC Joint Committee, whose assistance is gratefully acknowledged.

Note

1. The primary tool used for data collection was the case study – written material, interviews and observations. Our interview design used open-ended, semi-structured, in-depth sessions, involving between one and three sessions per individual, depending on the circumstances and the material covered. Interviews were conducted with representatives from all organizational levels. Clearly this research is open to several criticisms of which subsequent work will need to take account. First, it was conceived as an initial 'mapping' exercise rather than an attempt to measure in detail; however, the development of more accurate metrics of change and some method of correlating their impact on organizational performance is an important priority. A second limitation was that the range of indicative dimensions of change was limited to our initial selection; there may well be other aspects of the pattern which should be added to the list and tested. The sample size was also relatively small, although it did cover a wide range of examples of integrated AMT in a variety of organizational settings; further work could extend this coverage and/or take a more structured sample.

PART III

CONCLUSION

11

Managing People in a Time of Technical Change: Conclusions and Implications

Jon Clark

This volume and its contributions start from two basic assumptions: that technical change is now an unavoidable and pervasive fact of organizational life, and that its effective adoption depends to a greater or lesser extent on the degree to which its human resource implications are understood and acted upon. The aim of this chapter is to draw some general conclusions and practical implications about the connections between technical and organizational change, the most important personnel/HR issues arising from advanced technical change, and the role of general managers, line managers and personnel specialists in managing its introduction and operation. The discussion will be structured under five main headings:

- Technical change and organizational change: unpacking the connections
- Personnel issues and HRM: adaptive strategies and policy contradictions
- Line managers and technical change: linking strategic HRM and operational requirements
- Employee acceptance and resistance: the symbolic importance of technical change
- Personnel specialists and advanced technical change: achieving a voice for personnel/HR issues.

Technical Change and Organizational Change: Unpacking the Connections

Although it is often difficult to isolate the influence of technical change from that of other factors such as product market competition, recession, or company restructuring, many contributors to this volume have demonstrated specific connections between technical change and organizational change in the widest sense. Some of the most interesting evidence was discussed in Chapter 10 by John Bessant, who presented findings from twenty-eight companies using advanced manufacturing technology (AMT). He found that the successful use of AMT was directly associated with certain specific organizational arrangements and personnel policies. These included: new forms of organization design such as flatter management hierarchies and cross-functional project teams; new forms of supportive first-line management; flexible work practices and teamworking; mechanisms for ensuring employee involvement in 'continuous improvement'/total quality systems; redesign of reward systems and tight links with appraisal; more focused recruitment/selection criteria and procedures; high levels of continuous training and development. While these were not always the direct result of technical change, the characteristics of advanced technology – particularly in its more integrated, systemic forms – did suggest an 'underlying trajectory' of change in the direction of various forms of organizational integration such as teamworking, enlarged multi-skilled jobs and cross-functional organizational structures.

This kind of 'soft determinism' (Clark and Staunton, 1989; quoted by Bessant, p. 207 above) in the fit between advanced manufacturing technology and organizational arrangements was also in evidence in some of the more detailed one-company case studies. However, in these studies it was also apparent that differences in particular technologies and the primary tasks of organizations (for example, producing body panels, assembling printed circuit boards, processing insurance policies) could lead to quite different working practices in areas such as self-management or self-supervision. At Pirelli Aberdare, for example (Chapter 6), while the daily work schedule was predetermined by production planners and downloaded automatically to the shopfloor, production tasks still remained highly complex and there was a need for multi-skilled and often multi-employee intervention to deal with unpredictable events. As a result, it was not always possible to trace problems or faults directly to one machine or individual or to institute a management control system based on close monitoring of individual performance. Against this background, production employees worked under a system of 'self-supervision' which gave them a high level of autonomy in operational decision-making, both as individuals and team members. A similar kind of 'technological imperative' could be detected at Hardy Spicer (Chapter 4), where the need to maintain the continuous flow of integrated production lines required operators to take all first-level decisions at the point of production in order to keep the line running.

In contrast, every single task associated with the assembly of printed circuit boards at K-Electric (Chapter 7) could be broken down into standard times, and precise targets could be set for the insertion of each individual component. For example, each operator in the panels section was expected to insert on average around ten components on a board every 30 seconds. The advanced technology also made it possible for faults in the assembly of individual components to be traced back directly to individual employees. In this case the particular technology and primary task facilitated the institution of a tightly controlled system of surveillance in which individual 'self-managed' performance was measured automatically and displayed publicly, both to the individual and their work team. In all these cases, the particular form of advanced technology had a determinate influence on the nature of organizational arrangements.

The relation between technical and organizational change was, however, not always of such a 'deterministic' kind. In the Hardy Spicer case (Chapter 4), the introduction of cell manufacture allowed much greater scope for managers and work teams to design organizational arrangements independent of any technical imperatives. One clear implication of all these cases is that those people who have responsibility for, or wish to influence, personnel issues under conditions of advanced technical change need to acquire a detailed appreciation of the particular technology and task when considering the choice of the most appropriate organizational arrangements. However, a review of the current courses, conferences and publications associated with the British Institute of Personnel Management indicates that it does not regard the management of technology as an important element in the training and development of professional personnel managers. Indeed, a recent study has concluded that British personnel managers are even failing to exploit the strategic uses of advanced technology for their own personnel information systems, mainly because of a lack of information technology skills and knowledge (IPM, 1992). This general lack of IT awareness and knowledge amongst personnel specialists is clearly an important factor contributing to their apparent marginality in processes of technical change (a similar point has been made by Karen Legge, see Appendix to Legge, 1989b).

Finally, a number of case studies have underlined the general importance of management information systems in ensuring that the full organizational implications of advanced technical change are realized. In Chapter 8 we saw how the introduction of on-line processing of policies in an insurance company was not backed up by an effective management information system to secure accurate real-time data on staff workloads. As a result staffing arrangements were based on inadequate data, and backlogs increased significantly, with major consequences not only for the attitude of staff towards advanced technical change, but also for the efficiency of the whole operation and the quality of customer service. This contrasted with K-Electric (Chapter 7), where a sophisticated computer-based management information system enabled the production of real-time information on operator performance and tight control of product quality – all part of a worldwide company strategy.

Personnel Issues and HRM: Adaptive Strategies and Policy Contradictions

One of the features which is held to distinguish HRM from more traditional approaches to personnel management is the emphasis on a *strategic* approach to the management of human resources (see Chapter 1). The case study contributions to this volume give clear indications about the components and potential internal contradictions of a strategic approach towards managing the human resource under conditions of advanced technical change.

First, if we view strategic behaviour not as a discrete decision or set of decisions, but as an incremental process of decision-making and adaptation over time and space, there is some evidence that personnel/HR issues may play a more important role in the management of advanced technical change than might appear at first sight. In the Hardy Spicer case, for example (Chapter 4), the long history of cooperation between management and trade unions and the existence of a well-trained and motivated workforce committed to the adoption of new technology were vital 'antecedent' factors in the company's decision to invest in advanced technical change on a brownfield site. At the same time, in considering organizational arrangements appropriate to the new technology, senior managers (including the personnel director) rejected some of the main human resource recommendations of its appointed consultants – for example, to opt for more direct controlling forms of supervision and to reduce the reliance on trade unions as a channel for communication with the workforce – because they wished to build on the climate of good employee relations which had been created over the years with the active involvement and leadership of the specialist personnel function. In this case, the influence of personnel issues in the development of both HR and wider business strategy was significant, but it preceded the formal decision to invest in new technology. The Hardy Spicer case is also a cautionary tale warning against the mechanistic application of particular models of HRM without regard for the specific strengths and weaknesses of individual companies.

Secondly, the case studies have given an indication of the most important personnel issues in the introduction of advanced technical change, irrespective of whether it is personnel specialists, non-specialists with responsibility for personnel issues, or general/line managers who are the champions of these issues. They can be grouped conveniently into three main types: organization design; work structuring; and HRM/personnel issues in the narrow sense.

Interestingly, the four HRM/personnel issues – selection, appraisal, reward and development – whose tight integration is often regarded as the true hallmark of strategic HRM (Devanna et al, 1984: 41; see also Storey, 1989b: 6–7) were highly prominent factors in the management of advanced technical change, although the extent to which case study companies actually implemented policies in these areas in an integrated and coherent way was highly uneven. Of the four issues, however, selection of the 'appropriate' staff (not just in technical but also attitudinal and behavioural terms) was a particular priority in all organizations, as was the training and development of staff to work with the new systems and to keep abreast of constant modifications and enhancements.

If we turn to work structuring, changes in supervision, the creation of semi-autonomous work teams (self-supervision) and enhanced functional flexibility were generally the most important technology-related trends. However, some organizations initially underestimated the disadvantages of full flexibility in patterns of working and subsequently introduced limitations to allow staff to play to their strengths and acquire ownership in particular areas of work (see Chapters 4 and 6). As to organization design, the three most important trends were the breakdown of traditional departmental or occupational boundaries, delayering and 'lean' staffing levels, although again, as with increased flexibility, if they were pursued too assiduously, they sometimes became counterproductive and began to inhibit the goals of commitment and quality which they were partly intended to advance. Finally, one issue held to be characteristic of an HRM approach figured prominently in all our case study companies, namely managing the managers, whether this involved the specification of their new roles or their selection, training and development. We will return to this issue below.

Thirdly, while there did appear to be significant advantages in establishing an interrelated set of human resource policies at an early stage (as suggested by normative models of 'strategic' HRM), there was extensive evidence that different policies could come into direct conflict with one another, often at subsequent stages in the process of change. In the financial services case, for example (Chapter 8), we saw how a proactive HR policy to gain support for advanced technical change – the redesign of jobs to prevent occupational deskilling and downgrading – was negated by a separate cost-driven policy to freeze recruitment which increased staff workloads substantially and generated a negative reaction to technical change. In Pirelli also (see Chapter 6), it was apparent that tight staffing levels in the commercial and accounts areas meant that it was not possible to release staff for training to achieve the flexibility that the tight staffing levels appeared to require. In many cases, in fact, lean or tight staffing levels – one of the hallmarks and promises of advanced technical change – made it difficult to release staff both for initial on-the-job training and technical updating, thus conflicting with the policies towards flexibility and multi-skilling. Also, in the Hardy Spicer, Venture Pressings and Pirelli cases (see Chapters 4, 5 and 6), initial intentions to introduce full flexibility amongst production staff conflicted with the need to generate commitment and ownership of particular work areas, leading line management in each case to modify the full flexibility policy at a later stage. As Chris Hendry has argued (Chapter 4), the ability to make such modifications is the true hallmark of strategic behaviour.

Line Managers and Technical Change: Linking Strategic HRM and Operational Requirements

In the previous section we touched a number of times on the question of implementing at establishment level strategies and policies conceived at a senior level within organizations. In multi-site organizations, the gap between conception and implementation is often exacerbated by the spatial distance between head office, divisional and establishment levels. In some organizations, too, this problem is exacerbated by a higher turnover in senior and middle management, which makes it harder to ensure continuity and consistency in the management of advanced technical change. John Child (1985) has argued that the discontinuity between different levels and timescales of managerial action is best conceived in terms of an 'attenuation' between (corporate) strategy and its implementation. This attenuation, he suggests, creates scope for 'variability' in the 'tightness of coupling' between senior management intentions and operational realities and requirements. In the generality of organizations, establishing the links between strategy and implementation – or rather adapting strategy to meet operational requirements – is likely to fall to those employees who have responsibility for managing day-to-day workplace operations: factory and office managers, manufacturing and administration managers, shop and branch managers, first-line managers, supervisors and team leaders.

How does advanced technical change affect their role in the management of human resources? Unfortunately we have few detailed data on which to make an assessment. However, advanced technical change is capable of providing greater transparency and speed of information flows (on everything from financial and work performance to absenteeism) and of accelerating the trend towards a reduction in the number of hierarchical levels in work organizations (delayering). In contrast to earlier gloomy predictions about the erosion or even demise of middle and first-line management, advanced technical change appears to have led to a broadening of their range of responsibilities and an increase in their direct accountability, not only for operational performance, but also for personnel and employee relations matters (on this see Dopson and Stewart, 1990; Daniel and Millward, Chapter 3, this volume).

If we extrapolate from the evidence presented in Chapters 4–10, advanced technical change does indeed appear to require a new breed of line managers who are both technically proficient at their jobs and also the main 'owners' and champions of personnel/HR policy at establishment level. Our studies suggest that they are likely to be facilitators rather than controllers, decision-makers rather than administrators, problem-solvers rather than fire-fighters, and people with the vision and ability to think strategically and adapt strategies and policies to meet operational requirements (see Storey, 1992a: Chs 7 and 8, for more general evidence and discussion of this question).

Does this new breed of line manager actually exist in the generality of organizations introducing advanced technical change, or are they the exception rather than the rule? Bluntly, we cannot be sure. What evidence we have, however, suggests that three types of line manager are currently co-existing in various mixes in companies introducing advanced technical change: (i) **old-style time-served supervisors and middle managers** with no formal qualifications who have risen through the ranks and achieved their position in middle age mainly by virtue of their knowledge of the job; (ii) **new-style team leaders and line managers** in their late twenties to early forties who have technical qualifications (usually through the completion of further education courses linked to on-the-job training) and proven managerial skills (acquired through practical experience and attendance at short courses); and (iii) **the 'young virgins'**, university or college graduates in their twenties with high levels of academic knowledge but little or no experience of shopfloor work and little or no training in – or understanding of – human resource management. One of the most pressing challenges highlighted by advanced technical change is the need to devise job specifications, and recruit and manage the new breed of line managers, who will unite the strengths and avoid the weaknesses of these three types. The possible role of personnel specialists in meeting this challenge will be discussed in the final section of this chapter. Before we look at this, it is important to take into account evidence on the employee experience of technical change and its practical implications for managers.

Employee Acceptance and Resistance: the Symbolic Importance of Technical Change

In the late 1970s and early 1980s, at the time microelectronics-based information technologies were beginning to be introduced more widely into work processes, there was much talk of the likelihood of employee *resistance* to technical change. However, one of the most surprising findings from the WIRS surveys of 1984 and 1990 was the persistent and widespread *support* for advanced technical change amongst both manual and non-manual employees (see Chapter 3). Investment in new technology, it appears, is associated by employees with competitive advantage, optimism and success. It has a *symbolic* importance way beyond its actual effects on quality, efficiency or jobs.

Further research may qualify this finding to a greater or lesser extent. For example, survey evidence based on questions about recent experiences of technical change may be distorted by the fact that the respondents have all successfully survived the change, whereas the voice of the 'losers' – those not selected to work with the new technology and/or those who have taken early retirement or been made redundant – may not have been heard. The finding of substantial employee support for technical change may be simply the 'survivors' story'. Also, it is possible that the survey method is not as sensitive to worker resistance as techniques such as non-participant observation (see Chapter 8, which used this technique and uncovered a range of forms of resistance). In addition, employee (and management) responses may not be uniformly positive over time, but may vary at different stages in the process of change. Both managers and researchers need to look more closely at the nature of such processual variations in experiences of technical change.

Although these possible qualifications need to be taken seriously, however, they are unlikely to refute the general validity of the remarkably robust survey findings on positive worker support for technical change. Indeed, one of the main reasons advanced as to why specialist personnel managers play only a marginal role in technical change is the general lack of resistance to change from the workforce and therefore the absence of any need for personnel specialists to engage in conflict resolution or negotiations (see Chapter 3). However, the absence of conflict does not absolve managers of the need to devise new organizational and personnel arrangements appropriate to the new technology or to generate commitment to them. The danger of assuming that personnel/HR issues are only of secondary importance is particularly acute where collective employee representation at establishment level is weak or even non-existent (see Chapter 9). We are thus faced with a paradox: the two main institutionalized 'voices' of personnel/HR issues in work organizations, specialist personnel managers and employee representative bodies (trade unions etc.), appear to play only a marginal role in technical change in the generality of organizations, and yet many advanced technical changes appear to have failed because of lack of appropriate organizational arrangements and due consideration of human resource issues. This paradox will be addressed in the final section of this chapter.

Personnel Specialists and Advanced Technical Change: Achieving a Voice for Personnel/HR Issues

The most obvious reason why specialist personnel managers play only a marginal role in the introduction of advanced technical change is that – in relation to the UK, at least – only around a quarter of workplaces with over twenty-five employees actually have a specialist personnel manager (defined as someone who spends half or more of their time on personnel and employee relations matters). Even where there are on-site personnel managers, the evidence suggests that they are tending to confine themselves to an ever-narrower range of employee relations concerns, for example in the field of employment law (see Chapter 3). In relation to advanced technical change, Sewell and Wilkinson (Chapter 7) found a similar narrowing of personnel expertise, which at K-Electric was largely confined to the provision of 'rational instruments of selection' – such as psychometric, aptitude and dexterity tests – for use in assessing the suitability of staff for new technology.

In contrast to the generality of cases, three one-company case studies in this volume (see Chapters 4, 5 and 6) present counter-examples of how specialist personnel/HR managers *can* play a prominent and important role in the management of technical change, *particularly in the early stages of implementation and planning for implementation*. The following are some of the characteristics of these cases:

- The companies had an established and recognized tradition of professional personnel management prior to the introduction of advanced technical change
- Senior personnel specialists shared the overall business and personnel approach of the chief executive officer or site manager, with whom they worked extremely closely on a day-to-day basis
- They established an informal role with the chief executive officer or site manager as a kind of 'organizational adviser' or general 'eyes and ears' – a role which was one of the main bases of their wider influence and legitimacy
- They were the senior managers in the company or site with the widest knowledge of best personnel practice, particularly through past experience and access to specialist networks (personal and institutional connections, professional journals)
- They were willing to take the new technology seriously and to design 'technology-driven' personnel policies where appropriate
- They championed the importance of high quality training as central to the successful implementation and operation of advanced technical change
- They were instrumental, together with general managers, in the selection of the line managers to manage the new technology
- They recognized the need to secure the involvement of general and line managers in providing day-to-day continuity and 'ownership' of human resource policies.

How might we conceptualize these characteristics in terms of Storey's typology of styles of human resource management (see Chapters 2 and 9 for discussion)? Broadly they represent a cross between the **change-maker** (strategic and interventionist) and **advisory** (strategic and non-interventionist) types. They were certainly strategic in that they were involved as equal partners with general and line managers in designing a set of (more or less interrelated) personnel policies for advanced technical change. However, whether they were 'interventionist' or not is less important than the fact that they were able to be involved in devising a framework for human resource change by virtue of two main factors: *their strong links with the chief executive officer or site manager* (that is, the main organizational power-holder) and *their distinctive knowledge and experience of personnel issues and current best practice*. To use Legge's terminology (discussed in Chapters 1 and 2), they were 'conformist innovators' in that they were concerned to make personnel/HR policies fit overall business and technical needs, but also 'deviant innovators' in that they brought to bear specialist knowledge in the personnel and human resource field. This allowed them to make a unique contribution to the evolution of overall management strategy, not just on narrower personnel/HR issues, but also in areas such as organization design and work structuring. Interestingly, although all were involved in managing relations with trade unions, their most important 'interventionist' role was within management policy-making. Their activity at the planning stage of technical change, was, in this sense, **strategic**, **advisory** and **interventionist** within the senior management team. At later stages of technical change, however, they tended to leave the management of technology to general and line managers, reverting to a more low key role (in Storey's terms, as handmaidens, regulators and advisers).

It should be noted that the three companies in which these personnel managers operated were all large, multi-site private sector firms in manufacturing, and thus in no way typical of the generality of UK organizations (see Table 3.4, p. 50 above). However, they are exemplar cases which provide insights into some of the practical conditions which could enable personnel specialists to achieve similar involvement. It is also interesting to note that, while in two of the three cases, greenfield sites provided a good 'opportunity structure' for strategic personnel involvement, the third was a brownfield site which allowed for an equally effective strategic involvement, albeit one which built more on past practices than anticipated futures. Also, two of the three companies were UK-owned, whereas most of the evidence (see Chapter 1) suggests that it is foreign-owned companies which are distinctive in giving a high profile to personnel specialists.

Practical Implications

What are the main practical implications of this discussion? First, there is general agreement that general and line managers are the most important agents of human resource issues in implementing technical change and managing the technology once it is implemented. Indeed, many of the problems associated with technical change arise only after its introduction and are then dealt with by line managers as 'process' problems without specialist personnel involvement. If this is to be the pattern in the future, and all the evidence suggests that it will be, personnel/HR considerations and capabilities will clearly need to be much more prominent in the job accountabilities, selection and management of general and line managers.

Secondly, there is also strong evidence that the benefits of advanced technical change will only be fully realized if appropriate organizational and work arrangements are put in place and a strategic approach is adopted to the management of human resources, *in particular to the management of middle and first-line managers*. In many ways it is irrelevant who is the champion, innovator and guardian of human resource issues. However, if it is to be general managers together with a new breed of line managers, their performance in this area – and the actual outcomes in matters of organization design, work structuring and human resource policies – will need to be regularly reviewed, preferably by someone with specialist knowledge, understanding and experience of personnel issues.

Evidence from the Pirelli case study (Chapter 6) is instructive here, because it demonstrates what can happen to these issues when there is an absence of continuity in specialist personnel management. With four different personnel managers in the first five years of the new factory and often significant gaps between appointments, some human resource issues which had been deemed to be central to the overall business strategy for the new factory (such as the development of an appraisal/performance review system and a comprehensive system of training for flexibility across the plant) were either not, or only partially and unevenly, implemented in the first 3–4 years of operation. In practice, general and line managers were so preoccupied with ironing out technical faults and getting the automated factory up and running that they failed to give priority to HR issues, issues in which in any case they had no claim to specialist expertise or knowledge. This experience underlines the need for someone or some mechanism to ensure that there is a 'voice' for HR issues at all levels in the organization and that managerial performance on these issues and the actual personnel/HR outcomes are subject to a regular 'audit' or review, both during the implementation of technical change and after it has had time to settle down.

Whether this role of 'auditor' (over and above that of change-maker, adviser, handmaiden and regulator) is carried out by a general manager with personnel responsibilities or a professional personnel specialist will depend on many factors, including the size of workplace, the priority accorded to personnel/HR issues, and the personality and objectives of the managers concerned. Whatever the circumstances, however, the challenge facing organizations considering or actually undergoing technical change is how to develop the mechanisms and the people to ensure that these issues are taken seriously, treated coherently and adapted and improved continually to meet changing requirements. The question for specialist personnel managers is whether they have the ambition and expertise to play a major role in this endeavour as the wider voice of organizational, work and human resource issues, or whether they wish to follow the recent UK trend of retreating into ever-narrower technical specialisms (employment law, recruitment techniques). In this sense, the relation between personnel management, human resource management and technical change raises fundamental questions about the whole future of the personnel profession.

Acknowledgement

This chapter is a development of ideas that arose out of discussions between the contributors at a workshop held at the University of Warwick in September 1992.

Bibliography

Ackroyd, S., Burrell, G., Hughes, M. and Whitaker, A. (1988) 'The Japanization of British industry?', *Industrial Relations Journal*, 19 (1): 11–23

Armstrong, P. (1988) 'The personnel profession in the age of management accountancy', *Personnel Review*, 17 (1): 25–31

Armstrong, P. (1989) 'Limits and possibilities for HRM in an age of management accountancy', in Storey (1989a), pp. 154–66

Atkinson, J. (1989) 'Four stages of adjustment to the demographic downturn', *Personnel Management*, 21 (8): 20–4

Atkinson, J. and Meager, N. (1986) *Changing Working Patterns: How Companies Achieve Flexibility to Meet New Needs*. Report prepared by the Institute of Manpower Studies for the National Economic Development Office. London: NEDO

Bamber, G. (1988) 'Technological change and unions', in Hyman and Streeck (1988), pp. 204–19

Barras, R. and Swann, J. (1983) *The Adoption and Impact of Information Technology in the UK Insurance Industry*. London: Technical Change Centre

Bassett, P. (1986) *Strike Free*. Oxford: Blackwell

Batstone, E., Gourlay, S., Levie, H. and Moore, R. (1987) *New Technology and the Process of Labour Regulation*. Oxford: Clarendon Press

Beaumont, P. (1986) 'Industrial relations policies in high tech firms', *New Technology, Work and Employment*, 1 (2): 152–9

Beaumont, P. (1987) *The Decline of Trade Union Organisation*. Aldershot: Gower

Beaumont, P. and Harris, R. (1988) 'High technology industries and non-union establishments in Britain', *Relations Industrielles*, 43 (4): 829–46

Beaumont, P. and Townley, B. (1985) 'Greenfield sites, new plants and work practices', in V. Hammond (ed), *Current Research in Management*. London: Frances Pinter, pp. 163–79

Bell, R.M. (1972) *Changing Technology and Manpower Requirements in the Engineering Industry*. Falmer: Sussex University Press

Bessant, J. (1983) 'Making IT fit', in G. Winch (ed), *Information Technology and Manufacturing Processes*. London: Rossendale, pp. 14–31

Bessant, J. (1985) 'The integration barrier', *Robotica*, 4 (3): 97–103

Bessant, J. (1991) *Managing Advanced Manufacturing Technology: The Challenge of the Fifth Wave*. Manchester: NCC/Blackwell

Bessant, J., Burnell, J., Webb, S. and Harding, R. (1992) 'Continuous improvement in UK manufacturing'. Paper for the British Academy of Management, Bradford, September

Bessant, J., Levy, P., Ley, C., Smith S. and Tranfield, D. (1992) 'Organisation design for factory 2000', *International Journal of Human Factors in Manufacturing*, 2 (2): 95–125

Blau, P. (1990) 'Structural constraints and opportunities: Merton's contribution to general theory', in J. Clark, C. Modgil and S. Modgil (eds), *Robert K. Merton: Consensus and Controversy*. London: Falmer Press, pp. 141–55

Boreham, P. (1983) 'Indetermination: professional knowledge, organization and control', *Sociological Review*, 31 (4): 693–78

Bowen, W. (1989) 'The puny pay-off from office computers', in Forester (1989), pp. 267–71

Braverman, H. (1974) *Labor and Monopoly Capital*. New York: Monthly Review Press

Brödner, P. (1985) *Fabrik 2000. Alternative Entwicklungspfade in die Zukunft der Fabrik*. Berlin: Edition Sigma

Buchanan, D. (1989) 'Principles and practice in work design', in Sisson (1989a), pp. 78–100

Burnes, B. (1988a) 'New technology and job design; the case of CNC', *New Technology, Work and Employment*, 3 (2): 100–11

Burnes, B. (1988b) 'Integrating technology, integrating people', *Production Engineer*, 67 (8): 54–5

Butchart, R. (1987) 'A new UK definition of the high technology industries', *Economic Trends*, No. 400, February, pp. 82–8

Child, J. (1985) 'Managerial strategies, new technology and the labour process', in D. Knights, H. Willmott and D. Collinson (eds), *Job Redesign*. Aldershot: Gower, pp. 107–41

Child, J. (1987) 'Organizational design for advanced manufacturing technology', in T. Wall, C. Clegg and N. Kemp (eds), *The Human Side of Advanced Manufacturing Technology*. Chichester: Wiley, pp. 101–35

Child, J., Fores, M., Glover, I. and Lawrence, P. (1983) 'A price to pay? Professionalism and work organization in Britain and West Germany', *Sociology*, 17 (1): 63–78

Child, J. and Fulk, J. (1982) 'Maintenance of occupational control', *Work and Occupations*, 9 (2): 155–92

Child, J. and Tarbuck, M. (1985) 'The introduction of new technology: management initiative and union response in British banks', *Industrial Relations Journal*, 16 (3): 19–33

Clark, J., McLoughlin, I., Rose, H. and King, R. (1988) *The Process of Technological Change: New Technology and Social Choice in the Workplace*. Cambridge: Cambridge University Press

Clark, P. and Staunton, N. (1989) *Innovation and Technology in Organisations*. London: Routledge

Clegg, C. and Kemp, N. (1986) 'Information technology: Personnel, where are you?', *Personnel Review*, 15 (1): 8–15

Cohen, S. and Taylor, L. (1992) *Escape Attempts*. London: Routledge

Collinson, D. (1987a) 'Who controls selection?', *Personnel Management*, 27 (5): 32–5

Collinson, D. (1987b) 'A question of equal opportunities: a survey of staff in a large insurance company', *Personnel Review*, 16 (1): 19–29

Collinson, D. (1991) '"Poachers turned gamekeepers": are personnel managers one of the barriers to equal opportunities?', *Human Resource Management Journal*, 1 (3): 58–76

Collinson, D. (1992) 'The realities of recruitment', in P. Frost, V. Mitchell and W. Nord (eds), *HRM Reality: Putting Competence in Context*. Cincinatti, Ohio: South-Western Publishing, pp. 143–54

Collinson, D. (1993) 'Strategies of resistance: power, knowledge and subjectivity in the workplace', in J. Jermier, W. Nord and D. Knights (eds), *Resistance and Power in Organizations*. London: Routledge

Collinson, D., Knights, D. and Collinson, M. (1990) *Managing to Discriminate*. London: Routledge

Coopey, F. and Hartley, J. (1991) 'HRM and the Concept of Multiple Commitments', *Human Resource Management Journal*, 1 (3): 18–32

Cressey, P. and MacInnes, J. (1980) 'Working for Ford: industrial democracy and the control of labour', *Capital and Class*, 11: 5–33

Cressey, P. and Scott, P. (1992) 'Employment, technology and industrial relations in UK clearing banks: is the honeymoon over?', *New Technology, Work and Employment*, 7 (2): 83–96

Cross, M. (1988) 'Changes in working practices in UK manufacturing 1981–88', *Industrial Relations Review and Report*, No. 415, May, pp. 2–10

Daly, F. (1991) 'Technology may be the tool, but people provide the power', *Plant Engineering and Maintenance*, 14 (7): 1–10

Daniel, W.W. (1987) *Workplace Industrial Relations and Technical Change*. London: Frances Pinter and Policy Studies Institute

Daniel, W.W. and Hogarth, T. (1990), 'Worker support for technical change', *New Technology, Work and Employment*, 5 (2): 82–93

Daniel, W.W. and McIntosh, N. (1972) *The Right to Manage?* London: Macdonald

Daniel, W.W. and Millward N. (1983) *Workplace Industrial Relations in Britain: The DE/PSI/ ESRC Survey*. London: Heinemann (2nd edn, 1984, Aldershot: Gower)

Davies, A. (1986) *Industrial Relations and New Technology*. London: Croom Helm

Davis, D. (1988) 'Technology and deskilling: the case of five principal trade areas in New South Wales', *New Technology, Work and Employment*, 3 (1): 47–55

Dent, H. (1990) 'Organizing for the productivity leap: the inevitable automation of management', *Small Business Reports*, 15 (9): 31–44

Devanna, M., Fombrun, C. and Tichy, M. (1984) 'A framework for strategic human resource management', in Fombrun et al (1984), pp. 33–51

Dopson, S. and Stewart, R. (1990) 'What is happening to middle management?', *British Journal of Management*, 1 (1): 3–16

Dore, R. (1986) *Flexible Rigidities*. London: Athlone Press

Drucker, P. (1988) 'The coming of the new organization', *Harvard Business Review*, 66 (1): 45–53

Edwards, P. (1985) 'Managing labour relations through the recession', *Employee Relations*, 7 (2): 3–7

Edwards, P. (1987) *Managing the Factory*. Oxford: Blackwell

Edwards, P. (1989) 'The three faces of discipline', in Sisson (1989a), pp. 296–325

Elger, T. (1991) 'Task flexibility and the intensification of labour in UK manufacturing in the 1980s', in Pollert (1991a), pp. 46–66

Ettlie, J. (1988) *Taking Charge of Manufacturing*. San Francisco: Jossey-Bass

Fombrun, C., Tichy, N. and Devanna, M. (1984) *Strategic Human Resource Management*. New York: John Wiley

Forester, T. (ed) (1989) *Computers in the Human Context*. Oxford: Blackwell

Foulkes, F. (1980) *Personnel Policies in Large Non-Union Companies*. New York: Prentice-Hall

Fowler, A. (1987) 'When chief executives discover HRM', *Personnel Management*, 19 (3): 3

Francis, A. (1986) *New Technology at Work*. Oxford: Clarendon Press

Francis, A. and Willman, P. (1980) 'Micro processors: impact and response', *Personnel Review*, 9 (2): 9–16

Freeman, C. and Perez, C. (1989) 'Structural crises of adjustment, business cycles and investment behaviour', in G. Dosi (ed), *Technical Change and Economic Theory*. London: Frances Pinter, pp. 38–67

Freeman, R. and Medoff, R. (1984) *What Do Unions Do?* New York: Basic Books

Friedman, A. and Cornford, D. (1989) *Computer Systems Development: History, Organization and Implementation*. Chichester: Wiley

Garrahan, P. and Stewart, P. (1992) *The Nissan Enigma*. London: Mansell

Geary, J. (1992) 'Pay, control and commitment: linking appraisal and reward', *Human Resource Management Journal*, 2 (4): 36–54

Gleave, S. and Oliver, N. (1990) 'Human resources management in Japanese manufacturing companies in the UK: 5 case studies', *Journal of General Management*, 16 (1): 54–68

Goffman, E. (1959) *The Presentation of Self in Everyday Life*. Harmondsworth: Penguin

Goffman, E. (1968) *Asylums*. Harmondsworth: Penguin

Goodman, J. (1989) 'Industrial relations and restructuring in manufacturing: three case studies in the United Kingdom', *International Labour Review*, 128 (5): 601–20

Goss, D. (1991) *Small Business and Society*. London: Routledge

Guest, D. (1987) 'Human resource management and industrial relations', *Journal of Management Studies*, 24 (2): 503–21

Guest, D. (1989) 'Human resource management: its implications for industrial relations and trade unions', in Storey (1989a), pp. 41–55

Guest, D. (1991) 'Personnel management: the end of orthodoxy?', *British Journal of Industrial Relations*, 29 (2): 149–76

Guest, D. (1992) 'Employee commitment and control', in J. Hartley and G. Stephenson (eds), *Employment Relations*. Oxford: Blackwell, pp. 111–35

Guest, D. and Dewe, P. (1991) 'Company or trade union: which wins workers' allegiance?' *British Journal of Industrial Relations*, 29 (1): 75–96

Hage, J. (1980) *Theories of Organization*. New York: John Wiley

Hall, R. (1968) 'Professionalization and bureaucratization', *American Sociological Review*, 33 (1): 92–104

Haug, M. (1973) 'Deprofessionalization: an alternative hypothesis for the future', in P. Halmos (ed), *Professionalization and Social Change. Sociological Review Monograph*, pp. 195–212

Hayes, R. and Abernathy, W. (1980) 'Managing our way to economic decline', *Harvard Business Review*, July/August, pp. 67–77.

Hayes, R., Wheelwright, S. and Clark, K. (1988) *Dynamic Manufacturing: Creating the Learning Organization*. New York: Free Press

Hendry, C. (1990) 'New technology, new careers: the impact of company employment policy', *New Technology, Work and Employment*, 5 (1): 31–43

Hendry, C. (1991) 'Manufacturing change at Belma joints', in K. Legge, C. Clegg and N. Kemp (eds), *Case Studies in Information Technology, People and Organisations*. Manchester and Oxford: NCC/Blackwell, pp. 35–47

Hendry, C. and Pettigrew, A. (1986) 'The practice of strategic human resource management', *Personnel Review*, 15 (5): 3–8

Hendry, C. and Pettigrew, A. (1987) 'Banking on HRM to respond to change', *Personnel Management*, 19 (11): 29–32

Hendry, C. and Pettigrew, A. (1988) 'Multiskilling in the round', *Personnel Management*, 20 (4): 36–43

Hendry, C. and Pettigrew, A. (1990) 'Human resource management: an agenda for research', *International Journal of Human Resource Management*, 1 (1): 17–43

Hendry, C., Pettigrew, A. and Sparrow, P. (1988) 'Changing patterns of human resource management', *Personnel Management*, 20 (11): 37–41

Hill, S. (1991a) 'How do you manage a flexible firm? The total quality model', *Work Employment and Society*, 5 (3): 397–416

Hill, S. (1991b) 'Why quality circles failed but TQM might succeed', *British Journal of Industrial Relations*, 29 (4): 541–68

Hollway, W. (1990) *Work Psychology and Organizational Behaviour*. London: Sage

Huczynski, M. and Buchanan, D. (1991) *Organizational Behaviour*, 2nd rev. edn. New York: Prentice-Hall

Hyman, R. (1987) 'Strategy or structure? Capital, labour and control', *Work, Employment and Society*, 1 (1): 25–55

Hyman, R. (1991) 'Plus ça change? The theory of production and the production of theory', in Pollert (1991a), pp. 259–83

Hyman, R. and Streeck, W. (eds) (1988) *New Technology and Industrial Relations*. Oxford:Blackwell

IDS (1984) *An Alternative Approach*. London: Incomes Data Services, IDS Study No. 314

IDS (1990) *Flexibility in the 1990s*. London: Incomes Data Services, IDS Study No. 454

IDS (1992) *Skill-Based Pay*. London: Incomes Data Services, IDS Study No. 500

Imai, K. (1987) *Kaizen*. New York: Random House

IPM (1992) 'Potential of computers not realised', *Personnel Management Plus* (Journal of the Institute of Personnel Management), 3 (10): 7

IRRR (1984) 'A greenfield agreement 15 years on', in *Industrial Relations Review and Report*, No. 314, pp. 6–10

IRRR (1985a) 'NEK Cables: innovation on a greenfield site', in *Industrial Relations Review and Report*, No. 335, pp. 5–8

IRRR (1985b) 'Nissan: a deal for teamwork and flexibility?', in *Industrial Relations Review and Report*, No. 344, pp. 2–7

IRRR (1986a) 'Change in a traditional environment – the CWS experience', in *Industrial Relations Review and Report*, No. 361, pp. 10–15

IRRR (1986b) 'Nissan: a catalyst for change?', in *Industrial Relations Review and Report*, No. 379, pp. 8–12

IRRR (1987a) 'Komatsu – the first year of a new start', in *Industrial Relations Review and Report*, No. 391, pp. 2–6

IRRR (1987b) 'A greenfield strategy for Ind Coope's Burton Brewery', in *Industrial Relations Review and Report*, No. 394, pp. 2–8

IRRR (1987c) 'BICC optical cables unit goes "Into 2000"', in *Industrial Relations Review and Report*, No. 398, pp. 12–16

IRRR (1988) 'Flexible teamworking at Unigate's greenfield site', in *Industrial Relations Review and Report*, No. 430, pp. 8–10

IRRR (1990) 'New employee relations policies at Dundee Textiles', in *Industrial Relations Review and Report*, No. 459, pp. 12–14

IRRR (1991) 'Bosch: an industrial relations strategy for a new start-up', in *Industrial Relations Review and Report*, No. 501, pp. 4–10

Jaikumar, R. (1986) 'Post-industrial manufacturing', *Harvard Business Review*, 64 (6): 69–76

Jenkins, R. (1986) *Racism and Recruitment*. Cambridge: Cambridge University Press

Johnson, T. (1972) *Professions and Power*. London: Macmillan

Jones, B. (1982) 'Destruction or redistribution of engineering skills', in S. Wood (ed), *The Degradation of Work?* London: Hutchinson, pp. 179–200

Jones B. (1988) 'Work and flexible automation in Britain: A review of developments and possibilities', *Work, Employment and Society*, 2 (4): 451–86

Juravich, T. (1985) *Chaos on the Shopfloor: A Worker's View of Quality, Productivity and Management*. Philadelphia: Temple University Press

Kanter, R. (1984) *The Change Masters*. London: Allen and Unwin

Kaplinsky, R. and Hoffman, K. (1992) *Transnational Corporations and the Transfer of New Management Practices in Developing Countries*. Report prepared for the United Nations Center on Transnational Corporations, New York, April

Keenoy, T. (1990a) 'HRM: A case of the wolf in sheep's clothing?', *Personnel Review*, 19 (2): 3–9

Keenoy, T. (1990b) 'Human resource management: rhetoric, reality and contradiction', *International Journal of Human Resource Management*, 1 (3): 363–84

Keenoy, T. (1990c) 'HRM and work values in Britain'. Paper presented to the second international conference of the International Society for the Study of Work and Organizational Values, Prague, 19–22 August

Keep, E. (1989) 'A training scandal?', in Sisson (1989a), pp. 177–202

Kern, H. and Schumann, M. (1984) *Das Ende der Arbeitsteilung?* Munich: Beck

Kerr, S., von Glinow, M. and Schriesheim, J. (1977) 'Issues in the study of professionals and organizations: the case of scientists and engineers', *Organizational Behavior and Human Performance*, 18 (2): 329–45

Klegon, D. (1978) 'The sociology of professions: an emerging perspective', *Sociology of Work and Occupations*, 5 (3): 259–83

Knights, D. and Willmott, H. (eds) (1988) *New Technology and the Labour Process*. London: Macmillan.

Kochan, T., McKersie, R. and Katz, H. (1986) *The Transformation of American Industrial Relations*. New York: Basic Books

Kondo, D. (1990) *Crafting Selves: Power, Discourse and Identity in a Japanese Factory*. Chicago, Ill.: Chicago University Press

Lamming, R. (1992) *Beyond Partnership*. London: Prentice-Hall

Larson, M. (1977) *The Rise of Professionalism*. Berkeley, Ca: University of California Press

Latreille, P. (1992) 'Unions and the inter-establishment adoption of new microelectronic technologies in the British private manufacturing sector', *Oxford Bulletin of Economics and Statistics*, 54 (1), pp. 31–51

Lawrence, P. and Dyer, D. (1982) *Renewing American Industry*. New York: Free Press

Lee, D. (1981) 'Skill, craft and class: a theoretical critique and a critical case', *Sociology*, 15 (1): 56–78

Legge, K. (1978) *Power, Innovation and Problem-Solving in Personnel Management*. London: McGraw-Hill

Legge, K. (1989a) 'Human resource management – A critical analysis', in Storey (1989a), pp. 19–40

Legge, K. (1989b) *Information Technology: Personnel Management's Lost Opportunity? Personnel Review* Monograph, 18 (5)

Linstead, S. (1985) 'Breaking the purity rule: industrial sabotage and the symbolic process', *Personnel Review*, 14 (3): 12–19

Liu, M., Denis, H., Kolodny, H. and Stymme, B. (1990) 'Organisation design for technological change', *Human Relations*, 43 (1): 7–22

Lloyd, C. (1989) 'Restructuring in the West Midlands' clothing industry', *New Technology, Work and Employment*, 4 (2): 100–7

MacInnes, J. (1988) 'New technology in Scotbank: gender, class and work', in Hyman and Streeck (1988), pp. 128–40

McLoughlin, I. and Clark, J. (1988) *Technological Change at Work*. Milton Keynes: Open University Press

McLoughlin, I. and Clark, J. (1993) *Technological Change at Work*, 2nd rev. edn. Milton Keynes: Open University Press

McLoughlin, I. and Gourlay, S. (1990) 'Innovation and change in ROSELAND: a survey of high tech establishments'. Occasional Paper No. 12, Kingston Business School

McLoughlin, I. and Gourlay, S. (1991) 'Transformed employee relations? Employee attitudes in non-union firms', *Human Resource Management Journal*, 2 (1): 8–28

McLoughlin, I. and Gourlay, S. (1992) 'Enterprise without unions: managing employment relations in non-union firms', *Journal of Management Studies*, 29 (5): 669–91

McLoughlin, I. and Gourlay, S. (1994) *Enterprise Without Unions: Industrial Relations in the Non-Union Firm*. Milton Keynes: Open University Press

Marchington, M. and Harrison, E. (1991) 'Customers, competitors and choice: employee relations in food retailing', *Industrial Relations Journal*, 23 (4): 286–99

Marchington, M. and Parker, P. (1990) *Changing Patterns of Employee Relations*. London: Harvester Wheatsheaf

Marginson, P. (1989) 'Employment flexibility in large companies: change and continuity', *Industrial Relations Journal*, 20 (2): 101–9

Marginson, P., Edwards, P., Martin, R., Purcell, J. and Sisson, K. (1988) *Beyond the Workplace: Managing Industrial Relations in Multi-Plant Enterprises*. Oxford: Blackwell

Marsden, D. and Thompson, M. (1990) 'Flexibility agreements and their significance in the increase in productivity in British manufacturing since 1980', *Work, Employment and Society*, 4 (1): 83–104

Martin, J. (1990) 'Deconstructing organizational taboos: the suppression of gender conflict in organizations', *Organization Science*, 1 (4): 339–59

Martin, R. (1981) *New Technology and Industrial Relations in Fleet Street*. London: Oxford University Press

Martin, R. (1988) 'Technological change and manual work', in D. Gallie (ed), *Employment in Britain*. Oxford: Blackwell, pp. 102–27

Melcher, A., Acar, W., DuMont, P. and Khouja, M. (1990) 'Standard maintaining and continuous improvement systems: experiences and comparisons', *Interfaces*, 20 (3): 24–40

Miles, I., Rush, H., Turner, K. and Bessant, J. (1988) *Information Horizons*. London: Edward Elgar

Miller, D. and Friesen, P. (1984) *Organizations: A Quantum View*. Englewood Cliffs, NJ: Prentice-Hall

Miller, E. and Rice, K. (1967) *Systems of Organization*. London: Tavistock

Miller, G. (1967) 'Professionals in bureaucracy: alienation among industrial scientists and engineers', *American Sociological Review*, 32 (5): 760–1

Miller, P. (1989) 'Strategic HRM: What it is and what it isn't', *Personnel Management*, 21 (2): 46–51

Millward, N. and Stevens, M. (1986) *British Workplace Industrial Relations 1980–1984: The DE/ESRC/PSI/ACAS Surveys*. Aldershot: Gower

Millward, N. and Stevens, M. (1988) 'Union density in the regions', *Employment Gazette*, 96 (5): 286–95

Millward, N., Stevens, M., Smart, D. and Hawes, W. (1992) *Workplace Industrial Relations in Transition: the ED/ESRC/PSI/ACAS Surveys*. Aldershot: Dartmouth Publishing

Mintzberg, H. (1978) 'Patterns in strategy formation', *Management Science*, 24 (9): 934–48

Mintzberg, H. (1989) *Mintzberg on Management*. New York: Free Press

Morgan, G. (1986) *Images of Organization*. London: Sage

Morris, J., Munday, M. and Wilkinson, B. (1992) 'Japanese investment in Wales: economic and social consequences'. Unpublished report, Cardiff Business School

Morris, T. and Wood, S. (1991) 'Testing the survey method: continuity and change in British industrial relations', *Work, Employment and Society*, 5 (2): 259–82

Mumford, E. (1969) *Computers: Planning and Personnel Management*. London: Institute of Personnel Management

Mumford, E. (1972) *Job Satisfaction: A Study of Computer Specialists*. London: Longman

Nelson, R. and Winter, S. (1982) *An Evolutionary Theory of Economic Change*. Boston: Harvard University Press

Newell, H. (1991) 'Field of dreams: evidence of "new" employee relations in greenfield sites'. DPhil dissertation, University of Oxford

Noble, D. (1984) *Forces of Production*. New York: Knopf

Northcott, J. and Rogers, P. (1984) *Microelectronics in British Industry: Patterns of Change*. London: Policy Studies Institute

Northcott, J. and Walling, A. (1988) *The Impact of Microelectronics: Diffusion, Benefits and Problems in British Industry*. London: Policy Studies Institute

Oliver, N. and Wilkinson, B. (1988) *The Japanization of British Industry*. Oxford: Blackwell

Oliver, N. and Wilkinson, B. (1989) 'Japanese manufacturing techniques and personnel and industrial relations practice in Britain: evidence and implications', *British Journal of Industrial Relations*, 27 (1): 73–91

Oppenheimer, M. (1973) 'The proletarianization of the professional', in P. Halmos (ed), *Professionalization and Social Change*. *Sociological Review* Monograph, pp. 213–27

O'Reilly, J. (1992) 'Where do you draw the line? Functional flexibility, training and skill in Britain and France', *Work, Employment and Society*, 6 (3): 369–96

Owens, T. (1991) 'The self-managing work team', *Small Business Reports*, 16 (2): 53–65

Pascale, R. and Athos, A. (1981) *The Art of Japanese Management*. Harmondsworth: Penguin

Peters, T. and Waterman, R. (1982) *In Search of Excellence*. New York: Harper and Row

Pettigrew, A. (1990) 'Longitudinal field research on change: theory and practice', *Organization Science*, 1 (3): 267–92

Pettigrew, A., Sparrow, P. and Hendry, C. (1988) 'The forces that trigger training', *Personnel Management*, 20 (12): 28–32

Pettigrew, A. and Whipp, R. (1991) *Managing Change for Competitive Success*. Oxford: Blackwell

Phillimore, A. (1989) 'Flexible specialization, work organization and skills', *New Technology, Work and Employment*, 4 (2): 79–91

Piore, M. and Sabel, C. (1982) *The Second Industrial Divide: Possibilities for Prosperity*. New York: Basic Books

Pollert, A. (ed) (1991a) *Farewell to Flexibility?* Oxford: Blackwell

Pollert, A. (1991b) 'The orthodoxy of flexibility', in Pollert (1991a), pp. 3–31

Popham, P. (1992) 'Turning Japanese', *Independent Magazine*, 12 September, pp. 24–30

Porter, M. (1985) *Competitive Advantage*. New York: Free Press

Pottinger, J. (1989) 'Engineering change through pay', *Personnel Management*, 21 (9): 73–4

Prais, S. (1981) *Productivity and Industrial Structure*. Cambridge: Cambridge University Press

Preece, D. (1989) *Managing the Adoption of New Technology*. London: Routledge

Preece, D. and Harrison, M. (1988) 'The contribution of personnel specialists to technology-related organizational change', *Personnel Review*, 17 (1): 13–19

Price, R. (1988) 'Information, consultation and the control of new technology', in Hyman and Streeck (1988), pp. 249–62

Purcell, J. (1987) 'Mapping management styles in employee relations', *Journal of Management Studies*, 24 (2): 205–23

Purcell, J. (1989) 'The impact of corporate strategy on human resource management', in Storey (1989a), pp. 67–91

Purcell, J. and Sisson, K. (1983) 'Strategies and practice in the management of industrial relations', in G.S. Bain (ed), *Industrial Relations in Britain*. Oxford: Blackwell, pp. 95–120

Raelin, J. (1985) *The Clash of Cultures: Managers and Professionals*. Boston, Mass.: Harvard University Press

Rainbird, H. (1990) *Training Matters: Union Perspectives on Industrial Restructuring and Training*. Oxford: Blackwell

Rajan, A. (1984) *New Technology and Employment in Insurance, Banking and Building Societies*. Aldershot: Gower

Reitsperger, W. (1986) 'British employees: responding to Japanese management philosophies', *Journal of Management Studies*, 23 (5): 563–78

Ritzer, G. (1972) *Man and His Work: Conflict and Change*. New York: Meredith Corporation

Roberts, B.C. (1987) 'Review' of Daniel (1987), *British Journal of Industrial Relations*, 25 (3): 475–8

Rolfe, H. (1986) 'Skill, de-skilling and new technology in the non-manual labour process', *New Technology, Work and Employment*, 1 (1): 37–49

Rothwell, S. (1985) 'Company employment policies and new technology', *Industrial Relations Journal*, 16 (3): 43–51

Saks, M. (1983) 'Removing the blinkers: a critique of recent contributions to the sociology of professions', *Sociological Review*, 31 (1): 1–21

Schonberger, R. (1985) *World Class Manufacturing*. New York: Free Press

Schuler, R. (1989) 'Strategic human resource management and industrial relations', *Human Relations*, 42 (2): 157–84

Scott, P. (1985) 'Automated machining systems and the role of engineering craft skills', in H. Bullinger (ed), *Proceedings of the Second International Conference on Human Factors in Manufacturing*. Bedford: IFS Publications, pp. 121–30

Sewell, G. and Wilkinson, B. (1992a) 'Someone to watch over me: surveillance, discipline and the just-in-time labour process', *Sociology*, 26 (2): 271–89

Sewell, G. and Wilkinson, B. (1992b) 'Empowerment or emasculation? A tale of shopfloor surveillance in a total quality organisation', in P. Blyton and P. Turnbull (eds), *New Perspectives on Human Resource Management*. London: Sage, pp. 97–115

Shenkar, O. (1988) 'Blue, white and steel collar: a case study of robot introduction', *New Technology, Work and Employment*, 3 (1): 66–73

Sisson, K. (ed) (1989a) *Personnel Management in Britain*. Oxford: Blackwell

Sisson, K. (1989b) 'Personnel management in transition?', in Sisson (1989a), pp. 22–52

Sisson, K. (1989c) 'Personnel management in perspective', in Sisson (1989a), pp. 3–21

Smith, S. (1988) 'How much change at the store? The impact of new technology and labour processes on managers and staff in retail', in Knights and Willmott (1988), pp. 143–63

Sorge, A. and Streeck, W. (1988) 'Industrial relations and technical change: the case for an extended perspective', in Hyman and Streeck (1988), pp. 19–47

Sproull, A. and MacInnes, J. (1987) 'Patterns of union recognition in Scottish electronics', *British Journal of Industrial Relations*, 25 (3): 335–8

Sproull, A. and MacInnes, J. (1988) 'Union recognition, single union agreements and employment change in Scottish electronics', *Industrial Relations Journal*, 20 (1): 33–46

Starkey, K. and McKinley, A. (1988) *Organisational Innovation*. Aldershot: Avebury/Gower

Stopford, J. and Baden-Fuller, C. (1990) 'Corporate rejuvenation', *Journal of Management Studies*, 27 (4): 399–415

Storey, J. (1987) 'The management of new office technology: choice, control and social structure in the insurance industry', *Journal of Management Studies*, 24 (1): 43–62

Storey, J. (ed) (1989a) *New Perspectives on Human Resource Management*. London: Routledge

Storey, J. (1989b) 'Introduction: from personnel management to human resource management', in Storey (1989a), pp. 1–18

Storey, J. (1992a) *Developments in the Management of Human Resources*. Oxford: Blackwell

Storey, J. (1992b) 'HRM in action: the truth is out at last', *Personnel Management*, 24 (4): 28–31

Storey, J. and Sisson, K. (1989) 'Looking to the future', in Storey (1989a), pp. 167–83

Sturdy, A. (1990) 'Clerical consent: an analysis of social relations in insurance work'. PhD thesis, School of Management, University of Manchester Institute of Science and Technology

Takamiya, M. (1981) 'Japanese multinationals in Europe: international operations and their public policy implications', *Columbia Journal of World Business*, 16 (2): 5–17

Torrington, D. (1989) 'Human resource management and the personnel function', in Storey (1989a), pp. 56–66

Torrington, D. and Hall, L. (1987) *Personnel Management: A New Approach*. London: Prentice-Hall

Torrington, D., Mackay, L. and Hall, L. (1985) 'The changing nature of personnel management', *Employee Relations*, 7 (5): 10–16

Trevor, M. (1988) *Toshiba's New British Company: Competitiveness Through Innovation in Industry*. London: Policy Studies Institute

TUC (1979) *Employment and Technology*. London: Trades Union Congress

Tynan, O. (1986) 'The Work Research Unit and its role in change', *New Technology, Work and Employment*, 1 (2): 185–6

Tyson, S. (1987) 'The management of the personnel function', *Journal of Management Studies*, 24 (2): 523–32

Tyson, S. and Fell, A. (1986) *Evaluating the Personnel Function*. London: Hutchinson

Voss, C. (1986) 'Success and failure in advanced manufacturing technology'. Working Paper, University of Warwick Business School

Walton, R.E. and Lawrence, P.R. (1985) *Human Resource Management: Trends and Challenges*, Boston, Mass.: Harvard Business School Press

Watson, T. (1977) *The Personnel Managers*. London: Routledge

Whitaker, A. (1986) 'Managerial strategy and industrial relations: a case study of plant relocation', *Journal of Management Studies*, 23 (6): 657–78

Wickens, P. (1987) *The Road to Nissan*. London: Macmillan

Wiedemeyer, M. (1989) 'New technology in West Germany: the employment debate', *New Technology, Work and Employment*, 4 (1): 54–65

Wilensky, H. (1964) 'The professionalization of everyone?', *American Journal of Sociology*, 70 (2): 137–58

Wilkinson, B. (1983) *The Shopfloor Politics of New Technology*. London: Heinemann

Wilkinson, B. and Oliver, N. (1990) 'Japanese influences on British industrial culture', in S. Clegg and G. Redding (eds), *Capitalism in Contrasting Cultures*. Berlin: de Gruyter, pp. 333–54

Williams, R. and Steward, F. (1985) 'Technology agreements in Britain: a survey 1977–83', *Industrial Relations Journal*, 16 (3): 58–73

Willman, P. (1987a) 'New technology and industrial relations – a review of the literature'. Research Paper No. 56. London: Department of Employment

Willman, P. (1987b) 'Industrial relations issues in advanced manufacturing technology', in T. Wall, C. Clegg and N. Kemp (eds), *The Human Side of Advanced Manufacturing Technology*. Chichester: Wiley, pp. 135–52

Willman, P. and Winch, G. (1985) *Innovation and Management Control: Labour Relations at BL Cars*. Cambridge: Cambridge University Press

Wilson, F. (1988) 'Computer numerical control and constraints', in Knights and Willmott (1988), pp. 66–90

Winch, G., Voss, C. and Twigg, D. (1991) 'Organization design for integrating technologies'. Research paper, University of Warwick Business School

Winner L. (1977) *Autonomous Technology*. Cambridge, Mass.: MIT Press

Wobbe, W. (1992) 'Advanced manufacturing and anthropocentric production systems in the European Community', in P. Brödner (ed), *Ergonomics of Hybrid Automation Systems*. Amsterdam: Elsevier, pp. 1–8

Womack, J., Jones, D., Daniel, T. and Roos, D. (1990) *The Machine that Changed the World*. New York: Rawson Associates

Yeandle, D. and Clark, J. (1989a) 'A personnel strategy for an automated factory', *Personnel Management*, 21 (6): 51–5

Yeandle, D. and Clark, J. (1989b) 'Growing a compatible IR set-up: Pirelli General's single union agreement in South Wales', *Personnel Management*, 21 (7): 36–9

Yu, C. and Wilkinson, B. (1989) 'Pay and appraisal in Japanese companies in Britain'. Japanese Management Research Unit Working Paper No. 8, Cardiff Business School

Zammuto, R. and O'Connor, E. (1992) 'Gaining advanced manufacturing technologies' benefits: The roles of organization design and culture', *Academy of Management Review*, 17 (4): 701–29

Index

Note: Page references in italics indicate tables.